IAN FLEMING'S
INSPIRATION

For Charles. My inspiration.

IAN FLEMING'S INSPIRATION

THE TRUTH BEHIND THE BOOKS

EDWARD ABEL SMITH

PEN & SWORD
HISTORY

AN IMPRINT OF PEN & SWORD BOOKS LTD.
YORKSHIRE – PHILADELPHIA

First published in Great Britain in 2020 by
PEN AND SWORD HISTORY
An imprint of
Pen & Sword Books Ltd
Yorkshire – Philadelphia

ISBN 978 1 52675 769 2

A CIP catalogue record for this book is available from the British Library.

Typeset in Times New Roman 11.5/14 by
Aura Technology and Software Services, India.
Printed and bound in the UK by TJ International Ltd.

Pen & Sword Books Limited incorporates the imprints of Atlas, Archaeology,
Aviation, Discovery, Family History, Fiction, History, Maritime, Military,
Military Classics, Politics, Select, Transport, True Crime, Air World,
Frontline Publishing, Leo Cooper, Remember When, Seaforth Publishing,
The Praetorian Press, Wharncliffe Local History, Wharncliffe Transport,
Wharncliffe True Crime and White Owl.

For a complete list of Pen & Sword titles please contact
PEN & SWORD BOOKS LIMITED
47 Church Street, Barnsley, South Yorkshire, S70 2AS, England
E-mail: enquiries@pen-and-sword.co.uk
Website: www.pen-and-sword.co.uk

Or
PEN AND SWORD BOOKS
1950 Lawrence Rd, Havertown, PA 19083, USA
E-mail: Uspen-and-sword@casematepublishers.com
Website: www.penandswordbooks.com

Contents

Acknowledgements

There are many people I would like to thank for making this book possible. Firstly, to Jonathan Wright from Pen & Sword for commissioning this book and giving me the platform to work on a project about such a fascinating topic. Thanks must also go to Alice Wright, Lori Jones, Charlie Simpson, Emily Robinson and Laura Hirst from Pen & Sword for their dedicated support through the writing and editing process. I owe much gratitude to my wonderful copy editor, Stephen Carver, whose incredible hard work has made this book what it is. His expertise, counsel and patience have been hugely appreciated, and he has been such a pleasure to work with.

Many thanks to all those who helped me with my research or made introductions and enquiries on my behalf to people relevant to this book: Dorothy, Michael, Julian, Catherine, Peregrine, Matthew, Sarah and Henry to name a few.

This is now the second time my father has had to put up with reading through early drafts of my manuscripts, and his corrections, advice and encouragement are greatly appreciated. Special thanks also to my mother for her endless support for this, and my other projects.

Finally, I would not have been able to write this book without the constant motivation and inspiration from my wife, who has had to put up with me either being away at various archives and libraries researching, or chained to my desk writing for days on end. I cannot thank her enough for her unwavering support.

Foreword

I have always loved James Bond. Ever since I was nine years old, when a friend showed me my first Bond movie, *Octopussy*, I was hooked. As a child, unsurprisingly, it was the films in the Bond franchise that were my fascination. But getting older, I started to enjoy the books more and soon realised that although the most recent film at the time of writing, *Spectre* (released in 2015) grossed $880 million worldwide, sixty-two years after the first book *Casino Royale* was published, almost all of the original characteristics which make Bond so popular today still remain.

There is no doubt that the films, which have so far generated over $7 billion and represent the fourth most popular film franchise ever – behind Marvel, *Star Wars* and *Harry Potter* – have been the most successful elements of Bond. However, if it were not for the creation of this iconic character by Ian Fleming, to which the films remain surprisingly loyal to this day, it could easily be argued that they would never have been such a phenomenon. These characteristics include traditional British wit, the mysteriousness of the spy world, exotic locations and fascinating people, mainly women. Ultimately, when one reads or watches James Bond, one is transported to a place of escapism and excitement.

The question is, therefore, where did these traits for Bond come from? There is obviously a large element of fiction in all of them, but when looking into the background of Ian Fleming, we see so many of the Bond features in him, gained from his personal experiences.

James Bond is at the centre of the British Secret Service, as Fleming was during the Second World War. Bond travels to exotic locations, in which he thrives, as Fleming did throughout his life, most notably Jamaica. Bond has a dry British sense of humour, which Fleming arguably had too much of. The same can be said for Fleming's interest in and passion for the women in his life, which is the characteristic for which Bond is possibly most famous.

Fleming was also an incredibly well-connected man, through his family, his professional connections and the people he would go on to befriend. Many of these fascinating characters, some of whom remain to this day household names, are the basis for most of Bond's friends and enemies. Fleming was very open about the fact that he would take his plots from real life, no matter how bizarre they might seem.

Fleming's first biographer, John Pearson, believed that 'James Bond is not really a character in this book. He is a mouthpiece for the man who inhabits him, a dummy for himself to hang clothes on, a zombie to perform the dreams of violence and daring which fascinate his creator'.[1] It is astonishing, when one puts the Bond author's own life up against that of his fictional creation, how much they cross over with each other. Whether it be the central plot of one of the Bond stories, simply the food 007 eats or the feeling he gets when driving down a road, they are all based on real experiences.

Each chapter of this book is named after the James Bond novel or short story to which the influence in Fleming's life relates. Although Chapter One is named after the first novel, *Casino Royale,* the chapters are, in the most part, chronological to Fleming's life rather than the order in which the books were written.

Sources for this book have been taken from various places, in particular from military archives around Britain, as well as over sixty books either about Fleming or the parts of history in which he was involved. Obviously, the Bond novels provided much of the narrative to this story.

There are many excellent works written about Ian Fleming and I am delighted to add to this library, which I have no doubt will never stop growing.

Part One

War

Chapter 1

Casino Royale

'Scent and smoke and sweat hit the taste buds with an acid thwack at three o'clock in the morning'.[1] No, that was not right. What about: 'Scent and smoke and sweat can suddenly combine together and hit the taste buds with an acid shock at three o'clock in the morning.'[2] Not right either, that was too drawn out. 'The scent and smoke and sweat of a casino are nauseating at three in the morning.'[3] That was the one.

After stumbling a few times with his opening line, Ian Fleming was away from the blocks and powering through his first novel. In *Casino Royale*, published in 1953 by Jonathan Cape, we meet the fictional spy for the first time, sent to a French casino to beat the bankrupt international criminal, Le Chiffre, in a high stakes game of baccarat. Despite Bond winning in the game, he is betrayed by fellow agent Vesper Lynd, captured and tortured. Fleming's several tries at opening his first foray into novel writing are a good metaphor to represent his early life: quite a few attempts at different things, before finally finding his feet.

Ian Lancaster Fleming was born on 28 May 1908 in the affluent London district of Mayfair, at 27 Green Street, just off Park Lane. His father, Valentine (Val) Fleming, was Conservative MP for Henley from 1910 until his death in 1917. *Who's Who* listed his hobbies as 'deerstalking, salmon-fishing' and 'fox-hunting', adding that he also 'hunts a pack of basset hounds'.[4] Despite exclusively having countryside interests, Val did not marry a tweed-wearing, horse-riding daughter of an Earl, as many would have predicted. Instead, Ian's mother was the beautiful bohemian Evelyn (Eve) St. Croix Rose, a strong-willed and intimidating woman who few could handle other than her husband. Val and Eve had four sons – Peter, Ian, Richard and Michael – between 1907 and 1913. It was said that Val had a particular soft spot for his second son, whom he affectionately called 'Johnny'. All the children got very little time with their father, who after the declaration of war in 1914 signed up to C Squadron of the

Queen's Own Oxfordshire Hussars, where he quickly rose to the rank of Major before being killed by enemy action in 1917.

In his obituary in *The Times*, written by none other than Winston Churchill, he is described as having a 'lovable and charming personality' and being:

> one of those younger Conservatives who easily and naturally combine loyalty to the party ties with a broad liberal outlook upon affairs and a total absence of class prejudice ... He was a man of thoughtful and tolerant opinions, which were not the less strongly or clearly held because they were not loudly or frequently asserted. The violence of faction and the fierce tumults which swayed our political life up to the very threshold of the Great War, caused him a keen distress. He could not share the extravagant passions with which the rival parties confronted each other. He felt that neither was wholly right in policy and that both were wrong in mood.[5]

For the rest of his life, Ian Fleming kept a framed copy of this in his house.

Fleming and his brothers had worshipped their father, nicknaming him 'Mokie' as it rhymed with 'smoky', because of his endless puffing on a pipe. For the rest of their childhood, the boys would pray each evening that God should make them more like Mokie. Much has been made of the fact that Fleming grew up without a father figure in his life, although any influences from this were fiercely dismissed by him. We discover when reading his novels that James Bond is an orphan, having lost his parents in a mountaineering accident. Although Fleming lost one parent rather than two, the impact on him was so great he felt completely isolated – as he imagined an orphan would – when his father did not return home from the war.

His mother did not let her children forget their father, nor his Scottish roots. When they were children, Eve would continually remind her boys to 'never forget you're a Scot'.[6] For Fleming, his Christian name was as Scottish as they came and he would always refer to himself as, at least in part, a Scot. Lancaster as a middle name came from Eve's adamant claim to be the descendent of John of Gaunt, the third son of Edward III, who became the Duke of Lancaster. Eve wanted to instil in her children 'the importance of ancestry', especially as she was acting as both their mother and father.[7]

His childhood home between Henley-on-Thames and Oxford, constructed by his grandfather four years before Fleming was born, was called Joyce Grove. He was brought up comfortably, if not luxuriously, within British middle-class society until, at the age of six, he was shipped off to Durnford Preparatory School in Dorset.

With future World War II intelligence colleagues such as Sir Stephen Hastings and Nicholas Elliott among the school's alumni, Durnford should have suited Fleming, but he detested the place. In a series of heartbreaking letters sent to his mother, a nine-year-old Ian wrote repeatedly how he was sorry not to be enjoying school. Although there with his older brother Peter, he was miserable, which was one of the only things he had in common with the other pupils who all found the harsh environment intolerable. Blessed relief from the hellish Durnford came in 1921, when at the age of twelve, Fleming moved to Eton College, the school his father and uncle had attended. With a huge sense of freedom away from the prison-like preparatory school, it is fair to say that Fleming's time at Eton was not a huge academic success.

With not enough attention given to study and far too much shown towards women, he was underperforming in the classroom from day one. However, he did find his feet on the sports pitch, a skill that he planted firmly in James Bond. In 1924, sixteen-year-old Ian won seven out of ten events at Eton's junior sports competition, a record that remains in place to this day. When he advanced into senior sports, he held the title of *Victor Ludorum*, the 'winner of the games', for two consecutive years, again a record which has yet to be beaten. Perhaps what drove Fleming to sporting success was the feeling of being caught in the shadow of his older brother Peter, who had edited the *Eton College Chronicle* before leaving for Oxford top of his class. Peter would go on to be a celebrated author and marry the world-famous actress, Celia Johnson. His desire for success was summed up by his lifelong friend Ivar Bryce, who was a contemporary at Eton: 'While not desperately competitive he would try violently to run the fastest and furthest, to jump the longest and highest, to climb the steepest … and in every way expend the last drop of a furious energy'.[8]

Unfortunately for Fleming, this admiration from his pals was not enough to appease his housemaster, E.V. Slater, who did not feel his attitude was in line with Eton's motto of *Floreat Etona*, 'Let Eton flourish'. Fleming would openly admit that he had no interest in the academic curriculum, which he felt was irrelevant. It was this type of attitude, however, which meant the jury was out on his character. On one hand, he completely disregarded everything in the classroom, but on the other he was a huge success in sport. One of his teachers, Ernan Forbes Dennis, was more positive than his housemaster, saying in a school report that Ian 'has excellent taste ... and a desire both for truth and knowledge. He is virile and ambitious, generous and kind-hearted'.[9] As a young adult, Fleming was tall, dark and very handsome, but had broken his nose while playing football at school – so badly that he required an operation to fix it – altering his near-perfect complexion. His slightly crooked nose added something of a rugged look. His friend Alan Schneider agreed it was the touch which Fleming was missing, later remarking that 'I thought this made him look like a handsome pirate'.[10] When creating his action hero in *Casino Royale*, Fleming decided to give Bond something subtly different in the guise of a thick scar that ran down his cheek making him look a little like a pirate. Fleming writes that similar to himself, Bond suffers from a congested nose due to the amount of smoke in the casino. In the same way, Ian's broken nose caused this very affect when in confined places with lots of smokers and was something he often complained about.

Leaving Eton a term early – like James Bond, who was expelled for a sexual encounter with a maid – Fleming did not have the necessary grades needed to get into the Royal Military College at Sandhurst. For the Fleming family, a career in His Majesty's Service was an absolute must. Therefore, his mother immediately sent him to a special school for intensive studying. Run by former army officer Major Trevor, this proved miraculously successful and Fleming was duly accepted into Sandhurst after only a few months of concentrated education, finishing sixth in the national entry exam. It would seem that things were starting to look up for nineteen-year-old Ian, who quickly settled into the routine of training to be an army officer. However, with a theme that would often appear in his life, Fleming's head was turned by a beautiful woman. The lady in question – Peggy Barnard – was a young local girl to whom he had taken a shine after they met at the Sandhurst sports day. Fleming asked her to stay for dinner, but she refused due to a long-standing arrangement with another man. Reacting badly to this rejection, Fleming went to Soho and found a woman of dubious virtue and subsequently caught gonorrhoea. A man with this disease was seen to be far below the standards required of a British Army Officer, and Fleming was immediately thrown out of Sandhurst.

It was Eve who again bailed her second son out of trouble, first sending him to a clinic to rid him of his 'clap' and then off to Austria. With her intention that Fleming should enter the Foreign Office, she paid for her wayward son to go to the Tennerhof in Kitzbühel, a school to help language skills and prepare men to enter to diplomatic service. It has been claimed by some biographers that each night Fleming 'was out with a different girl, and he must have slept with most of the girls in the town in a short while'.[11] This, to the relief of his mother, was not the case and Tennerhof actually suited Fleming. The wife of the headmaster, Phillis Bottom, was said to have encouraged Fleming to write for the first time at the age of nineteen. Years later, he sent her a lovely letter attributing much of his success with James Bond to her influence on him.

He was soon studying modules at Munich University and the University of Geneva. It was here he met Monique Panchaud de Bottens, a local woman he fell in love with and to whom he was briefly engaged. This behaviour was a far cry from the claims that he was always sleeping around town. But Fleming's mother pulled the strings, and not approving of Monique's humble beginnings, insisted that they break off their engagement. Her continued involvement in her son's affairs grated so badly on him that it would serve as the catalyst to his pushing away any woman of authority in his adult life.

Fleming was not going to live up to his mother's expectations of being an army officer, but her second choice was now in grasping distance, as he prepared to take his Foreign Office exams. It is a popular myth that he failed the tests spectacularly; this is untrue, as he finished seventh out of sixty-two, and it was only the top five who were accepted. Nevertheless, a fail was a fail, and he scored particularly badly in in his English exam, only getting twenty marks out of a possible hundred. By this point, despairing slightly, Eve called in a favour from Sir Roderick Jones, head of Reuters News Agency, to get Fleming some employment. With the army and Colonial Service down, it was now a case of getting her son into anything she deemed respectable. Her connections proved successful and in October 1931 Fleming was given a six-month trial at the firm on a starting salary of £150 a year. He proved a useful asset, quickly being offered the permanent position as a sub-editor and journalist for Reuters News Agency, earning £206.5s a year. From here, his career grew – at least for the next two years – so much so that his salary had doubled to £300 per year. Of his time in this industry he acquired much knowledge, in particular he learned how to write quickly and accurately. He commented years later that Reuters were in fact known to fire people for inaccuracies or being slow.

As he settled into life in London, Fleming's tastes became more sophisticated. In particular, the food and drink he would consume were becoming more extravagant as he got older. Fleming got a lot of enjoyment out of passing this trait onto James Bond, who explained to Vesper in *Casino Royale* that investing time in choosing what to eat and drink provided him with never-ending pleasure, as it made his meals so much more interesting. In a time where the effects of rationing were still being felt around Britain, one of the most appealing aspects of Fleming's writing was the detailed description of all the delicious food Bond consumes around the world.

Probably his biggest achievement at Reuters was Fleming's coverage of the show trial of six British engineers in Soviet Russia. On 25 January 1933, the secretary of British engineering firm Metropolitan-Vickers, Anna Kutusova, was grabbed and bundled into a waiting car while on her way to work. From this moment, a web of speculation was sown, which culminated in the wrongful arrest of six employees, all accused of espionage and spying. The story attracted worldwide attention, not least from Britain, whose six civilian citizens were now facing possible execution in Russia. Despite Reuters having a correspondent in Moscow, Robin Kinkead, the powers that be felt he needed support, so decided to give Fleming a chance at something big. Kinkead received a telegram from his London boss Bernard Rickatson-Hatt saying 'I am sending you Ian Fleming. One of our ablest young men to help coverage of trail'.[12] This was the break that Fleming had wanted. It was also the first time he was able to demonstrate his ability as an excellent writer. His leading article – written in the style of an epic novel – was received with much enthusiasm in London.

Fleming even requested an interview with Joseph Stalin, who refused, albeit in a handwritten letter of apology. This note was something of a souvenir for Fleming, who, according to his brother Peter, would show it 'on a number of occasions to use as a kind of super-visa to bluff his way out of awkward situations'.[13]

The trip was a huge boost for Fleming's career, with a fellow journalist who met him telegramming back to Reuters:

> Should like you to know that we fellow journalists of Ian Fleming whom none of us had ever met before his appearance here cover Met-Vickers trial not only consider him a pukha [*sic*] chap personally but have extremely high opinion of his journalistic ability ... He has given us all a run for our money.[14]

Not only did this trip give Fleming the pedestal he needed to stand on and prove his ability as a writer, it also gave him his first taste of Russia, which would become the arch nemesis of James Bond. While in Moscow, Fleming witnessed the underhand activities of the Communist State, which influenced his creation of criminal organisation SMERSH, whose task as described in *Casino Royale* was to sniff out any forms of treachery within the Soviet Secret Service. Anyone discovered to be acting outside of his or her jurisdiction would subsequently be eliminated by operatives in the organisation. The show trial that Fleming had reported on was the outcome of a parodied state, which SMERSH epitomised.

Although his bosses at Reuters shared the 'high opinion of his journalistic ability', Fleming was restless. There was always a sense that he was not fulfilling his family expectations of working in his forefathers' industry, banking. Underlying that, he lived an extravagant lifestyle and needed more money to be able to fund it. Fleming's grandfather had been the Scottish financier Robert Fleming, one of seven children, who founded the Scottish American Investment Trust and the merchant bank Robert Fleming & Co. Such was the poverty he grew up in, five of his six brothers died from living in impoverished conditions. Becoming a self-made millionaire, by the time of his death in 1933, Robert had crossed the Atlantic no fewer than 128 times to America, where his business success was booming. Fleming's grandfather, who rivalled J.Pierpont Morgan and Jacob Schiff, had the same words of advice to give anyone who asked for it: 'Lairn to say no, laddie. Lairn to say no'.[15]

Eve was adamant that Fleming should follow the tradition of his grandfather and father and enter the business. Not least because he was displaying the taste for an expensive lifestyle, and his mother knew that there were few professions that would sustain this. Despite the fact that he came from a wealthy family, and Fleming's grandfather had made a small fortune, the terms of Val's will meant that Ian and his brothers would not receive any of it until Eve either died or remarried. Therefore, they had money in reaching distance, but for the present time, they would need to make their own ends meet. Giving in to the forceful wishes of his mother, Fleming joined the merchant bank Cull & Co in October 1933, before becoming a stockbroker in 1935 at Rowe and Pitman, where he was appointed as a partner. This was an exceptional position to be offered, which was thanks mainly to his association with Robert Fleming. For Fleming, not only was he offered a position he was twenty years too inexperinced, his remuneration was much higher than he had ever aniticipated. This was especially the case as Fleming did not possess any of his grandfather's natural financial flair. In fact, soon after he joined Rowe and Pitman, one colleague at the firm believed that 'as a stockbroker old Ian really must have been among the world's worst'.[16]

The work involved much wining and dining of clients, which Fleming took to instantly. Another colleague recalled how he 'would take a great deal of trouble to make sure that the food was as good as he could get. Over the lobster or the tornadoes he would start talking rather knowledgeably about what he called the "strategy of investments"'.[17] This type of work was not conducive to a healthy lifestyle, but was not something that worried Fleming, who at this point was smoking 400 custom-made Morland cigarettes, blended from three types of Turkish tobacco and emblazoned with three gold rings, each week. In *Casino Royale*, Bond has a similar habit, albeit slightly worse, smoking over seventy cigarettes of the same blend each day. Fleming was also drinking like a fish, mostly gin, which he would consume by the bottle. When his doctor suggested that a bottle of gin per day was having adverse effects on his health, he moved to having a bottle of Old Grandad bourbon instead. His ability to hold his drink was something Fleming was particularly proud of, as he saw it as a sign of strength. James Bond is given the same power; for example in *Casino Royale*, in one card game alone, Bond drinks a vodka martini, a carafe of vodka, two entire bottles of champagne and finally a large brandy. Although even Fleming would struggle with this quantity in one sitting, he was able to outdrink most of his friends.

With more money now at his fingertips, Fleming bought himself a flat at 22A Ebury Street, which suited his criteria that the location was easily accessible from the City and Chelsea, but not too close to Fitzrovia.

It was during this period that Fleming got his first taste of spying. Curiously, in 1939, he was approached by the Foreign Office to carry out an assignment in Russia. The reasons behind their choice remain somewhat of a mystery, but it is likely that given his sudden rise to celebrity, at least for a few hours, during the show trial in Moscow, he would be perfect for the job. Seconded temporarily to *The Times* as his cover, Fleming was sent to Russia to write a special intelligence report.

While in Moscow, Fleming was a sponge, absorbing everything he could to take back for his debrief in the Foreign Office, believing himself to be completely inconspicuous. He unofficially teamed up with a *Daily Express* correspondent, Sefton Delmer, who recalled that as soon as he saw Fleming 'I knew he was on some intelligence job ... he made such a determined show of typing away whenever the Russians were looking'.[18] On their return from Moscow aboard the Warsaw Express, while Fleming watched the countryside fly past, Delmer was busy trying to memorise his notes. He intended to then tear them into tiny pieces and throw them out of the window, in case he was arrested. Fleming mockingly enquired why his friend did not plan to eat them – a practice he believed was common among spies – making light of Delmer's paranoia. Delmer would have the last laugh, as the train was stopped at the border, and the men were searched thoroughly. Fleming was found to be carrying a carton of latex contraceptives in his possession, which he later claimed were for chemical testing by experts, but were likely also for personal use. As the Russian guards examined the condoms in some detail, Delmer turned to a concerned looking Fleming and commented, 'You should have swallowed them,' before walking off and leaving his friend to face the music alone.[19]

*

With his comfortable upbringing, and his taste for expensive food, drink and cigarettes, Fleming created much of James Bond in his own image. Not just his looks, but also his hobbies and passions. Fleming enjoyed gambling, though he admitted he would usually end up playing for minimal amounts of money, in part due to his available funds but also his lack of practice. Fleming makes sure Bond is infinitely better than him at gambling, claiming that Bond had never yet lost a game of cards while playing at such high stakes as in *Casino Royale*.

Another passion for Fleming was his cars. He loved everything about the machines, especially the feeling they gave him when driven at speed. He recorded the pleasure he felt in 1927 when he drove a three-litre Bugatti on a stretch of road outside Henley, reaching the dizzying speed of over 100 mph for the first time. Describing cars as a long-lasting interest of his, Fleming made sure that Bond was not only as passionate as he, but equally well equipped. The cars became a staple for James Bond in the books, and arguably one of the most famous traits of the agent in the film franchise. Fleming was clear in *Casino Royale* that Bond's only real personal hobby was his car, which like his creator, Bond drove with incredible skill and pleasure.

It was passions such as his cars, gambling, fine dining, golf and sex that gave Fleming his pleasure in life. In the most part though, he was not a happy person, and this was threaded into James Bond's character, whose life was always described as a mixture of adrenalin and melancholy. Fleming's biographer, John Pearson, recalled him as a man with a 'sad, sardonic smile as he clenched the Dunhill holder between his battered teeth, and drew heavily upon his umpteenth Morland's Special of the morning'.[20]

Clearly, from his early life, there are many personal experiences which Fleming used to create Bond, but there were many other people who influenced his creation. It is impossible to trace any one person that the character was based on, although there have been many assertions. Similarly, his name comes from various places and there are many claims from people for suggesting it. When he set about writing *Casino Royale*, Fleming told his friend C.H. Forster that to create a name for his hero, he would simply think of two names of students from his school and then swap their Christian names around. When Forster told Fleming that the first two names from his school register had been James Aitken and Harry Bond, Fleming apparently got excited, claiming that James Bond was the type of name he was looking for. Whether this was the source or not, Fleming said years after creating Bond that he had wanted the dullest and most mundane sounding name he could find, albeit one that was suitably British and masculine. Although he struggled to find the right name initially, he knew an extravagant name – for example Peregrine Maltravers – would not work for his mysterious government spy and assassin.

Historian Ben Macintyre agreed with Fleming's thoughts on this topic: 'With no offence to Peregrines worldwide, this is not a name women tend to go to bed with on first acquaintance'.[21] It is no doubt of great relief to all enthusiasts of Fleming's work that the lead character was not one, 'Bond, Peregrine Bond.'

The most likely and commonly known reason for the name James Bond came from the author of *Field Guide to Birds of the West Indies*. This was a favourite book of Flemings and sat on his desk in his Jamaican home, 'Goldeneye'. Its author, the real James Bond, made contact with Fleming through his wife years later. She wrote to Fleming that 'I told my JB he could sue you for defamation of character' but cheerfully concluded that the Bond books are 'too much fun for that'. Homage to the ornithologist James Bond was paid in the film *Die Another Day*, when Pierce Brosnan is seen holding a copy of the book, with the author's name scratched out. Fleming actually met the real James Bond on one occasion, where he offered – in return for the use of the name 'James Bond' – the unlimited use of the name Ian Fleming for when he discovered a new species of bird. Fleming joked that Bond should wait until he found a species that was really ugly and dispicable, so he would truely be getting his own back. Fortunately for Fleming, the real James Bond never did.

Fleming's life to this point provided him with all the inspiration he needed to create the character of James Bond. He had decided on his looks, his hobbies and his personality. Now, Fleming needed to learn about sabotage and spying to put his new creation into action. Luckily, with the outbreak of war looming, he was about to be offered the perfect opportunity.

Chapter 2

For Your Eyes Only

The short story 'For Your Eyes Only', published on 11 April 1960, sees James Bond sent to Jamaica to avenge the killing of a couple called the Havelocks. They are friends with the leader of the Secret Service, Admiral Sir Miles Messervy KCMG, more commonly known as M, to the extent that M had served as best man at their wedding. For Bond's eighth literary outing, he is not officially on a mission, but rather carrying out a favour for the man he hero worships, M, who in turn trusts Bond to carry out this personal task. Bond is able to find the Havelocks' murderer, von Hammerstein, who he kills. Throughout this short story, the reader has a detailed view of Bond's relationship with M. Although the character can be traced to a few people, including Fleming's own mother, who was would sign her letters with an M, and the leader of the Special Operation Executive (SOE), Colin Gubbins, the person with the closest resemblance is the head of the Naval Intelligence Division (NID), Rear Admiral Godfrey. It was Godfrey who would fill the void created in Fleming's life by the death of his father.

If one were to ask about Godfrey, a description which would not be associated with him was that of an appeaser. This he shared with many, not least the former Chancellor of the Exchequer Winston Churchill, who said in a speech in 1940 that each neutral country 'hopes that if he feeds the crocodile enough, the crocodile will eat him last'.[1] Godfrey felt that politicians through the 1930s were bowing down to the pressure coming from Germany. Aggrieved by the terms of the Treaty of Versailles in 1919, Germany had effectively taken the full burden of guilt for the Great War and was now paying the hefty sum of £6.6 billion (the equivalent of £2.9 trillion at the time of writing) in damages. Godfrey was appalled by what he saw in Germany, as out of the deep depression and gloom came Austrian-born Nazi Party leader Adolf Hitler. Seen as the only offering of salvation, the Great War veteran rose quickly in the government to the position of Chancellor in 1933, before assuming the role of Führer a year later. On 12 March 1938 Hitler marched into Austria with very little resistance in the *Anschluss* annexation.

It was not long until further land would fall to Hitler, handed over by the British Prime Minister, Neville Chamberlain, an ardent appeaser. At the Munich Conference on 29 September 1938, European leaders agreed to break the Treaty of Versailles and allow the Germans control of the Sudetenland bordering Germany and Czechoslovakia, which had been confiscated in 1919. Hitler, who was present, demanded that 'the oppression of three and a half million Germans in Czechoslovakia cease and that the inalienable right to self-determination take its place'.[2] Czech President Edvard Beneš was not invited to the conference, despite a large chunk of his country being placed on the negotiating table. He and his people had no choice but to fall in line. Neville Chamberlain returned from the conference, in his mind, victorious. At Heston Aerodrome, he produced a piece of paper that he waved in the air saying that this 'Anglo-German Naval Agreement is symbolic of the desire of our two peoples never to go to war with one another again. This is ... peace with honour'.[3] Critics of Chamberlain were far reaching, from the political elite like Winston Churchill, to Russian President Joseph Stalin and the lesser known like Rear Admiral Godfrey.

Chamberlain's notion of peace was far from the reality, and it soon started to slip through his fingers like sand. By Monday, 22 May 1939, the Foreign Ministers of Fascist Italy and Nazi Germany signed the 'Pact of Steel', stating that they would unite against Great Britain and France militarily, economically and in wartime production. It was becoming ever clearer that another war was looming.

*

Two days after the Pact of Steel, on Wednesday, 24 May 1939 at the Carlton Grill in London, Ian Fleming arrived for a mysterious lunch. He had been invited by an acquaintance, Admiral Aubrey Hugh-Smith, the brother of Lancelot 'Lancy' Hugh Smith, with whom he worked at Rowe and Pitman at the time. When Fleming arrived, Hugh-Smith introduced him to his other guest, a fifty-one-year-old man with a long face that wore the constant look of displeasure. This expression would be the basis for the character of 'M', as would the personality of the man who wore it. This was Rear Admiral John Godfrey, who had recently been appointed Director of Naval Intelligence on 24 January 1939.

14

John Henry Godfrey was born on 10 July 1888 in Handsworth. Growing up in an affluent family, he attended King Edward's School in Birmingham. He then moved to Bradfield College, where he studied alongside many other future and prominent members of the armed forces, of which he would become one of the most established. With his heart set on life in the navy, at the age of eighteen Godfrey enlisted at the Britannia Royal Naval College in Dartmouth. When the Great War broke out, aged twenty-seven, Godfrey was ordered to serve on HMS *Euryalus*. He watched from afar as the Battle of Heligoland Bight unfolded in 1914 in the south-eastern part of the North Sea, which was the first naval battle of the war. Although HMS *Euryalus* was in the vicinity, sitting in reserve on the Dutch coast, she did not take part in any action. Later that year, HMS *Euryalus* was assigned to 7th Cruiser Squadron in the English Channel along with HMS *Aboukir,* HMS *Cressy* and HMS *Hogue.* On 22 September 1914, while Godfrey's ship had returned to port to recoal, her three sister ships were sunk by one of Germany's 329 submarines, killing 1,135 British sailors. Such was the luck of war, HMS *Euryalus* and everyone aboard left the scene without a scratch, unlike the vast majority of their fleet who were making their way to the bottom of the ocean.

From 1915, Godfrey was promoted onto the staff of the Commander-in-Chief in the Mediterranean aboard HMS *Repulse*, where he remained for the rest of the war. Like Godfrey, the fictional M is said to have also served on this ship. After the conflict concluded, he was promoted again, this time to Deputy Director at the Royal Navy Staff College, before moving into the intelligence space, assuming the role of Director of Naval Intelligence (DNI). Here was a man seen to be going places in the navy and his superiors were keen that he continue to prove himself.

His predecessor in the role, Admiral Sir Reginald Hall, became a close confident and went on to provide regular council to Godfrey. On the topic, Godfrey recalled that 'to no one am I more indebted than Reggie Hall, the DNI during the Kaiser's war. He came to see me (when I was appointed DNI) and thereafter very unobtrusively offered me full access to his great store of knowledge and judgement on this strange commodity, intelligence, about which I then knew hardly anything'.[4] Hall had used a stockbroker called Claud Serocold as his personal assistant during World War I. This lead the new Director of Naval Intelligence to decide he should hire someone in Serocold's image.

This is slightly surprising as, although Godfrey did trust Hall's opinion, he did not rate many in his predecessor's team. Godfrey remarked in his diary when he first arrived at his new post in early 1939 that it was full of 'retired officers who had not found active employment in civilian life and were practically unworkable through neglect of their brains'.[5] Nevertheless, taking the advice from Hall, Godfrey turned to some of his influential friends to ask for potential candidates for the role of his personal assistant. Specifically, he sought help from the Governor of the Bank of England, Montagu Norman, Head of Barings Bank, Edward Peacock, and Chairman of Hambros Bank, Olaf Hambro. Through family connections, Montagu Norman had put Ian Fleming's name forward as the perfect candidate; he had the right military background in his family and despised his role in banking, so would likely jump at the chance of a new career. Godfrey needed to choose carefully, as he was 'an uncompromising, precise, short-tempered and loyal older man' who was notoriously very difficult to work for.[6] However, he was self-aware enough to know that he needed to not only find someone he could tolerate, but more importantly someone who would put up with his volatile style. Author Kingsley Amis calculated that throughout the Bond books, the most common words used to describe M are 'angry', 'brutal', 'cold', 'curt', 'dry', 'gruff', 'stern' and 'testy'. By the accounts of those who worked for Godfrey, these adjectives certainly rang true.

Over their lunch at the Carlton Grill, the role was described to Fleming, who later recalled that Godfrey's criteria was for a multilingual man of roughly his age, who had a good grasp of how the City worked. Godfrey explained that Fleming had been recommended to him as someone who ticked all of these boxes. Fleming failed to disclose over lunch that he was a far cry from the skills Godfrey had described. It was true that although Fleming was a decent linguist, speaking French and German fluently with Russian coming on well, his understanding of the City, London's financial district, was almost non-existent as he had no interest in learning anything about it whatsoever. Nevertheless, he used one of his most powerful traits, his charm. His ability to win over everyone and anyone he wanted when he tried was a mannerism that would hold him in good stead in the coming years. He was particularly good at socialising with older men, something which he had practiced throughout his childhood. After lunch was over, Fleming received the following letter from a secretary within the Admiralty:

> Sir,
>
> I am commanded by my Lords Commissioners of the Admiralty to thank you for the offer of your services to the Admiralty and to inform you that as they would probably desire to avail themselves of your offer should hostilities break out. My Lords have given directions that you should be earmarked for service under the Admiralty in the event of emergency.
>
> I am, sir, your obedient servant.
> N. Macleod.[7]

In short, Fleming had got the job, albeit, he had not applied for it or even signalled his interest in pursuing it over lunch. Although a naval salary for Fleming's proposed rank was a far cry from how much he would need to keep living his extravagant lifestyle, something about the position appealed to him. Not least because he got on with Godfrey and liked the prospect of adventure the role offered, this was also the first time in his professional life that someone had wanted him, and without his mother's influence.

Fleming duly joined the Royal Naval Volunteer Reserve (RNVR) on 1 June 1939 as a Lieutenant but was quickly promoted by Godfrey to the rank of Commander, a title he would use for the rest of his life and assigned to his creation James Bond. In an obituary written by M when Bond is thought to be dead, Fleming writes in a rather mocking tone that Bond was quickly promoted from Lieutenant to Commander within the Special Branch of the RNVR, thanks mainly to the value and satisfaction he provided to his superiors.

In his new role, Fleming immediately started by writing reports for the Admiral, which Godfrey insisted should 'aim at three virtues. First, it should have impact. Second, it should be unambiguous … Third, it should have the brevity that comes only from clear intention'. His new personal assistant did this with ease and was soon entrusted with more work. He also used Fleming to represent him at important routine interdepartmental conferences. But Fleming's role was far wider reaching than either man had anticipated.

Within the structure of Naval Intelligence, Fleming worked in department NID 17 in an office called Room 39, which was Godfrey's personal staff, 'responsible that the most important items of intelligence other than those of a purely operational nature, are brought to [DNI's] attention'.[8] Fleming was now the eyes and ears of his boss, becoming essentially his gatekeeper. Documents would arrive on his desk with two zeros on the front, meaning they were of the most sensitive nature. This was where Fleming got the idea for Bond's codename, 007. He explained in an interview with *Playboy* years later that, the double-0 prefix first came to mind for him while working at the Admiralty, as he noticed that all top-secret signals had the double-0 prefix written on the front. At the time, Fleming did not realise that this would later become one of the main identifying features of his world-famous hero.

In a move that few in his position would ever dare to do, Fleming would stop papers going to his boss because he viewed them as irrelevant. On several occasions he would scribble the words 'no importance' on a memo, and have it taken back to the officer who had written it, most likely of a more senior rank than Fleming.[9] Working from Room 38 and 39 in the Admiralty – based directly on the Mall, close to the Prime Minister's residence at No. 10 Downing Street and the Foreign Office – Godfrey immediately gravitated towards his new personal assistant. He trusted Fleming over everyone else, stating 'my idea was that I would tell Ian everything so that if anything happened to me there would be one man who would know what was going on – he could ensure the continuity of the department'.[10]

Fleming's lifelong refusal to accept authority, mainly born out of his mother's continual interference, would have caused most junior officers serious problems in the Navy. He told Godfrey from the start that he would not refer to him as 'Sir' despite the fact that everyone else did. Instead of being irritated by the insubordination of his thirty-one-year-old assistant, Godfrey appreciated that Fleming 'would not hesitate to argue against a senior officer if he thought that officer was wrong'.[11] In an establishment of 'yes men', here was someone who would give his honest opinion. Both men grew to respect each other hugely, which is reflected by the many times Fleming wrote of Bond's admiration, respect and in some cases even love for M. This summed up exactly his feeling for Godfrey, which would remain the same for the rest of his life. After Fleming died, Godfrey was not as complimentary about his fictional self, saying that Fleming 'turned me into that unsavoury character, M' and that 'The end result did not convince or thrill'.[12]

Work was fast paced, exciting and stressful for Fleming and his colleagues. One of the secretaries, Mrs Stewart, who joined NID after Fleming in November 1942, recalled her routine of 9.30am to 12.45pm spent working 'at high pressure ... almost always operational work involving the rapid assessment of signals and dispositions'. From 12.45pm to 2.00pm there was time to have 'a noisy, unrestful, but generally nutritious and satisfying lunch'. The remainder of the day until 7.00pm was taken up with longer term research projects before heading to the canteen for dinner, which 'must without exception have been one of the most drab, unattractive and unimaginative wartime institutions in Britain'. She would then return to the office to tackle further tasks until 11.00pm, which would call for another visit to the canteen for 'a half cooked Welsh rarebit and a cup of coffee', before more work and then finally the mercy of bed.[13] Although Fleming worked in the same building – described by one visitor as 'baize' with 'tall westerly windows' which 'were crisscrossed with sticky tape to reduce splinters from bomb blast' – the canteen was not somewhere he often frequented.[14] Instead, he would usually dine out with Godfrey, so important private naval conversations could continue.

For Fleming, the job got him right into the centre of the intelligence service, including all the most secret operations. Thanks to this, he found the war above all, incredibly exciting. This included being the main liaison officer for the NID with the other two armed services, the Army and Royal Air Force. The three intelligence arms, although run independently, were centrally governed by the Special Operations Executive, known as the SOE. After the Dunkirk evacuation on 17 July 1940, in a desperate attempt to withstand the Nazi war machine, the newly appointed British Prime Minister, Winston Churchill, and his War Cabinet set up the Combined Operations Headquarters, which had 'complete discretion over instruction in combined operations for the three services, with full control'.[15] Churchill appointed his close ally and personal friend Admiral Sir Roger Keyes as Director of Combined Operations. Keyes immediately set about reorganising the different offshoot intelligence services. Within one week, upon the advice of Keyes, the War Cabinet established the SOE 'to co-ordinate all action, by way of subversion and sabotage, against the enemy overseas'.[16]

This new organisation was formed of propaganda unit 'Department EH', the sabotage operation created by SIS, 'Section D' and the War Office's research department 'MI(R)'.

Known outside of its inner circles as the Inter Services Research Bureau or simply SO2, the SOE was the only British Secret Service organisation to be terminated at the end of the war. According to historian Brian Lett, 'officially SOE did not exist, and it operated on a strict "need to know" basis, both in its relations with the three Armed Services, and within its own ranks'.[17] The SOE was held under the political management of Hugh Dalton, Minister of Economic Warfare, who according to his diary was told by Churchill after his appointment to 'now, set Europe ablaze'.[18] Dalton's first agenda item was to appoint someone to operationally lead this organisation. He knew exactly who should do such a task, a man who would go on to be one of the most influential people in Fleming's life during the war, a forty-five-year-old 'short wiry Scottish Highlander' called Major General Sir Colin McVean Gubbins, known simply as M.

Born in Japan in 1896, Gubbins was the offspring of an English diplomat father and a Highland Scot mother. With his father in such a profession, Gubbins grew up with his grandparents on the harsh but beautiful Isle of Mull, while his parents lived and travelled to all corners of the world. Having been privately educated at Cheltenham College, Gubbins attended the Royal Military Academy in Woolwich and was soon commissioned into the Royal Artillery at the start of the Great War. His fierce fighting was recognised with the prestigious Military Cross after he courageously led a rescue party to drag wounded members of his gun detachment to safety, while under heavy shelling. After his heroic act in 1915, he was shot in the neck the following year, but only spent eleven days in hospital before returning to the front line. Then, within another year, he was caught in a mustard gas attack near Arras resulting in another short spell in hospital, but was quickly back in action. It was only in 1918 that he suffered too badly to be able to remain in the trenches. However, his pain was not from enemy hostility, but rather from body lice, which caused him to get the dreaded 'trench fever' from which he would only recover once being shipped back to Britain. Regaining health from this disease was in no way certain, and many of the one million sufferers during the war did not survive, or if they did, it left lasting effects. For Gubbins, the road to recovery took some time, but he returned to full health and in 1919 he was sent overseas, first to Russia and then to Ireland in 1921.

Known for his linguistic skills, Gubbins competently spoke French, Russian and Urdu, which made him particularly popular with his military employers. As another war loomed, in 1939 he was recruited into the War Office's Research Division. His remit was to create guides on underhand warfare, small enough that they 'could be consumed in less than two minutes, if swallowed with a large glass of water' to prevent them falling into enemy hands. He wrote three: *The Art of Guerrilla Warfare*, *The Partisan Leader's Handbook* and *How to Use High Explosives*. He later commented that the task was somewhat of a challenge as 'there was not a single book to be found in any library in any language which dealt with the subject[s]' he was writing about. Instead, according to historian Giles Milton, he drew inspiration from 'Sinn Fein and T.E. Lawrence of Arabia, as well as from Al Capone and his Chicago Gangsters'.[19]

When the Second World War began, the War Office immediately sent Gubbins to Warsaw as the Country Head of Intelligence. This assignment was short lived, as the Nazis soon arrived in Poland and he was forced to flee. He was then sent to Norway under a similar guise, this time tasked with setting up a special defensive commando unit, following many of the principles he had put onto paper in his guides. The team he created in Norway began doing all they could to delay the Nazi advance. Soon, with the fall of the country looming, he returned to Britain where he became the Director of Operations and Training under Dalton for the SOE. Within the space of four years, he would go on to be promoted, replacing Charles Hambro in September 1943 as Head of SOE.

Gubbins was an enthusiast of technology and equipment, so set about establishing a research department. This consisted of various laboratories which designed and manufactured essential pieces of equipment for agents to use in the field. Run by Charles Fraser-Smith, the types of inventions his department came up with would include escape saws for captured spies concealed in buttons, signet rings and a pipe. He also created cameras hidden in cigarette lighters and garlic-laced chocolate, given to spies landing in France so their breath smelt suitably local. Possibly the most famous of their inventions was the 'explosive turd', which was an above-ground land mine. With the advantage of not needing to be buried, this weapon was easy for saboteurs to deploy and was incredibly realistic, having been designed based on specimens from London zoo. Over the course of the war, Fraser-Smith would go on to commission over 300 firms around London to build various gadgets for his agents.

As an abrupt and decisive man, Gubbins' personality was personified within the organisation, where he complemented its reputation perfectly. Described by other intelligence bodies as 'an upstart organisation', the SOE was immediately looked upon with suspicion and jealousy by the other departments it now ultimately controlled. This was a new organisation, favoured by Churchill, who swooped into the intelligence world and instantly took charge. They had not earned their stripes, and this was continually made clear to all in the department throughout the war. Along with Gubbins, the primary recruits came from all walks of life, from city workers to journalists and engineers. With no military instinct, almost all the earlier recruits did not conform to hierarchy or bureaucratic conventions. Of course, this added further fuel to the anti-SOE fire.

Gubbins quickly gained an unsavoury reputation among his counterparts in the intelligence world, in particular the Secret Intelligence Service, known as SIS or MI6. According to the historian Keith Jeffery, SIS is 'the oldest continuous surviving foreign intelligence-gathering organisation in the world'. Founded in October 1909, it 'grew from modest beginnings' to a point where its intelligence was the best in the world.[20] At this time, SIS was run by Stewart Menzies, simply known as C. Although the SIS was completely independent of the SOE – as the two organisations had competing objectives – their paths were inescapably tangled. With the former focused purely on silent intelligence gathering and the latter on loud sabotage operations, fulfilling Churchill's request to 'set Europe ablaze', their conflicting agendas were bound to clash, and they regularly did. Alan Hillgarth, Naval Attaché in Madrid, with whom Fleming would go on to work closely during the war, explained that 'when SOE was formed as a separate entity from SIS, there was inevitably rivalry between them. Though their functions were different, there were unavoidable instances of trespass'. He added that one 'cannot carry out clandestine operations without intelligence to guide you, and you cannot help acquiring intelligence in the course of proceedings'.[21]

The several arms of sabotage and intelligence therefore needed to put their differences aside and start working together. For Godfrey, this was a task that not only was he very bad at, it was something he had absolutely no interest in doing whatsoever. He made little effort to disguise his resentment of Gubbins' organisation. He despised the SOE, something he was not quiet about:

> I have been in conflict with [the SOE] again and again on one subject or another, and have often been exasperated to the point of despair by some folly … This is not to say they have not been doing a sound job of work in the past, but the need for self-advertising in order to gain recognition, and a tendency to boast due to their inferiority complex, had tended to obscure the real value of their work.[22]

As always, he therefore turned to his personal assistant. Godfrey reflected that Fleming learnt 'that intelligence may be a sticky commodity which sometimes needs sugar coating and that the purveyor of bad tidings is unwelcome'. This was a somewhat ironic statement for the Director of Naval Intelligence to make, as he had little concept of how to sugar coat anything. Godfrey went on further, lecturing Fleming on 'how to reconcile sugar coating and bad tidings with speed', adding it was 'an aptitude possessed by few'.[23] A trait which Fleming soon picked up on was that of Godfrey's occasional waffling, something which he bestowed upon his fictional creation of M, who according to Bond in 'For Your Eyes Only' was prone to talking around the topic, rather than getting to the point.

It was in 1941 that Fleming first met the Head of SOE. This was a monumental meeting, the image of the man standing in front of him – tall and balding with a chiselled face, firm moustache and bushy eyebrows – would, along with Godfrey, inspire the creation of Fleming's fictional secret service boss. Descriptions of Gubbins' features appear throughout the Bond series, especially in 'For Your Eyes Only', where, for example, Fleming describes his grey-blue eyes in considerable and intricate detail. Of course, most famous was his use of the codename M, to which the character is almost exclusively known.

Similar to Godfrey, Gubbins lacked the charm and diplomacy that Fleming displayed so effortlessly. In 'For Your Eyes Only', it is revealed that like both men, 'M did not give a damn for the susceptibilities of any Ministry and thought nothing of going behind their backs'.[24] Fleming, on the other hand, was willing to play the game, which he did to win over his boss's biggest rival. Setting about building his relationship with the SOE, initially Fleming suggested having weekly meetings with Lieutenant Colonel Taylor, whose respective role was to liaise with the intelligence arms of the three armed forces. But soon Fleming was granted direct access to M himself, beginning in January 1941, and continuing through the war. A colleague of Fleming's observed that 'Godfrey was quite happy to leave much of the liaison work that was necessary to Ian Fleming' and made little attempt to intervene.[25] Fleming was quickly carving out a role for himself much larger than either he or his boss had ever envisaged.

Fleming was clever in his dealings with the two departments. He would play the sides off on each other, making Gubbins and Taylor feel that he was leaning towards their way of thinking, and was not simply a spokesperson for the other side. However, he remained fiercely loyal to his naval boss and never crossed the line. Fleming had gained a lot of trust from Godfrey to have been given such responsibility.

So good was he at wooing Gubbins that at one point it was even suggested that Fleming should move over to the SOE and liaise back to the NID, hence doing his job but from the other side of the fence. This, it was implied, would help with the problem of poor communication between the two departments. Godfrey received a letter from Sir Frank Nelson, a member of Gubbins' team, proposing 'the ideal solution' to improve contact 'would be the transfer to SOE of an officer RN, of about the rank of commander, who has worked in the Plans Division at the Admiralty. Our idea would be to appoint this officer as a member of our special planning stuff [who] directs, supervises and checks all plans for our various operations'.[26] Godfrey was having none of it. He wrote back politely but firmly dismissing the idea and when he broached the subject with Fleming directly, he was pleased to hear that his personal assistant would not have entertained the idea either. This further bonded the two men and Godfrey grew increasingly reliant and fond of Fleming, later commenting that he should have had his job with 'I his naval advisor'.[27]

As of September 1942, Fleming's remit was further expanded to include Joint Intelligence Committee work, daily situation reports as well as a side project of writing ideas for potential espionage operations for NID. Fleming's nephew Fergus described his uncle's time in the war as 'one of ingenuity and daring', producing schemes which were 'notable for their imagination'.[28]

On 29 September 1939, days after war had been declared, Godfrey issued a long-anticipated document to intelligence chiefs, written by his personal assistant, just four months after employing him. With another war now starting, the Allied Forces – initially consisting of France, Poland and Britain – needed to quickly get one step ahead of their enemy. Named the 'Trout Memo', Fleming's document listed ways for 'bamboozling the Germans at sea' through 'deception, ruses de guerre, passing on false information and so on'. A big fan of fly-fishing, Godfrey had the memo named accordingly as he felt the document, like a fisherman, 'casts patiently all day. He frequently changes his venue and his lures. If he has frightened a fish he may give the mater a rest for half-an-hour, but his main endeavour, is to attract fish by something he sends out from his boat'.[29]

The Trout Memo served as a bible for espionage activity within NID, containing fifty-one ingenious ways of 'introducing ideas into the heads of the Germans' through false information. There were suggestions such as 'setting adrift tins of explosive disguised as food' which had 'instructions on the outside in many languages' in the hope that 'hungry enemy sailors or submariners would pick them up, try to heat the tins, and blow themselves up'. Other ideas devised by Fleming included 'dropping footballs painted with luminous paint to attract submarines' and 'distributing messages cursing Hitler's Reich in bottles from a fictitious U-boat captain to cause unrest among the enemy'.[30]

Although most of the ideas in the Trout Memo would be kicked into the long grass as the war progressed, there was one which caught the imagination of Charles Cholmondeley, a twenty-five-year-old secondee into the security service from the Royal Air Force, nearly four years later. Number 28 was headed 'A suggestion' and 'not a nice one' in which 'A corpse dressed as an airman, with [false] despatches in his pockets, could be dropped on the coast, supposedly from a parachute that had failed'. The concept was further fleshed out to explain that 'there is no difficulty in obtaining corpses at the Naval Hospital, but, of course, it would have to be a fresh one'.[31]

In April 1943, Cholmondeley borrowed the idea for what would be one of World War II's most infamous and successful deception plans, *Operation Mincemeat*. Dropping the dead body of tramp Glyndwr Michael dressed as a naval officer off the coast of Huelva, it was washed ashore with papers purporting that the Allies intended to invade Greece and Sardinia, rather than the expected target of Sicily. The Nazis fell for the ruse spectacularly, moving troops away from Sicily, which remained the target for the invasion named *Operation Husky* and was successfully taken after the landing on 9 July 1943.

*

Writing the Trout Memo for Fleming had been a pleasure – although it would be another four years before he would see the fruits of his labour bear out in *Operation Mincemeat* – as this was the type of intelligence he enjoyed. Since playing sport at school, he had not felt enjoyment like this, and he was eager to continue challenging himself.

On 10 May 1940, the code word 'Danzig' was sent down all Nazi radio waves, signalling the start of Hitler's invasion of the Netherlands, Belgium and France. Within days, German troops were advancing quickly towards France and its capital. It was only a matter of time before the crumbling French army would fall. But the French Navy was a different matter, as boats and sailors are much simpler to move than vehicles and soldiers. It was deemed that naval vessels falling into the hands of the enemy were far more dangerous than army or air force losses. As later shown following the Dunkirk evacuation, the Germans were far superior to the British in terms of infantry and air force; the latter was 1.5 million men strong and during the conflict Germany would produce nearly 120,000 planes. Germany's weakness, if they had one, was their navy of just fifty-seven overwater vessels compared to Britain's 368. With the outcome of the war in the balance, the French navy falling into the hands of the Germans could be the tipping weight to their victory of Europe.

The man in charge of the French Navy was François Darlan, a much-loved Admiral of the Fleet. It was essential for the Admiralty to keep communication open with Darlan, who held the key to his fleet, as the fate of France unfolded. Darlan had withdrawn from his Paris headquarters to Chateau d'Artigny near Tours. Although he had allowed Captain C. S. Holland to accompany him as the British Admiralty representative, Holland was struggling to persuade Darlan to flee France to England, taking his navy with him. The immediate issue faced by the British was that all communication between Darlan, through Holland to London, had been from Paris. Godfrey was concerned that if, or more likely when, Paris fell, communication would be cut off and therefore the ability for Holland to pass on messages and agreements from London would be severed. Holland had his work cut out, as Darlan was far from devoted to Britain, with him even reminding Churchill at dinner some years before that his own great-grandfather had been killed at Trafalgar. The only concession he had so far agreed was that just two of the 189 ships in the French Fleet, the *Richelieu* and the *Jean Bart*, could 'go to England if the risk from the air is too serious'.[32] As for the remaining 187 ships, they were staying where they were.

To keep the communication lines with Darlan open, Fleming suggested that he and a wireless operator should travel immediately to France. Here they could get as close as possible to Darlan's new headquarters and be on hand for Holland should he need to send or receive messages from the Admiralty. Years later, Fleming recalled that the only reason for him to suggest this was to escape the stuffy nature of Room 39 and get the chance to endulge in some French culture.

Godfrey eagerly agreed and on 13 June 1940 Fleming landed at Le Bourget airfield near Paris. Here, he somehow acquired a radio operator from the vicinity, which in itself was an impressive feat, 'the nature of which [Godfrey] never understood'.[33] Fleming was even able to obtain an official letter from the Air Ministry requesting that 'Lieutenant I.L. Fleming be given return passage by air to London on any date that suited him'. With his wireless operator in tow, the recently turned thirty-three-year-old Fleming made his way to Tours and set up camp outside Chateau d'Artigny.

Two days after his arrival, Fleming passed his first message to Darlan urging him yet again to 'bring over your fleet' to Britain and explaining that 'preparations were already being made to receive [him] and his ships'. Darlan's reply to Fleming, which he in turn sent back to the Admiralty, was that 'the French Admiralty is grateful for these preparations ... but is not counting on using them except in the last resort. For the moment the war at sea will go on as before'.[34] Fleming had his own ingenious solution, which was to offer Darlan the Isle of Wight as French territory for the war, and so would keep the fleet out of the hands of the Germans. The idea was suggested but not considered.

Only a matter of hours after Darlan's reply German bombers began to ruthlessly target his chateau. Forced to flee, Darlan and his inner circle headed for the coast in his staff car, while his remaining staff scrambled to destroy anything of strategic value the Luftwaffe bombs had left intact. Fleming had intended to give chase and keep the communication channel open with Darlan until the last second, but instructions radioed from London were for him to divert to Bordeaux where he was to make himself available there in assisting the evacuation of France. In particular, there were certain objects that either needed returning to Britain or destroying so as not to fall into enemy hands. He was confronted when arriving at the port by a chaotic mass of British nationals, refugees, and officials. Even the British Ambassador, having fled his Embassy in Paris, was there.

Fleming met a young man called Peter Smithers who similarly had been diverted to the port to carry out the same task. Smithers briefed Fleming that they were to prepare the evacuation of vital supplies. The two men set about collecting said supplies, which turned out to be a large pile of rusting aircraft engines and spare parts. For the first of many times in the war, Fleming's powers of persuasion came to good use. Trying to convince the captain of one of the fleeing ships to make room for what looked like scrap metal, which would need to take the place of people, was no easy task. However, mixing his charm with the official nature of his uniform and orders, the engines were loaded onto the ship, having been concealed in several dozen packing cases, and set sail to safety.

With their cargo on its way to Britain, Fleming and Smithers toured the now abandoned seaside town, looking for anything of value which should be destroyed before the Germans arrived. Searching the British Consulate, they were astonished to find piles of papers which had been overlooked when everything else was burnt. Working late into the night, they spent hours taking stacks of valuable data from the building into the courtyard where a large fire now blazed. Only when they were satisfied early the next morning that everything of value had been burnt did they make their way to the dock to board one of the remaining ships.

At the port, Fleming found himself at the back of a queue of hundreds of men, women and children all desperately trying to board one of the last ships. For Fleming and Smithers, it would not be an issue for them to jump the queue to the front and get a space thanks of their official position. However, the plight of all these refugees became the personal concern of the two men, who would not leave until they found a solution. Just outside the estuary were eight civilian boats, with their captains refusing to set sail because of the dangers they feared would confront them at sea. Again, Fleming switched into charm mode, mixed with a voice of authority expected of a British Naval Officer and demanded that the boats be used to carry the remaining people to safety. A 'torrent of argument, pleading, warning and command' ensued until the French captains reluctantly agreed to Fleming's demands.[35] He threatened one skipper who raised conern of his own safety, that if the Germans did not sink his ship, Fleming would ensure the Royal Air Force or Royal Navy would do the honours.

As the refugees now boarded their boats and with the Germans fast approaching, Fleming and Smithers were taken to HMS *Arethusa*, which was waiting off Arachon. With the ship also housing the British Ambassador's party, they returned to the shores of Britain.

Although Darlan had promised that 'the French Fleet should never fall into German hands', the British government were not willing to take the risk.[36] Therefore, on 3 July 1940, Churchill ordered *Operation Grasp* and *Operation Catapult*, which were intended either capture or destroy the French Fleet. In Portsmouth, Plymouth and Alexandria in Egypt, the French vessels were captured with minimal fuss. But in Algeria, the demands by the British to surrender were not met, and therefore the fleet was destroyed by the British and 1,297 French sailors were killed.

Ian Fleming had the taste for action now and was chomping at the bit to be sent abroad again. He need not have worried, because the war was taking a direction which would require the personal assistant to the Director of Naval Intelligence to form another scheme, even more exciting than the last.

Chapter 3

From a View to a Kill

In Fleming's first published short story, 'From a View to a Kill', James Bond is sent to investigate the mysterious disappearance of a dispatch rider carrying top-secret documents through Versailles. Bond soon discovers that there is a hostile base hidden in rocks along the road, where three enemy saboteurs are living. This fantastical story, which many commented was too farfetched – even for James Bond – was in fact born out of an idea Fleming came up with at the start of the war.

After the alliance was formed between Italy and Germany, the British government were concerned that other countries with fascist leanings would join. In the early part of the war, it was highly anticipated that the leader of Spain, Francisco Franco, might opt to join the Axis Powers. Initially, he had not seemed a threat on account of only recently establishing himself properly as the country's leader after a long and bloody civil war. Although Franco was an adamant pro-Axis leader, he knew only too well that Spain's geographical location meant it could only feed itself from overseas trade, something that could easily be cut off thanks to the superiority of the British Navy. While this made him reluctant to join the Axis Powers, there were no guarantees, and more importantly, it was likely that if the Spanish did not pledge their allegiance and offer assistance to Hitler and Mussolini, the Axis Powers would simply invade.

The Allies knew that should Spain join the Italians and the Germans, not only would it seriously strengthen their enemy, it would also threaten the strategically located British Colony of Gibraltar.

Identified as one of the Pillars of Hercules, Gibraltar has always been of utmost importance for the British Navy. Having been besieged no fewer than fifteen times over the last 2000 years, Gibraltar's location at the southern point of Spain means it can control not only the entrance to the Mediterranean, but also provide easy access into Morocco and North Africa. The Axis Powers knew only too well the value of Gibraltar, and in particular the shipping channel into the Mediterranean. According to a local NID source, the Germans had observation posts erected on both sides of the Gibraltar Straights. It was explained in a report sent to London that these 'became so efficient that the information obtained from them, supplemented by reports from Italians in Spanish stations, from lighthouses, fishing boats and pilots, made it impossible, when visibility was good, for any ship to move in or out of Gibraltar, or through the Straights, unobserved'.[1]

If the Germans could get such information when Gibraltar was ruled by the British, surely there was no reason the British couldn't if it were to fall into enemy hands? It was essential that Britain had a plan to maintain communication and launch sabotage operations in Spain if needed. NID were the go-to department for such a task and the assignment landed on Godfrey's desk. Designing subversive operations would be ideal for his personal assistant, thought Godfrey. He had some hesitancy as he had only just sent Fleming to Morocco as his representative to inspect the Naval Intelligence operations in North Africa. Unlike his previous adventure through France, Fleming opted for a more Bond-like suit rather than his uniform, a navy-blue single-breasted two-piece, with a white shirt, dark knitted tie and black shoes. He now always travelled with a fountain pen containing a special cartridge, which would fire a cloud of tear gas when the clip was pressed, and a commando knife from Wilkinsons for protection.

The trip was nondescript, although when landing in Tangier, Fleming nearly caused a diplomatic storm by giving 'an enormous V sign on the main runway of the international airport'.[2] He was given a severe ticking off on his return by the Admiralty and was privy to the full extent of Godfrey's short temper for the first time. He was soon forgiven and a week later sent to Spain, arriving on 16 February 1941, having travelled through Lisbon first and then on to Madrid. He would be using a courier's passport issued from the Embassy in Madrid to ensure smooth travelling to and from the country. Although by this point Fleming was an established member of NID, as with his Tangier visit he opted to travel 'undercover' in civilian clothes, with his trusty tear gas pen and knife.

Fleming was in Spain to meet Alan Hillgarth, then Naval Attaché in Madrid. Hillgarth was well known to Godfrey, as they had skilfully managed the evacuation of British subjects together during one of the bloodiest periods of Spanish civil war in 1938. The operation was hinged on the collection of men and women by HMS *Repulse*, Godfrey's battle cruiser at the time. So impressed was Godfrey, and with a reference from Winston Churchill to his name – who described him as a 'very good [man] equipped with a profound knowledge of Spanish affairs'– Hillgarth was offered the post of Naval Attaché in Spain.

Fleming was graciously hosted by Hillgarth and his wife Mary in their private Spanish residence. He was immediately impressed by his host, writing back to Godfrey on the evening of his arrival that Hillgarth was a competent operative and someone who would likely prove useful to NID. Fleming got on well with the couple, greatly enjoying their hospitality, and after a few days in Madrid the three travelled on to Gibraltar by air.

It was on this flight that Fleming and Hillgarth first discussed the foundations of what would be *Operation Golden Eye,* which served as inspiration for his short story, 'From a View to a Kill'. Fleming would also later name his Jamaican house after the operation. For the next week the two men fleshed out their plan to ensure that if Spain were to fall, whether voluntarily or through invasion, an undercover team could remain in Gibraltar to monitor the situation and in some cases, be a platform from which sabotage missions could be conducted.

To achieve this, *Operation Golden Eye* would loosely be broken down into three sections. First was the core plan of being able to launch sabotage attacks against the enemy; secondly there were *XY Operations*, the plan to demolish naval facilities and oil stocks in various Spanish ports as an invasion was unfolding; and thirdly, *Operation Tracer*, which was an elaborate scheme to monitor the area when under enemy control. *Operation Golden Eye* was further divided into two subgroups, taking into consideration the different eventualities, *Operation Sprinkler* and *Operation Sconce*. The former was to be deployed under the eventuality that Spain resisted following an invasion and the latter if Spain willingly joined the war or did not resist an invasion.

With the bare bones of a plan in place, Hillgarth and Fleming established a temporary *Operation Golden Eye* liaison office in Gibraltar, which would consist of ten naval officers with a designated NID commander in change and a demolition officer on standby. After only being in Gibraltar for a matter of days, already several requests for personnel were cabled to London and quickly accepted.

Having visited Tangier a matter of weeks before, Fleming suggested *Operation Golden Eye's* head office should be based there. This was in part because they needed somewhere to manage proceedings even if Gibraltar were to fall, but mainly, Fleming had been impressed by a man he had met – H.L. Greenleaves – who was an agent given the cover of an Assistant Press Attaché and later Vice-Consul in Tangier. Thanks to Fleming's recommendation, Greenleaves was chosen to lead operations on the ground. In order to carry out sabotage, fifty Spaniards would be selected and sent to Britain for training. Fleming was happy for their course to be varied, as long as they would be able to inhibit as many German communications as possible and generally make life disagreeable for the invading troops.

As *XY Operations* would have such a large number of targets, spanning ports across Cadiz, Malaga, Huelva, Seville, Lisbon, Balearics, Cartagena and Alicante, a further 250 men would be required to be trained and deployed.

In just a week, over 300 men had been assigned to *Operation Golden Eye,* which was off to a flying start. Planning, however, was temporarily put on hold, as Fleming and Hillgarth were instructed to make contact with an unexpected VIP due to arrive in Gibraltar, Hillgarth in his capacity as Naval Attaché and Fleming on behalf of the DNI. The man they were set to meet was Colonel William Donovan, chief of the USA intelligence section, who was touring the Mediterranean and Middle East for three months. Such was his importance to the Anglo-American relationship and the war effort, he was escorted by Churchill's personal representative, Colonel Vivian Dykes.

Godfrey wrote to Commander-in-Chief of the Mediterranean Fleet, Admiral Cunningham, saying 'There is no doubt that we can achieve infinitely more through Donovan than through any other individual' and suggesting 'he is very receptive and should be made fully aware of our requirements and deficiencies and can be trusted to represent our needs in the right quarters and in the right way in the USA'.[3] It was over to his personal assistant to secure the relationship.

On 24 February, Donovan arrived in Gibraltar. That evening, he was due to dine with Fleming, Hillgarth and Dykes, but unfortunately needed to cancel at the last minute because of a problem with his eye. The other men carried on without their honoured guest, eating a delicious dinner intend for Donovan and staying in the luxurious Government House. Dykes and Fleming sat next to each other for the meal and got along handsomely. Dykes recorded in his diary that Fleming 'was on the Reuter's staff before the war' and that 'he told me some interesting experiences', adding that he 'was inclined to knock it back too', referring to his heavy drinking.[4]

The next day, with Donovan restored to health, the party travelled back to Madrid. Saying his goodbyes to the Hillgarths, from Madrid Fleming went on to Tangier, where he did not repeat his gesture from his previous visit. After spending a day in the newly established *Operation Golden Eye* office with Greenleaves, Fleming flew to Lisbon and then back to London. Upon his return, Fleming dined with his friend Peter Smithers. He was particularly coy around the reason for his trip, saying he had been on a top secret mission abroad – that proved great fun – but the details of which he could only tell after the war.

The stops in Tangier and Lisbon were both related to the new plan he was putting in place, writing to Hillgarth how, while is Lisbon, he had been in conversations around the inclusion of Portugal in *Operation Golden Eye*, which had generally been met with positivity. He also thanked his new friend for his hospitality, saying how impressed he had been by Hillgarth and that having his team based in Britain's last European stronghold would be a huge asset to them winning the war.

*

Possibly the part of *Operation Golden Eye* that Fleming was most involved was the third part, *Operation Tracer*, a farfetched scheme that he thought would likely never be put into practice. This was the concept that men should be left behind hidden in Gibraltar if it fell, monitoring shipping traffic and spying on the enemy, concealed within one of the many tunnels and chambers in the Rock of Gibraltar.

So confidential was this operation, even more so than any other aspect of *Operation Golden Eye*, Godfrey insisted on discussing it outside of Room 39. He decided the only location he could trust was his own flat at 36 Curzon Street, Mayfair. The first meeting, the date of which was not recorded, nor minutes from the meeting taken, was held in the late summer of 1941, with the Head of NID 3, Colonel Cordeaux, Fleming and Godfrey in attendance. At the meeting, they decided that Commander Geoffrey Birley from the Gibraltar NID, along with two officers from the Royal Engineers, Colonel Fordham and Lieutenant Colonel Hay, were to be tasked with finding a suitable spot for the men to be stationed. After surveying multiple locations, Birley settled on a site within a tunnel system known as Lord Airey's Shelter, 1,350 feet above sea-level, named after former Governor of Gibraltar until 1870, Lord Richard Airey. On 4 November 1941, Birley submitted a full report on the location, which included suggestions for 'construction, camouflage, sanitary arrangements, wireless requirements, stores and crew'.[5]

On receipt of the report, the *Operation Tracer* inner circle gathered again at Godfrey's home. It was here they decided that construction should begin with haste, accepting Birley's recommendations. The target for completion was 15 February 1942, a mere four months away. They requested that a chamber should be burrowed into the rock off the main tunnel measuring 57,600 cubic feet. There would be two lookout stations with twelve six-inch viewing slits – which also provided the only ventilation – one looking east over the Mediterranean and the other looking west on the Straits of Gibraltar. It was also agreed at this meeting that the optimum number of people to be sealed in this chamber would be six men. For the basic necessities of keeping these men alive, Godfrey consulted with Lord Horder, the world-renowned physician whose patients had included Edward VII and George VI, as well as former Prime Ministers Ramsay MacDonald and Bonar Law. He also treated Hugh Gaitskell, soon to be leader of the Labour Party, and the man who would end up having an affair with Fleming's future wife.

As an advisor within the Ministry of Food, Lord Horder was able to provide much practical advice, such as the requirement of 1,666 gallons of water per man to survive for a year. Godfrey sent orders to Birley that a 10,000-gallon water tank be inserted into the chamber, which would be sufficient for the six men. Horder also advised that there was a far more pressing concern than simply keeping the men alive with food, water, sanitary provisions and so on. He raised the physiological impact that such a mission might have. This was not a worry for Godfrey and Fleming, who like Bond – described as a 'blunt instrument' – had dehumanised the whole operation in their minds. However, Horder's concern had wider reaching consequences than the physical welfare of the men. He pointed out that if any of them were to 'lose their mind', not only would it impact the others in the rock, but the accuracy of the intelligence being provided would need to be called into question.

He suggested bringing in another expert, Commander Levick. Called out of retirement to help with *Operation Tracer*, Levick had been a surgeon in the Royal Navy from 1902, joining at the age of 26, until his retirement in 1917. In 1910 he was granted special permission to take a leave of absence from the navy to join Robert Falcon Scott's Terra Nova Expedition, as their acting surgeon and zoologist. It was on this expedition that Levick and five other men were forced to live in an ice cave on the aptly named Inexpressible Island for the entire winter of 1912. Levick remarked that 'the road to hell might be paved with good intentions, but it seemed probable that hell itself would be paved something after the style of Inexpressible Island'.[6] Levick was tasked with managing the psychological impacts of *Operation Tracer.*

Around Christmas 1941, Cordeaux visited Gibraltar on behalf of Godfrey and Fleming, where he found construction of the bunker in Lord Airey's Shelter was well underway, but far from ready. He reported back on 27 December 1941 that 'the selected chamber and adjoining compartments [were] many months from completion' and unlikely to meet the tight deadline.[7] This at least gave them time to focus on another area of concern: communication. Radio jamming was becoming more frequent and could cause serious problems to *Operation Tracer's* success.

Cordeaux, Godfrey and Fleming arranged to meet with the Navy's Deputy Director of Signals Directorate (DDSD), Captain Sandwith and Head of Section VIII, or simply known as the Controller Special Communications, Colonel Gambier Parry, who reported that a standard Mark 3 transmitter and an HRO Receiver would suffice. These would be operated by three small 12-volt batteries, which were chargeable by two generators, one propelled by bicycle the other by hand. This also provided essential exercise; Fleming borrowed this detail for 'From a View to a Kill', where the enemy used a pedal generator to power their cipher machines.[8]

The main obstacle that Sandwith and Gambier Parry raised was that of an aerial. The radio would not be able to operate without one and it would need to be erected outside the cavity. In 'From a View to a Kill', Fleming solves this problem by having an aerial fashioned as a rose-stalk that could be raised and lowered electronically from a bush. Unfortunately, technology of this sophistication did not exist in real life. Instead, a simple solution of 'a rod aerial 18 ft. long' would 'be thrust out through the aperture when required'. A radio which was already in operation in Gibraltar was taken to Lord Airey's Shelter for testing by two of Gambier Perry's staff. Meanwhile the recruitment drive for suitable men to take part in *Operation Tracer* began in earnest.

On the evening of 27 January 1942, Godfrey hosted another meeting at his flat for Fleming, Cordeaux, Horder and Levick. The latter two men had written a report on the conditions required to keep the six yet to be selected men in a state of physical and mental health, drawing on Levick's time in the Antarctic. His recommendations included 'the choice and psychology of the personnel, on exercise and recreation, clothing, ventilation, sanitation, food, alcohol, tobacco, and the disposal – by embalmment and cementing up – of anyone who died'.[9] He called on much of his experience from the *Terra Nova Expedition*, for example how they were always 'cheered up' by 'successful sing-songs'.[10] He went into vast detail, even the types of games the men should play and the books which should be provided, including Russian authors Leo Tolstoy and Fyodor Dostoyevsky.

Off the back of their recommendations, Godfrey agreed that the *Operation Tracer* crew should consist of one officer, two doctors and three telegraphist ratings. He put Horder in charge of finding the two doctors, while Fleming would consult with the Second Sea Lord to find the remaining four men. At Levick's suggestion, the men would be auditioned before final selection to test their capability to be confined for such a long time.

A site was selected at the Royal Naval Training Establishment in Shotley, also known as HMS *Ganges*, and a programme hastily put together to begin on 16 May 1942. Meanwhile, the search for suitable recruits was on. First to be selected was Surgeon Lieutenant Bruce Cooper. The son of a Durham doctor, Cooper had excelled in the RNVR, having volunteered in 1939, where he had served on Atlantic convoy duties, for which he was mentioned in despatches. 'I had a telephone call one day', recalled Cooper. It was from Commander Levick saying he needed a doctor 'to do something special'.

Levick explained in as little detail as possible what was required for a most secret and dangerous mission. Flattered to be asked, Cooper duly attended a meeting at the Admiralty a few days later. 'I cannot tell you what it's all about yet,' the Commander told Cooper at the meeting, 'but you will need an accomplice.'[11] Cooper accepted the offer on the spot.

Cooper's first choice was an old university friend called Arthur Milner. A civilian doctor, Milner was not very receptive, mainly, as

Cooper recalled, because 'he suffered from chronic seasickness'. Cooper convinced Milner that despite the fact that he was being asked to join the Royal Navy, he would never have to serve at sea. Milner reluctantly accepted, and the two doctors were given the rank of Surgeon-Lieutenant.

Three leading signalmen were selected by Sandwith and Gambier Parry, and on 30 April 1942, the five men were sent to Shotley to await the start of their training. This would be supervised by Levick, who would observe the men to confirm their compatibility for the task. A leader had yet to be chosen, although records show that one officer was also sent as a possible candidate, although it soon became apparent to Levick that he would not suffice. He reported that the potential leader 'felt unable to share a meal with ratings' because of his rank.[12] For six men to be confined for over a year in a tiny room, it would be nearly impossible for them not to share everything with each other, let alone their food. He was quickly replaced by the charismatic Executive Officer 'Windy Gale', who had no time for the traditions of rank.

On 16 May 1942, two months of training began in Shotley. A tiny hut on Romney Marsh was used in place of the bunker and the Thames Estuary was their spying ground. For sixty days, the six men reported by radio the comings and goings of ships through the estuary, while Levick watched over them closely, reporting on how well the men kept to their strict regime which included rotas for meals, exercise, sanity duties and keeping watch. Levick had produced a manual called *Notes on Hygiene and Fitness* which the men used during their trial run. The training was also a good opportunity to test the radio equipment and the amount of supplies which would be needed. By the middle of July 1942, Windy Gale and his team were released from their self-imposed prison cell and were granted two weeks leave to be spent with their families. All the men were subject to the Official Secrets Act, so could not divulge what they were being sent away to do.

On 1 August 1942, the *Operation Tracer* team made their way to Gibraltar, where they were put under the command of Commander Pyke-Nott. The construction of their hideout was nearly complete, with the wireless now trialled and tested, the water tank and the stores full. The six men were given 'cover' roles on various ships and bases around the area. They were waiting for the Germans to invade the rock, at which point they would immediately make their way to the chamber, where

Pyke-Nott's men would seal them in with vast quantities of concrete and the spying would begin.

During the next year, the men spent much of their time still training for *Operation Tracer,* while also performing their cover duties. Cooper recalled how he would finish work as a Surgeon-Lieutenant and head to the prestigious Rock Hotel, where he would change in the toilet into his *Tracer* outfit, a khaki army sergeant's uniform, before entering the tunnel, where the men would test their equipment and check supplies.

Although the concept was very promising, *Operation Tracer* would never be properly tested. With the change in direction of the war – as Gibraltar was no longer a target for Hitler, who was focusing his efforts further east – on 20 August 1943, Windy Gale and his men made their final training exercise in the chamber, before emptying the stores and concreting it shut.

Godfrey still hailed the operation a resounding success, even arranging to meet with the First Sea Lord, Admiral of the Fleet Dudley Pound, to suggest that 'in future an operation of this pattern should have a permanent place in the defences of all major harbours abroad'. 'I agree', responded Dudley, asking 'what about Colombo and Trincomalee and Malta?'[13]

Fleming playfully teases the reader with the concept of *Operation Tracer* in 'From a View to a Kill', stating tongue-in-cheek that the stay-behind spy's set up in his novel by a fictional enemy was far better than anything Britain had prepared in case of a German invasion. Either way, *Operation Golden Eye* was not the only work Fleming was engaged upon. Despite the intense nature of such an important scheme, Fleming was also able to focus on another plan he called *Operation Ruthless*, which would live up to its name.

Chapter 4

From Russia, with Love

From Russia, with Love, published on 8 April 1957, was the fifth novel written by Ian Fleming. The book follows the Soviet counter-espionage group known as SMERSH, which Fleming explains is the Soviet government's official murder organisation comprising of 40,000 men and women. The name SMERSH is derived from the Russian term "Smiert Spionam", which means "Death to Spies". The book outlines a plan by SMERSH to murder James Bond in revenge for his attacks on their operatives Le Chiffre (*Casino Royale*), Mr Big (*Live and Let Die*) and Hugo Drax (*Moonraker*). To conduct the killing, the Soviet organisation tempts Bond to Turkey with a Russian cypher machine, being carried by the apparently defecting SMERSH desk agent Tatiana Romanova.

Bond experts Ajay Chowdhury and Matthew Field were clear that the inspiration for the plot came from 'Fleming's knowledge of the Enigma device used by the Germans during World War II'.[1] The sheer desperation for such a cypher machine was brought to the attention of Fleming when, at the end of 1940, he started supporting the Government Code and Cypher School (GC & CS) at Bletchley Park. Described by a secretary who worked there as 'a desperately awful place', Bletchley Park was a fifty-eight acre estate in Buckinghamshire, chosen as it was deemed suitably far north of London, nearly fifty miles, to be outside the catchment area for enemy bombings, but equally easily accessible from the capital.[2] In the official records of the NID, it was remarked that 'Bletchley had no social amenities worth mentioning'.[3]

Eminent GC & CS worker Mavis Batey recalled that through the duration of the war, 'Ian Fleming would visit regularly, every two weeks or so, on naval business'.[4] The man he would meet with was Dilly Knox, who had recently set up the Enigma research centre, having been assistant to Alastair Denniston, Commander of GC & CS. According to historian Andrew Hodges, Knox, who was 'a classical scholar and Fellow of King's until the Great War', took instantly to Fleming and the two men built up a close relationship.[5] Knox and his colleagues were busy trying to break German codes. Most famously the Enigma code, which, when broken, allowed the British to see the communications to and from Nazi military intelligence, the German Abwehr. After the war, despite the highly secret nature of the work done by the GC & CS at Bletchley Park, Winston Churchill was forthright with his praise, describing their achievements as 'the single biggest contribution to Allied victory in the war against Nazi Germany'.[6]

The process for code-breaking was arduous and lengthy. For the Abwehr's Enigma, GC & CS would work through up to 4,000 messages intercepted each day, painstakingly cross referencing the codes with captured codebooks in an attempt to find a pattern and therefore crack the code. The coding machines, described to Bond in *From Russia, with Love* as very similar to the shape and size of a typewriter, had a series of wheels – between three and eight depending on the model – which needed setting in a particular order dependant on the month, day and time; information which would be found in one of the code books. In total, the Enigma machines allowed 16,900 possible permutations to the alphabet. This was only the prelude to the message actually being encrypted, a procedure called *Steckerbrett*. This was the process of the further jumbling of letters by the message operators, to the point that there were up to 140,000,000,000,000 different combinations. As historian Nicholas Rankin explained: 'The possible ways to jumble the twenty-six letters of the alphabet to encipher a message were being multiplied from mere hundreds and thousands into millions, billions and even trillions'.[7] Remarkably, the team at Bletchley Park were slowly and meticulously starting to make sense of the Enigma code.

However, as the winter of 1940 encroached, there was growing concern that the Adwehr's Enigma codes might not be the only messages that needed cracking, as the German Navy were starting to use a different coding system altogether, which had recently been made far more complex, meaning the code-breaking experts needed to start from scratch again. As with Enigma, the way to do this was to see the Navy codebooks or cypher machines, none of which by 12 September 1940 had been captured.

In a report by Charles Morgan, an author called out of civilian life to work at Bletchley Park, he wrote that 'the highest grade Naval cyphers were seldom accessible' going on to say that for a time Bletchley Park had something similar but 'the addition of a new disc to [the] machine' meant it was rendered ineffective.[8] In a letter from GC & CS, the importance is described:

> Did the authorities realise that, since the Germans did the dirt on their machine on June 1st, there was very little hope, if any, of [us] deciphering current, or even approximately current, enigma for months and months and months – if ever? Contrariwise, if we [captured some enemy codes] – even enough to give a clue to one days material, we could be pretty sure, after an initial delay, of keeping going from day to day from then on; nearly up-to-date if not quite, because the level of traffic now is so much higher and because the machinery has been so much improved. The initial delay would be in proportion to [the amount of enemy codes captured]. If the whole bag of tricks was [captured], there'd be no delay at all.[9]

In *From Russia, with Love*, Bond explains to Tatiana that the reason he wants the machine so badly is because the fictionalised Bletchley Park have heard of it, but they had not yet seen one. In 1940, code-breakers at Bletchley Park needed as many codebooks as possible and ideally a transmitting machine. A flimsy attempt had been made already in the guise of an order sent to all Naval Officers from Godfrey, which read:

> It is known that many German Naval Signals are enciphered on a machine … Any machine of this type found on board a German man-of-war should be carefully packed and forwarded to the Director of Naval Intelligence … It is important that the machine should not be touched or disturbed in any way, except as necessary for its removal and packing.[10]

When this led to nothing, Frank Birch, Head of Naval Intelligence at Bletchley Park, contacted Admiral Godfrey saying 'a successful pinch' offered 'the best chance' for the Navy to help win the war, Godfrey sent Fleming to meet Birch at GC & CS to assist in any way he could.[11]

Birch, who led a team of 200 individuals, including eighteen Royal Navy officers, known as NID 12A, knew of Fleming's growing reputation from *Operation Golden Eye* and was delighted that he was being listened to.

Having already built a friendship with Knox, Fleming needed little persuading by Birch to realise the importance of a pinch. He immediately set about making an extravagant plan to do just that – capture the whole bag of tricks. The operation which would take shape under his command went on to inspire the background story of *From Russia, with Love*.

Reviewing the book, the *Sunday Times* acknowledged that Fleming 'adds the pleasures of a credible plot to the excitement of extreme violence'.[12] The basis for this plot was, of course, a reality to him when planning what he called *Operation Ruthless*, an elaborate and ingenious scheme to ambush and capture a German Naval vessel. The plan was drawn up into three sections: Firstly, obtain a Luftwaffe aeroplane in good working order, find a crew who could fly it, transmit signals and speak German. These 'tough bachelor[s]' who must be competent swimmers would be dressed in Luftwaffe uniforms covered in blood and burn marks. [13] Secondly, deliberately crash the plane into the English Channel, giving off an SOS signal to the Germany Navy as they plummeted into the sea. Thirdly, await rescue by a nearby German crew, and once aboard their vessel, shoot them and dump their bodies overboard. When control of the boat had been taken, navigate it back to a British port, where their plunder could be delivered to Bletchley Park.

Such a mission was feasible because the Nazis had begun a new rescue operation in the English Channel, as pilots were in short supply. It had been generally accepted that the German rescue boats were 'too fast and too cautious to be caught with any certainty by an ordinary British motor torpedo boat'.[14] They would need taking by complete surprise.

What Fleming was devising amounted to a sophisticated form of piracy. A note at the end of the memorandum was added, to give a cover story for the assailants if they were captured:

> Since attackers will be wearing enemy uniform, they will be liable to be shot as [partisans] if captured and the incident might be a fruitful field for propaganda. Attackers' story will therefore be 'that it was done for a lark by a group of young hot-heads who thought the war was too tame and wanted to have a go at the Germans. They had

stolen a plane and equipment and had expected to get into trouble when they got back'. This will prevent suspicions that party was after more valuable booty.[15]

Some senior figures in SOE commented that this sounded more like a boarding school tale to a housemaster than a serious attempt to disguise a sabotage mission behind enemy lines. Nonetheless, this audacious and potentially flawed plan was given the green light by Godfrey, despite some understandable uncertainty around its chances of success and somewhat ludicrous cover story. In contrast, the team at Bletchley Park gave their full support thinking it a very ingenious plot.

Fleming set about putting the wheels in motion – he needed to procure a German aeroplane and Luftwaffe uniforms, recruit some brave German speaking pilots who could successfully crash an 8,200kg aircraft into the ice-cold sea without causing themselves any serious injuries. This, of course, would only be the start of their mission, as they would then need to signal to a Nazi boat to come to their rescue, hope to emerge from the near-freezing water to overcome the whole crew, then navigate their way back to Britain without being attacked en route.

First on Fleming's list was finding a suitable aeroplane, which needed to be clearly identified as German. Captured aeroplanes were surprisingly common, with a total of 356 taken from the enemy by 1945. With the help of Godfrey, Fleming managed to locate a Heinkel He 111 bomber. Often described as the wolf in a sheep's coat – as the Germans deceived the British into believing it was a civilian plane when under design – the bomber with its 'greenhouse glass' front became a familiar sight and sound over Britain, with 452 manufactured in the first year of conflict alone. The aircraft in question, *Werk* number 6853, had been shot down on a mission over the Firth of Forth in Scotland. The reason it caught Fleming's eye was that it had sustained minimal damage and had been repaired by the Royal Aircraft Establishment in Farnborough. Fleming had called in a favour from Lord Beaverbrook, a former business contact and at that time the Minister of Aircraft Production, in order to get the aeroplane released to him.

Group Captain H.J. Wilson, who had been given responsibility for looking after the captured German aircraft, was initially reluctant to part with it. According to Fleming's biographer Andrew Lycett, Wilson 'rather punctured the idea by stating that a crash landing in the Channel would collapse the Heinkel's Perspex nose, and that the crew would all drown'.[16] However, with a mixture of Fleming's skills of persuasion and the direct orders from Lord Beaverbrook, Wilson was forced to concede. He was also instructed to make a reinforced windscreen, which was attached to the front of the plane in the hope it would survive the impact. Wilson also suggested they 'inject oil into the exhaust so as to give the impression of an engine fire'.[17] With the aircraft now undergoing modification, Fleming was also able to get his hands on the necessary uniforms from the stores at Cardington in Bedford, taken from either captured or killed Luftwaffe men.

Fleming fleshed out his plan, now with the support of the Head of the Operational Intelligence Centre, Admiral Jock Clayton. Adding some further detail, he decided that the plane would tag along before dawn after a German air raid, seamlessly joining the convoy of Luftwaffe planes, before being 'shot down' by the fierce Royal Air Force. The target boat he wanted his men to capture was by this point agreed. He needed to be certain that they would be big enough to carry the correct coding machine and codebooks. However, he also needed to make sure the vessel was not too large, as the disguised aircrew needed to easily be able to overcome their rescuers, and not end up in a bloody shootout. Fleming turned to GC & CS where Frank Birch produced for him a three-page paper called 'Activities of German Naval Units in the Channel'. Fleming wrote in a report following his interaction with Birch that the most effective way of capturing a small or large minesweeper – called a Raumboot or Minenesuchboot – with its priceless cargo, was to stage the crash in the middle of the channel. This was, he explained, because the Germans would be forced to deploy a minesweeper for that type of journey.

Next, he needed a crew of five, a crack team with many of the traits he would later attribute to his fictional hero. They needed to be resourceful, confident, and brave to the point of near stupidity. Fleming thought he knew the perfect man for the job – himself. Although showing a slight sign of arrogance, he was desperate to be part of the action. Godfrey flatly refused, stating 'Ian was someone who simply could not fall into enemy hands because he was privy to everything'.[18]

Peter Smithers, a colleague at naval intelligence, remembered that, 'Ian constantly longed to be personally engaged in the excitement. He was of an essentially aggressive nature. It was the repression of all these desires by authority, quite rightly, which in my opinion fired the imagination engaged in his books'.[19] There was no shortage of the kind of men Fleming needed at SOE; he was amazed when he started to make enquiries that they actually existed, trained and prepared for this exact type of mission. He discovered that they even had gadgets such as .22 caliber one-shot guns, concealed within a cigarette. In *From Russia, with Love,* when Bond lights a cigarette, he thinks, 'if only it had been a trick one – magnesium flare or something … If only the service went in for these explosive toys!'[20] In reality, they did.

Disappointingly, as Fleming began recruiting for his mission, he was informed on 16 October 1940 by Godfrey that *Operation Ruthless* was being put on hold because of particularly bad weather in the English Channel. It was decided that the location should be moved to Portsmouth where conditions might be more favourable. In a letter from Frank Birch dated 20 October 1940, he wrote to Fleming that Alan Turing and Peter Twinn, from Bletchley Park, 'came to me like undertakers cheated of a nice corpse two days ago, all in a stew about the cancellation of *Operation Ruthless*'.[21]

Fleming responded immediately to say that *Operation Ruthless* had not be cancelled, and quite to the contrary, they were simply awaiting better circumstances for the mission to commence – namely the correct weather conditions – during a time of heavy bombing raids over Britain and when the correct German vessels were in the English Channel. The boys from Bletchley Park need not have worried at this point, as the next day on 21 October 1940 the Air Ministry released the following document: 'Full Air Ministry Instructions for *Operation Ruthless*: Official objective to obtain certain important Naval intelligence material known to be carried in German R&M boats, and certain other types of MTB [motor torpedo boat] used on sea security service and rescue work in the channel'.[22] Fleming was elated, but not for long.

Despite the sudden impetus behind the plan, it would never be followed through to fruition, as a memo from a command station in Dover stated: '*Operation Ruthless* postponed. Two reconnaissance flights by coastal command revealed no suitable craft operating at night … Suggest material and organisation should be dispersed'.[23] Ultimately, the overriding issue that caused the ambitious operation to be cancelled was purely the lack of suitable prey in the English Channel. It has since been argued that such a plan was doomed to failure, mostly because of the incredibly difficult task of landing a five-man plane at night in the perilous winter sea. In particular, as was pointed out to Fleming, a plane which was famed for having a greenhouse-style glass front would easily smash on impact, causing it to instantly sink.

Disappointed by the outcome of *Operation Ruthless*, Fleming was comforted by the realisation that he was onto something. It was at this point that he started planning a dedicated team to continually carry out such covert activity.

The desire for an Enigma device would stay with Fleming for the rest of the war, where on several occasions he would try other plans to capture them. It would also be something that he made his hero, James Bond, equally as desperate to get, thus creating the foundation for one of his best received novels.

Chapter 5

Diamonds Are Forever

Written in January and February 1955, *Diamonds Are Forever* is Fleming's fourth novel, in which 007 takes on a gang of diamond smugglers in America. Published the following year, the story follows Bond's undercover operation as 'Peter Franks', a burglar turned diamond smuggler, to infiltrate the Spangled Mob gang in New York. With the help of his trusted American ally Felix Leiter, Bond is able to kill the gang leaders and shut down the smuggling ring. Throughout the book, the reader is shown Fleming's in-depth knowledge of America, in particular New York. Fleming's literary advisor, William Plomer, was extremely complimentary about this: 'What I particularly like is the Bond's-eye-view of America. It is very rare nowadays to get any kind of book with fresh observation of the ordinary or extraordinary details of American life by an English eye'.[1]

Diamonds Are Forever is also the third time we meet Felix Leiter, a Central Intelligence Agency (CIA) man who proves to be an invaluable help to the success of Bond's mission.

'The CIA is fundamental to America's national security,' said President Barack Obama during a speech given at CIA headquarters in Langley on 20 April 2009. 'Here in the twenty-first century,' he continued, 'we've learned that the CIA is more important than ever ... You serve capably, courageously, and from here in Virginia to dangerous outposts around the globe, you make enormous sacrifices on our behalf.'

With over 20,000 employees and an annual budget of nearly $20 billion, the CIA is one of, if not the most well-established intelligence institutions in the world. But unbeknown to most, in 1941 the personal assistant to the Director of Naval Intelligence, Ian Fleming, would be fundamental to the creation of the CIA from scratch. He was nothing but complimentary about the American service through his books. His fictional agent often relied on them, with Bond regularly claiming thier people and equipment were the best in the world. Since his meeting with Colonel William Donovan, chief of the USA intelligence section, in early 1941 while working on *Operation Golden Eye*, Fleming had been central to the effort in building a better relationship with his American counterparts.

To strengthen ties, Fleming suggested to Godfrey that the two men should visit America, especially as he was hungry for a new challenge following the disappointment of *Operation Ruthless*. Somewhat reluctantly, Godfrey agreed, and a trip was planned. In a memo, it was recorded that the men were making their way overseas in order to 'establish closer relations with opposite numbers in the United States while recognising that liaison of this sort called for careful handling'.[2]

Fleming and Godfrey made their way to Lisbon by KLM, before embarking on a twenty-two-hour flying boat journey through the Azores and on to New York, the most convenient and quickest method of travel to the city at the time. They stayed in Lisbon for two nights at the Estoril Hotel, in part to wait for their connecting flight, but also to give the Director of Naval Intelligence time to inspect the operations in Portugal's capital city.

Their first day was packed with visits to the local NID offices, including the *Operation Golden Eye* liaison office. In the evening, their time was more relaxed, with their first night spent dining at the Aviz Hotel, proclaimed by *Life Magazine* to be 'the world's most sumptuous hotel'. After a busy second day, the men decided that they wouldn't push the boat out to the same extent as they had the previous night, opting to eat at their hotel, before hitting the town in search of a casino. They chose a grey-walled and melancholy looking building on the Tagus estuary, in which Godfrey and Fleming played baccarat against some bored looking Portuguese men.

This visit to Lisbon would prove useful for several reasons: it gave Godfrey a better understanding of his international offices, a task he had to this point delegated almost entirely to his trustworthy assistant. Also, it brought the two men closer together, allowing them to spend time bonding outside of the smoky Room 39 at the Admiralty. Finally, for Fleming, it was a time that remained planted in the back of his mind and would play out in his future Bond novels. Eleven years after this visit, he would sit down at his typewriter and begin *Casino Royale*. Godfrey recalled that on that evening, Fleming pointed at his Portuguese baccarat opposition and whispered to Godfrey, 'just suppose these fellows were German agents – what a coup it would be if we cleaned them out entirely'.[3] Although Casino Estoril's name was changed to Casino Royale, the basis for the story was born that evening.

The following morning, slightly blurry-eyed, Godfrey and Fleming made their way to the estuary of the Tagus, past the casino, and boarded their flying boat to the United States. With only twelve such vessels ever made operational, their NC18605 'Dixie Clipper', operated by Pan American, consisted of three passenger compartments with luxurious sofas and chairs, a dining lounge that served six course meals on the finest china, and comfy sleeping berths. In 1943, this plane would be used for the first ever presidential transatlantic flight, taking United States President Franklin D. Roosevelt to the Casablanca Conference. Fellow passengers ranged from the aristocracy through to the famous, including Coco Chanel's biggest business rival, Italian fashion designer Elsa Schiaparelli. The luxury and convenience of the flight was marred by the fact that it brought undue attention to Fleming and Godfrey, who were not on an official visit and therefore were travelling 'undercover' and out of uniform. Godfrey opted for a grey suit and matching waistcoat, while Fleming went for his usual dark blue two-piece. They described themselves on their immigration forms as 'government officials'.[4]

After landing on the water by La Guardia Field, they were greeted by a group of photographers, all there to capture a scoop of the elegant Madame Schiaparelli. A picture appeared in the newspaper the next day of the fashion designer dressed in a dark jacket, cravat and headscarf, behind whom are Fleming and Godfrey trying to make their way into the country unnoticed. Luckily, no one recognised them and their identity in the country remained protected. From the airport, they made their way to their hotel, St Regis, owned by Vincent Astor, who was himself helping the British in the intelligence space.

Their first stop was to meet with J. Edgar Hoover, the forty-six-year-old founder of the Federal Bureau of Investigation in 1935 and its Director until his death in 1972. The NID felt that the way to build a better working relationship with their American counterparts was to start at the top. They had therefore arranged to meet with Hoover, who welcomed them into his New York field headquarters in Foley Square. Hoover granted the men an audience which lasted just sixteen minutes, from 12.31 pm to 12.47 pm on 6 June 1941. Hoover was a well-built man who wore importance as if it were a suit and welcomed the two British men into his office. He listened attentively to what they had to say, before firmly explaining he had no interest in their objective.

Although they had no luck winning Hoover's support, they were able to get a feel for the size and scale of his operation, as he showed them around the FBI Laboratory and their famous Record Department, before taking the men to the shooting range in the basement. From this moment on, Fleming's love and fascination for guns was something that would continually grow throughout his life. His books provide a glimpse into the pleasure he would take from being around guns, whether it be the intimate details of their look, feel, sound or smell.

Their visit to the Foley Square office was not completely unproductive, as Hoover offered to introduce Godfrey and Fleming to Sir William 'Bill' Stephenson, the man who represented British Intelligence interests in the US, and who dealt with Hoover directly. Although disappointing, Fleming agreed that it made sense for Hoover to keep his communications with Stephenson rather than open another separate channel with NID.

Sir William, often known as 'Little Bill', had been raised in Iceland, having been adopted by a poor Icelandic mother and Scottish father. Volunteering for the 101st Overseas Battalion of the Canadian Expeditionary Force in January 1916, he was sent to Britain where he was transferred to the Canadian Engineering Training Depot. The following year, having been moved again to the Royal Flying Corps and sent to the front line in Europe in 1917, he racked up an impressive twelve kills in under six months, and according to his biography became known as 'Captain Machine-Gun'. Stephenson was shot down on 28 July 1918 behind enemy lines and sent to the Officer's Prison Camp, Holzminden, Lower Saxony. Not content with sitting out the war in prison, he escaped in October, making his way to British occupied land. He explained later that by that point 'the air war seemed crucial. The Germans were near collapse, but they still had good aircraft and pilots in reserve. Anyone on our side with first-hand experience of them was still needed'.[5] Once back on the right side, he was soon in the air once more, causing havoc with the enemy.

He received the Military Cross, which was cited in the *London Gazette* on 22 June 1918:

> For conspicuous gallantry and devotion to duty. When flying low and observing an open staff car on a road, he attacked it with such success that later it was seen lying in the ditch

upside down. During the same flight he caused a stampede amongst some enemy transport horses on a road. Previous to this he had destroyed a hostile scout and a two-seater plane. His work has been of the highest order, and he has shown the greatest courage and energy in engaging every kind of target.

After the war, Stephenson moved to Canada for a short while before returning to Britain where he built up a multi-million-pound industrial empire and married an exceptionally wealthy Tennessean tobacco heiress, Mary Simmons. It was during this period that Bill Stephenson began a strong friendship with opposition MP, Winston Churchill. From his travels and international business contacts, Stephenson witnessed the Nazi Party's secret manufacture of arms and military products – including the Heinkel He 111 bomber used for *Operation Ruthless* – all of which he fed back to Churchill. The War Cabinet, led by Neville Chamberlain, suspected that Churchill was being passed information, with Maurice Hankey – advisor to Chamberlain, having been part of Lloyd George's War Cabinet in World War I – writing to Churchill inviting him 'to communicate in confidence any special sources of intelligence on which your information is based'.[6] Churchill did not agree.

Grateful for his loyalty and support, after he succeeded Chamberlain as Prime Minister, Churchill sent Stephenson to America on 21 June 1940 to establish the British Security Coordination, known as the BSC, in the then neutral US. Working for no salary, his organisation coordinated between the SOE, SIS and MI5 and the American FBI and intelligence services. Under his official title and cover as British Passport Control Officer, Stephenson was set the remit of: 'the establishment of a secret organisation to investigate enemy activities and to institute adequate measures in the Western Hemisphere'; 'the procurement of certain essential supplies for Britain'; and 'the fostering of American intervention'. His brief was further expanded by Churchill to gain 'the assurance of American participation in secret activities throughout the world in the closest possible collaboration with the British.'[7] With over six million German speaking and four million Italian speaking people in America, many of whom had ties to the Axis Powers, Stephenson was to keep tabs on any foreign agents.

Based out of Room 3603 on the thirty-sixth floor of the Rockefeller Centre, 630 Fifth Avenue, he built a team of over 1,000 agents and support workers. Fleming would always remember Stephenson as a man who would never talk unless completely necessary, but when he did speak, his words would be treated as gospel. From their first meeting in Stephenson's office, Fleming was immediately taken by the man. As his biographer John Pearson wrote, 'For Fleming, Stephenson was almost everything a hero should be ... he was very tough ... he was very rich ... he was single-minded and patriotic and a man of few words'.[8] When Stephenson asked him to write a quote for the front cover of his autobigraphy many years later, Fleming boldly claimed that William Stephenson was the real-life version of James Bond. Perhaps more importantly, Fleming believed that his new friend mixed the greatest dry martinis he had ever had in America. As a nod to Stephenson, in *Diamonds Are Forever*, Bond is pleasantly surprised by the quality the 'medium dry Martini with a piece of lemon peel' that Felix Leiter orders him.[9] It is the Californian brand of Martini that makes the drink so good in America, explained Leiter. Fleming was full of praise for the drink, which would become a staple for Bond.

Another reason that the Director of Navel Intelligence's personal assistant got on so well with the Head of the British Security Coordination was because Stewart Menzies, 'C', in overall charge of British intelligence, despised Stephenson. In fact, Menzies had tried to persuade the Prime Minister not to appoint Stephenson at all. With the ever-growing tension between Godfrey and the heads of other intelligence organisations in Britain, a mutual dislike for C gave the men something of a conversation topic.

Stephenson remembered that 'from the start Ian was always fascinated by gadgets and equipment'.[10] This was something of a speciality for the BSC; as Stephenson later remarked, 'in those days we were building up our mechanical coding equipment which was ultimately handling thousands of messages a day'.[11] This was exactly the work that Fleming's friends at Bletchley Park were attempting to do, and which he spent much of his time during the war trying to assist. Stephenson also had set up 'Station M', a laboratory he declared could 'reproduce faultlessly the imprint of any typewriter on earth', hidden in a building purporting to be the Canadian Broadcasting Corporation.[12]

Fleming was delighted to be invited to take part in an operation to search the office of a suspected Japanese spy, coincidently based in the office on thirty-fifth storey of the Rockefeller building, just one floor below the BSC headquarters. The man in question worked for the Japanese Consul-General in New York and was suspected of sending intelligence messages back to Japan.

At 3 am, while most New Yorkers were fast asleep – a comfortable 8 am in Fleming's mind thanks to the time difference with London – Stephenson, two members of his staff and Fleming entered the Japanese Consul-General's office with duplicate keys and managed to crack the safe that housed the Japanese codebooks. These were in turn taken upstairs, copied and then returned. For Fleming this was 'a great and gleeful adventure' which would help shape his future career as an author.[13]

*

From New York, Godfrey and Fleming travelled to Washington, where NID had an office, as they were due to meet with General 'Wild Bill' Donovan. Described as a 'short, plump lawyer with the Southern drawl', Donovan was a well-known divorce lawyer who had been President Roosevelt's legal aide. Donovan was already known to Godfrey and had met his assistant while in Gibraltar. He was also a close friend and associate of Bill Stephenson, someone who for a long time had 'been coaching and pushing' him to the position of head of the soon to be created American Secret Service.[14]

Stephenson had identified that the main reason for the lack of cooperation between the US and British intelligence services was not due to a lack of trying, but more because of disorganisation. There was no central American body to coordinate all the intelligence, and most importantly decide what to share and with whom. Instead, the Navy, Army, State Department and the FBI all fought against each other and this rivalry meant they were not sharing information with each other, let alone their allies. Stephenson had spent the last two years grooming Donovan to create a central intelligence organisation to corral the others into order.

Stephenson used two of his close contacts – Sir William Wiseman, his predecessor as Head of British Intelligence Operations in America, and Arthur Hays Sulzberger, publisher of the *New York Times* – to broker a meeting between Godfrey and President Roosevelt. They managed to persuade the First Lady, Eleanor Roosevelt, to invite Godfrey to a private dinner at the White House, not knowing but assuming her husband would also be present. As Godfrey was at the helm of one of the oldest intelligence-gathering organisations in the world, Stephenson believed he would carry sufficient credibility with Roosevelt, who was still unconvinced by Donovan. On his arrival at the White House, Godfrey spent much time talking with the President who 'gave Godfrey a difficult time, but he listened attentively to DNI, who was able to put his various points across, not least his enthusiasm for a unified American intelligence service, under Donovan'.[15]

After his meal, the Admiral confided in his personal assistant that he was unsure whether he had done enough to sway Roosevelt. However, he need not have worried, as on 18 June 1941, according to his biographer, 'Donovan was received by the President and after a long discussion agreed to accept the office of Co-ordinator of Information, his duties to include the collection of all forms of intelligence and the planning of various cover offensive operations'.[16] It was this office that would later develop into the CIA from 1947. Before that point, the Co-ordinator of Information would be rebranded as the Office of Strategic Services (OSS).

To help get started, Donovan turned back to his mentor William Stephenson, who played a big part in the appointment, consulting him on 'search methods and constructions for the formation of such an organisation'. According to Ivar Bryce, who was working for Stephenson at the time, 'Little Bill gave wise advice and the offer of an expert [to] formulate the table of organisation required to set up an American service'.[17] The person Stephenson suggested was also the man who had helped Donovan secure the position in the first place, Admiral Godfrey.

Typical of Godfrey, who needed to leave Washington to attend appointments in Britain, he delegated the work to Fleming. Godfrey had enjoyed his time with Fleming, not only on a professional level but also personal. In his report, written upon his return, he was very flattering about his colleague: 'I could not have wished for a more agreeable companion than Ian Fleming ... I have never known him anything but buoyant, responsive and light-hearted, especially when things were going badly'.[18]

John Pearson wrote that while he remained in Washington after Godfrey's departure, 'Fleming went to ground for a couple of days' to do top secret work.[19] It was during this time Fleming was ordered to design the structure of a secret service organisation being created from scratch, using his experience of SIS, SOE and NID. Bryce recalled that Fleming 'had been whisked off to a room in the new annexe of the Embassy, locked in it with a pen and paper and the necessities of life, and had written, under armed guard around the clock, a document of some seventy pages covering every aspect of a giant secret intelligence and secret operational organisation'.[20]

Another close friend of Donovan's was David Eccles, who worked for the Ministry of Economic Warfare and had been called upon to steer the British efforts to keep Spain out of the war. He reported to the Foreign Office that 'in order not to break the continuity of collaboration between us and Bill' he had 'installed Ian Fleming in my bed at Bill's house. He knows much more about the details of intelligence work than I do'.[21]

Historians have over the years questioned how much, or little, Fleming had to do with the design of Donovan's new organisation. Fleming himself did not speak much about it, but did write in a letter dated March 1957 to historical author Colonel Rex Applegate and former colleague of Donovan that in 1941 he had spent time at Donovan's Washington house creating the original charter of the OSS. He had also written to Cornelius Ryan, author of *A Bridge Too Far*, who was rumoured to be writing the official biography of Donovan, offering to help and asking if Ryan were to come across his origional memorandum during his research, Fleming would be grateful for a copy.

In any case, two separate documents were produced by Fleming, the first focused purely on how an American intelligence service would cooperate with their British counterparts. In this paper Fleming recommended that the American operation 'should be under the protection of a strong government department and it should be insured by every means possible against political interference or control'. He suggested that all intelligence officers 'must have trained powers of observation, analysis and evaluation; absolute discretion, sobriety, devotion to duty; language and wide experience, and be aged about 40–50'.[22] Fleming even recommended that the new American organisation could work closely with the likes of Frank Birch at Bletchley Park, so 'all high grade cryptographic work should be carried out at Bletchley and Washington, thereby ensuring rapid collaboration between England and America'.[23] One member of the OSS later maintained that they 'owed everything to British services ... all manner of [material] used by secret services came to us'.[24]

A second memo, dated 27 June 1941, was more generic than its predecessor, stating broadly how the OSS should be structured.

It emphasised urgency in order that the new enterprise would be in a position 'to put up any kind of a show, should America come into the war in a month's time'.[25] Although the Axis Powers would not attack America for another six months, Fleming's urge to make the organisation operational as soon as possible meant it was sufficiently advanced to make an impact following the Japanese attack on Pearl Harbor on 7 December 1941.

What really stood out from both of these pieces was the language. Perhaps from his time in journalism, Fleming had learned how to adapt his style to different cultural nuances. Godfrey was particularly impressed, for Fleming 'ensured that everything was to the point, devoid of ambiguity and worded in a way that appealed to the Americans'.[26] In essence, Fleming had written a pitch, his language devoted to selling an idea.

A month after their first meeting with William Stephenson, on 18 July 1941, Fleming shared the good news with Godfrey that Donovan had been granted funding to the sum of $10 million to start operations within one month.[27] The department was authorised to officially carry out the following duties: secret intelligence, research and analysis, secret operations (including morale and physical subversion), strategic services, progression and development of weapons and equipment, contact with foreign nationality groups and liaison with other Government agencies. Fleming was particularly interested in the research part of this business, principally the gadgets they would go on to create. He especially liked the compasses concealed in golf balls they produced, which would be sent in Red Cross parcels to prisoners of war. As an avid golfer, Fleming went on to use this concept in *Diamonds Are Forever*, as Bond conceals diamonds in his Dunlop 65s, Fleming's personal favourite. But it was pointed out by SOE's gadget expert, Charles Fraser-Smith, that if 'any suspicious investigator tried to bounce balls they would have given the carrier away instantly' due to the extra weight.[28]

As was the case in Britain, rivalry between the new agency, the FBI and the BSC would be rife. Over the coming years this would come to fruition, as demonstrated in a letter dated 21 October 1943, in which Michael Wright from the British Embassy in Washington wrote to Peter Loxley in the Foreign Office describing how Hoover 'does not consistently maintain a level course, and has made things difficult for Stephenson from time to time … it is possible that at one time Stephenson put rather too many of his eggs in the Donovan basket, always expecting Donovan to win out completely in the general rivalry'.[29] Fleming threads a somewhat anti-Hoover sentiment through *Diamonds are Forever*, with throwaway comments about the FBI's lack of co-operation and how this caused a breakdown in relations with other intelligence agencies.

After nearly a month spent in the USA, Fleming came back to London. What had started as a diplomatic visit to help build ties with their opposite numbers in New York and Washington had resulted in Godfrey returning a successful kingmaker and Fleming as the kingdom designer. Donovan gave Fleming a .38 colt revolver engraved with 'for special services' in gratitude for his work. He would proudly show the weapon to his associates, telling them it was given to him by the father of the American Secret Service.

Throughout the rest of the war, Fleming often returned to America to see Stephenson and Donovan. He wrote years later in a letter how, during the war, he was a frequent visitor to the Rockefeller Centre. In fact, although it is not known how many times he made the journey across the Atlantic, he certainly became something of a fixture in America, spending several weeks at a time there, multiple times each year.

He grew intimately knowledgeable about the country. For example, when he met Donald McCormick – a Naval Lieutenant who would go on to write a biography of Fleming – in New York, he was able to warn his younger colleague of some of the inner workings of the city, details of which he could have only obtained by on the ground knowledge. He advised McCormick of the deadly threat in New York's less reputable bars. He went into considerable detail about a specific Belgian lady named Fifi, often found frequenting the Barbizon Plaza, who was a notorious spy being watched by the American Secret Service. Fleming even warned McCormick that, if she tempted him sexually, he should be prepared that the FBI would likely be listening in, if not watching him.[30]

Diamonds are Forever received much praise from critics, not least because of Fleming's vivid detail. Described by the *Spectator* as having 'brilliant descriptive powers', Fleming is able to make the reader feel they are in America with Bond. It is perhaps unsurprising how knowledgeable he was about the CIA, as, after all, it was Fleming who designed it.

Chapter 6

You Only Live Twice

The final book to be published in Fleming's lifetime, *You Only Live Twice*, sees Bond being sent to Japan to create ties with the Japanese intelligence services. While there, his mission changes dramatically, and instead he must infiltrate a mysterious castle, which is thought to house his nemesis, Ernst Stavro Blofeld. Described as a short fat man, Blofeld is the equivalent of Sherlock Holmes' Professor Moriarty. His name was based on Fleming's school friend, Tom Blofeld, whose son Henry became a well-known BBC cricket commentator.

As Blofeld is Bond's number one enemy, he has no choice but to kill him. The plan is to arrive by sea, climb a rock face into the castle, then murder Blofeld before returning to his boat. In true Bond style, he gets caught in the act and only narrowly escapes after killing Blofeld and destroying the castle. As with all of its predecessors, *You Only Live Twice* was a highly romanticised version of the author's own personal encounters. In this case, Fleming was using his experience from working on what was known as *Operation Postmaster*.

As one of the most celebrated secret operations to take place during World War II, *Operation Postmaster* only came to the public's attention several years after victory. Although it is now far from secret, what is often not reported is that Fleming was one of the masterminds behind the whole operation. Like all of his wartime endeavours, he was not on the front line, but rather pulling strings from London.

The operation was conceived after Bletchley Park provided intelligence of a boat in West African Spanish territory claiming to be neutral but in reality commanded by the 'violently pro-Nazi' Captain Specht, who was reportedly using the unblocked radio to feed the Abwehr 'with precise details of Allied shipping movements'.[1] The information was being sent to Berlin through a German fishing organisation in Las Palmas, Gran Canaria. Orders from the top of the British military were that this should be stopped immediately, in a way that would not cause unnecessary stress on the political situation between Britain and Spain. This was an ideal job for SOE, and a report about the situation landed on Colin Gubbins' desk. He set about the task of intercepting Captain Specht's ship. As this would be a maritime operation it was to be done in partnership with Naval Intelligence. Gubbins, known to most as M, therefore consulted Fleming, with whom he now had a good relationship, and the two worked together to plan and execute what would turn out to be one of the most daring raids of the war. Although Fleming would not be capturing a castle in the same way as Bond, the technique of doing so was remarkably similar.

At their briefing, it was explained to Fleming that in the harbour of Santa Isabel on the Island of Fernando Po sat two anchored ships. These were the *Duchessa d'Aosta*, captained by Specht, and the *Likomba*. It was likely that the two boats, although not seemingly providing an immediate threat apart from the use of an unblocked radio, could have been strategically placed there by the enemy. Not only because the *Likomba*, a German tug, would be of practical use to the Nazis, but the *Duchessa d'Aosta* was a valuable ship, possibly worth up to £150,000 at the time with a further £250,000 in cargo. They also held considerable manpower; the crew of the 7,872-ton *Duchessa d'Aosta* was forty-four strong and the 199-ton *Likomba* had two German officers onboard with a native crew.

With the briefing complete, Fleming and M set about building the right team to take on the task of intercepting these ships. To lead, M selected Gus March-Phillipps, who had recently returned from a close shave on the shores of Dunkirk. According to author Brian Lett, as a practicing Roman Catholic 'he believed fervently in God' which was 'followed closely by King and Country'. He was a devoted patriot who felt adamantly that serving his country was more important than his own wellbeing.

Having commissioned in 1928 into the Royal Artillery, March-Phillipps was immediately sent to India where he served for several years, rising to the rank of Lieutenant. A handsome, slim and lightly framed man of medium height with dark, slightly receding hair and piercing eyes, March-Phillipps had been bitten in the face by a horse as a child, which left him with scarring around the mouth. He quit the army in October 1932 aged twenty-four because he felt 'disillusioned with army life', becoming a successful novelist instead. When World War II broke out, he re-joined the army and was appointed as a staff officer in General Brookes' headquarters. As part of the British Expeditionary Force in 1939, he narrowly avoided death during the Dunkirk evacuation. Back in Britain, he was aching to get face to face with the enemy again. As his past showed, he was not one to enjoy the red tape required in the army, so the informal nature of SOE appealed to him.

On 23 January 1941, M interviewed March-Phillipps, who believed he was going for a role with the Inter Services Research Bureau (ISRB). The assessment went well, and needing no persuading, March-Phillipps was sworn into the SOE, joining on 5 March 1941. Technically, a post within the SOE would mean that he was no longer a member of the British Army, although former soldiers in the organisation retained their rank. March-Phillipps was given the code name of Agent W.01 with autonomy to build his own team. 'W' stood for West Africa, where they would be serving, and '01' for 'licensed and trained to kill'.

First to be recruited by March-Phillipps was Second Lieutenant Geoffrey Appleyard, who met M on 25 January 1941. The twenty-three-year-old Royal Army Service Corps (RASC) officer had first come across March-Phillipps at Dunkirk, when the latter landed on top of Appleyard as they both dived for cover from enemy shelling. The first words the two men said to each other came from March-Phillipps who shouted at Appleyard, 'I feel like a bloody coward, how about you?' From that point on the two men would remain friends and became the perfect complement to each other through the war.

Appleyard, from Leeds, was brought up in a comfortable middle-class family. After attending Bootham School, an independent Quaker boarding school in York, he gained a first-class degree in Engineering from Cambridge. Not only was Appleyard a highly intelligent young man, he was enviably sporty, having captained the English ski teams against Norway in 1938 and 1939, as well as being a skilled ice hockey player and water skier. He was also incredibly good looking, with tanned skin, blond hair and a muscled physique. The Army was a natural step for Appleyard, and he joined on a Supplementary Reserve commission on 1 April 1939. His mentality within the military was simple and consistent: 'It is not enough to do our duty, we must do more than our duty – everything that we can to the absolute limit'.[2] Within six months of joining up, the young Second Lieutenant found himself in northern France, where he was soon fleeing for his life, at which point he met March-Phillipps. Both men were successfully evacuated from the beaches of France, although Appleyard's rescue vessel was sunk on its next voyage, the day after it had taken him to safety. Like March-Phillipps, Appleyard was hired into the SOE, taking the rank of W.02.

It was not until 7 March 1941 that March-Phillipps actually met Fleming. Over the coming months, the two men spoke regularly to discuss their potential operation in West Africa. They had a shared vision for this group of SOE soldiers, which was to act as a small-scale raiding force that would be able to cause considerable disruption to the two enemy boats without the British government needing to take responsibility. If any of the men were captured, the authorities would deny any knowledge of March-Phillipps and his men, all of whom had to sign a declaration agreeing to this. They were to be prepared to undertake any type of subversive operations on both sea and land, without the protection granted by the Geneva Convention.

Sent to Anderson Manor, the new headquarters for the Small Scale Raiding Force (SSRF) in Poole on the south coast of England, March-Phillipps and Appleyard set about recruiting their own miniature army. They first hired Graham Hayes, Jan Nasmyth and Leslie Prout, the latter two men having already served with March-Phillipps in Europe. Prout was granted an emergency commission and became the third officer in this new force, being appointed as Lieutenant on 22 April 1941.

Their first task was to find a suitable mode of transport. This came in the guise of a converted Brixham trawler which had once been a fishing vessel before World War I called the *Maid Honor*. The sailing boat was an odd choice for a cutting-edge military force, not least because it only had one small auxiliary engine and was made entirely of wood, but the men felt that the speed and stealth of sailing outweighed the potential downsides. Also, March-Phillipps was keen to prove his theory that a wooden boat was advantageous as it would not be vulnerable to magnetic mines. In the words of Lieutenant Prout, 'having obtained agreement in principle to the proposal of small-scale raids, Gus … although having no authority to proceed … calmly requisitioned' the *Maid Honor*.[3] This was seen by his men as pulling off 'a feat only he could have got away with'.[4] At forty tonnes in weight, the seventy-foot boat would be kitted out as a 'Q-ship', meaning it would be sufficiently modified by the Director of Scientific Research at the SOE, Dr Dudley

M. Hewitt, to have as much advantage in combat as possible. As Brian Lett wrote, 'She was to have a crew of seven, and would be armed with a variety of concealed weapons. She had a two-pounder gun concealed in the dummy wheelhouse and carried 100 rounds for it. She was to carry 4 five-pounder spigot mortars, 4 Bren light machine guns, 4 Tommy guns, 6 rifles, and 36 hand grenades.'[5]

Adding to their team, now known as the Maid Honor Force, was Anders Lassen, a broad-shouldered, tall, blue-eyed man from Denmark who had, in part, been chosen for the SOE by M because he 'had stalked a stag on foot in the hills of South Morar, near the SOE Training Camp, and had killed it with his knife'.[6] Also part of the Maid Honor Force was seventeen-year-old Frank 'Buzz' Perkins, the Naval Reserve Denis Tottenham, Andres Desgranges from the Free French, East Surrey Regiment's chef Ernest Evison, proud Scot 'Haggis' Taylor, and Sergeant Major Tom Winter.

Now a unit of twelve men, the members of the Maid Honor Force were visited in Poole by Commander Ian Fleming on 1 June 1941. He was there to inspect the unit before requesting permission from the Admiralty to send his force overseas to begin their covert activities. There was some significant reluctance to allow SOE's men into West Africa, where tensions with the so-called neutral Spanish were high. Responsibility for persuading the naval powers fell to Fleming. Eight days of fraught conversation later, Fleming met with M on the evening of 22 July 1941, where he was able to present the Head of SOE with handwritten approval from Admiral Godfrey on behalf of the Admiralty. The next two days were full of planning conversations between M and Fleming on the details of the Maid Honor Force's mission, which would be to make their way south where they would, in one way or another, remove the communication channel with the Abwehr and put the *Duchessa d'Aosta* and the *Likomba* out of action.

Intelligence was starting to feed back to Fleming from the head of the SOE in West Africa – thirty-two-year-old Belgian Louis Frank – who had left Britain on 6 December 1940 along with six other members of the new W Section. Part of the advanced party included Lieutenant Victor Laversuch, Captain Richard Lippett, Captain John Eyre and Lieutenant Desmond Longe. The men were sent to Lagos on a hazardous journey, protected by the American Navy, and set up offices in Lagos Police Station. While there, they recruited a further SOE officer, Lieutenant

Charles Guise, to be known as W.10. Although he spoke limited Spanish, W.10 became the unit's undercover officer, travelling under the disguise of a diplomatic courier to Fernando Po on a small requisitioned river tug, the *Bamenda*.

Louis Frank informed M that Guise had reported 'an active organised German community of some forty on the mainland and island', continuing:

> The community have large commercial interests. They have a great deal of influence with the Spanish officials, whose Falangist ideology is akin to their own. They are active in propaganda work and they have an organised system of espionage ... The position of the courier is extremely delicate. He has only recently been appointed and is regarded with the greatest suspicion by the Spanish authorities.

He concluded that although Guise 'has done a great deal in a short time to establish satisfactory relations, the slightest mischance or false step might easily lead to a request for his recall'.[7] It was becoming clear that the network of pro-Nazi supporters was much larger and a bigger threat than anyone had anticipated.

*

On 12 August 1941, the men aboard the *Maid Honor* set sail on the 3,000-mile voyage from Poole to Freetown. The boat flew a Swedish flag as disguise. M had visited the Maid Honor Force on 10 August 1941 to bid them farewell and wish them luck. Hosting a lunch for the men, M sat at the end of the table 'like a much loved warlord presiding over a band of gangsters'.[8]

After a somewhat perilous journey, March-Phillipps' team arrived in Lagos, beyond Freetown, on 20 September 1941. They were greeted by Longe, who described the crew as 'a party of such delightful, enthusiastic and courageous men, prepared to face any task allotted to them, no matter the odds'.[9] Appleyard wrote that the camp they were welcomed into 'is for us a sort of holiday' as he relaxed on his sun bed.[10] Their journey was tougher than anyone had anticipated, so the respite was needed. But the challenges aboard the *Maid Honor* had definitely brought the unit together. This is seen in a letter from Appleyard to his sister on Christmas Eve of 1941:

> We are three officers on board – Gus (Captain), Graham and I. Then there is Tom Winter, who was a sergeant in Graham's parachute battalion. He was a special protégé of Graham's and the two always work together. Next come Andre Desgranges, who is my special protégé, works with me, and is one of the finest chaps with whom I have ever had anything to do … He was a deep sea diver in the French Navy before the war, and is also a good engineer … Also we have Andy Lassen – A Dane – who is a crack shot with any kind of weapon and a splendid seaman. Denis Tottenham, aged twenty-four, is a good seaman … Then there is Buzz Perkins, the youngest of the party, who is a very sound lad, very keen and willing and tough. Finally, there is Ernest Evison, the cook (whole time job when we are at sea), who in his job is invaluable and unbeatable … he is an excellent cook, trained in France and Switzerland.[11]

He failed to mention the other two members of the crew, acting quartermaster Leslie Prout and Haggis Taylor. This seems through error rather than any intent.

Although they had been granted permission to travel to West Africa and be based there, the Maid Honor Force were still struggling to gain the necessary permission to carry out the raid they wanted, to remove the *Duchessa d'Aosta* and the *Likomba* from the hands of the enemy. Fleming, M and March-Phillipps had always thought they would need to destroy the boats, but this would be too obviously a hostile tactic against Spain. From the rich intelligence provided by Guise, it became apparent that they could steal the boats instead. The suggestion excited M, who liked the idea of his men being able to 'strike the enemy and disappear completely, leaving no trace'.[12] Plans were altered, with the focus now being the acquisition of the vessels. The objective of what was now termed *Operation Postmaster* was to board and capture both the *Duchessa d'Aosta* and the *Likomba*. They would then be removed from the small harbour at Santa Isabel with as little fuss as possible.

The three leaders of *Operation Postmaster* were March-Phillipps, in command of the boats; on the ground in Lagos, Laversuch was in charge; and pulling the strings from London was Ian Fleming. On 15 October 1941, Laversuch left Lagos to travel to London where he met with M and Fleming. Together, they presented their proposed mission to the Foreign Office on 12 November, who reluctantly agreed to let the operation go ahead. Reporting a strong case back to Godfrey, Fleming gained even more reluctant permission from the Admiralty on 20 November. *Operation Postmaster* was now becoming a reality.

It was agreed that the Maid Honor Force would be responsible for carrying out the raid, but their namesake boat would play no part. Both target boats had been stationed in the port for some time, with the *Duchessa d'Aosta* being anchored for over sixteen months without its engines ever being started. It was therefore decided early in the planning phase that trying to use the boats' own means of power was simply not an option. Instead, two tugs, the *Vulcan* and the *Nuneaton* were chosen to tow the boats out of the harbour. Each tug came with an expert tugmaster, Commander Coker and Lieutenant Goodman. On his many trips through the harbour, Guise spent much time subtlety inspecting the anchor chains holding the *Duchessa d'Aosta* and the *Likomba* to determine the number of explosives which would be needed to blow them free.

For the operation to be a success, the Maid Honor Force needed to get as many enemy crew members off the boats as possible before they boarded. At the very least, it was important to get the officers off, as they were the most likely to organise resistance. Responsibility for creating a suitable distraction fell into the hands of Richard Lippett. His plan was simple; he would invite the officers to a dinner party, which had the advantage of not only getting them off their respective ships but would also suitably intoxicate them to make their chances of being able to form a last-minute resistance even slimmer.

Lippett first had to find a puppet he could control and who could unwittingly act as the host. For this role, he chose Abelino Zorilla, a local hardware store worker. Zorilla was told that a shipping company had approached Lippett to arrange some entertainment for the officers onboard the boats, as they were concerned about morale. Lippett himself explained to Zorilla that he could have nothing to do with such entertainment as it would be seen as him fraternising with the enemy. The lie was quickly accepted, and invites were duly sent out and acceptances received.

The operation had originally been scheduled for 22 December 1941, for the simple reason that this was the next moonless night. The Maid Honor Force would need to leave Lagos some time before, ideally four days, but travel delays caused them to depart behind schedule and the operation was delayed by a month until 14 January 1942. There were several advantages to this delay, not least because the operation was far from fully planned; it also meant the men could have a Christmas party. In letter home, Appleyard wrote, 'We had a grand Christmas dinner at night, with turkey and etceteras, plum pudding (on fire!), mince pies, etc, and all the additions of crackers, a Christmas tree, chocolates.'[13]

It was bad news for Lippett, who had to cancel his party and try to get something else arranged. Zorilla set to the task admirably, finding a new date and reissuing invites. He even ran a test party on 27 December to help add to the cover. Thirty people were in attendance at the Casino Terrace Restaurant, including Captain Specht and all of the officers from the *Duchessa d'Aosta*. The proceedings did not conclude until 4.00am the next morning.

The real party was now set for 14 January 1942. The preferred restaurant was the Valencia, due mainly to the fact it was inland from the port and therefore a fair distance for the officers to travel back to their boats should the alarm be raised. It also meant that any noise from the explosions required to blow the anchor chains would be muffled. However, with only two days to go until the operation, the Valencia cancelled the reservation due to the illness of the owner's wife. In its place, the Casino Terrace Restaurant was chosen as the next best option. Unfortunately for the Maid Honor Force, the restaurant was adjacent to the port, with a large terrace overlooking the *Duchessa d'Aosta* and the *Likomba*. Contingency planning was needed, so bright lights were erected on the terrace pointing inwards to obscure the view to the port. The local brothel was also asked to provide prostitutes to attend the party, because it was believed that if the women sat facing the port, the officers would be suitably distracted and unlikely to turn around.

While the party planning was underway, there was also the chance for Fleming to look at the issue of what to actually do with the boats when captured. He consulted with Admiral Willis, Flag Officer commanding 3rd Battle Squadron, on 5 January 1942. Immediately considering the mission to be of significant importance, Admiral Willis gave his support and offered the use of one of his fleet, HMS *Violet,* under the command of Lieutenant Herbert Nicholas, as the perfect vessel to officially 'capture' the *Duchessa d'Aosta* and the *Likomba* once at sea.

It was agreed that a fake message would be issued to HMS *Violet* saying two unidentified – believed to be enemy – vessels had been spotted in the ship's vicinity and they would be sent to intervene. The British would then release a statement to the BBC reading:

> The Admiralty announced tonight that early this afternoon a Naval Patrol ship intercepted off the West African coast two Axis vessels whose crews had mutinied and were attempting to reach the Vichy French port of Cotonou. Neither of these vessels, a cargo boat of some 8,000 tons and a tug of 200 tons, made any attempt to resist capture. One of the crew stated that the ships had been lying in Spanish territorial waters since 1939 and explained that, owing to some dissatisfaction with their living conditions and lack of pay, they had decided to take advantage of the absence of their senior officers to raise steam and slip out to sea under cover of darkness. The story throws interesting light on the low state of Axis morale abroad and also emphasises once more the unceasing vigilance of the Royal Navy.[14]

Further consideration was also given to the size of the Maid Honor Force, which only consisted of eleven men, with an additional six SOE officers. For extra support, March-Phillipps was sent to meet with the Governor of Nigeria, Sir Bernard Bourdillon. The Governor was only too happy to lend his support, providing seventeen local men to join the raiding force.

Selected from all corners of the Colonial Government, they consisted of four police officers, three working in education, three from the administrative branch, four members of the Public Works Department, one surveyor, one accountant and a doctor in case of casualties. Guise recalled to Fleming that they were 'as choice a collection of thugs as Nigeria can ever have seen'.[15] The men were all invited to attend a party on 32 Cameron Road in Lagos on 10 January, with no further detail provided. The party consisted of a briefing by March-Phillipps, requiring the men to take two weeks leave in order to volunteer for a secret mission, of which they were told it would be dangerous but of great national importance. All the men duly agreed to the terms, were kitted with black field-dress and taken to the *Vulcan* and *Nuneaton* in Apapa Dock in Lagos, where they joined the Maid Honor Force and SOE officers. The two boats and forty-one men, as well as a full complement of stokers and trimmers to run the barges, set sail for Santa Isabel Harbour at 4.40am on 11 January 1942.

The *Vulcan*, whose task it was to capture the *Duchessa d'Aosta*, was commanded by Mr T.C.T. Coker, with Lieutenant Duff as his deputy – a man who took to wearing full uniform from the waist up, but below he wore only his underpants to combat the heat. Coker had two engineers, Lieutenant Commanders Oldand and Duffy, and acting Quartermaster Dennis Tottenham from the Maid Honor Force. In military command were March-Phillipps and Appleyard, accompanied by Desgranges, Lassen, Prout, Evison and Taylor. Also aboard were four volunteers, including a medic, and an engine crew of thirteen black Africans to keep the steam tug operational. The ship had undergone some modification, with a landing board added to the port side of the guard rail, to act as a 'plank' for the men to mount the *Duchessa d'Aosta*.

Responsible for capturing the *Likomba* was the *Nuneaton*, a motorised tug commanded by Lieutenant Goodman and crewed by Nigerians O. Hanson and Olu David. Along with Hayes in command were Guise, Winter and Perkins from the Maid Honor Force. The remaining local volunteers accompanied them. No modifications were needed on the *Nuneaton*, as it was decided that two Folbot canoes, painted grey, would be used to board the enemy vessel.

The *Vulcan* 'wallowed along slowly' with the *Nuneaton* being towed 'dancing along behind her like a naughty puppy on a lead', according to a member of the Maid Honor Force. There were some difficulties on their journey, not least through their decision to tow the *Nuneaton*. At one stage, the boats drifted apart to the point they were nearly side by side rather than front and back. When the *Vulcan* was caught in the swell, dragging the *Nuneaton* with her, she almost capsized the smaller boat. As Lassen noticed what was unfolding, he jumped down from the wheelhouse with an axe and ran to the stern of the *Vulcan* to hack through the line, releasing the *Nuneaton* and preventing her from being dragged further under the water. Both boats had an enforced blackout during darkness, to avoid any enemy interception, but also added to their navigational challenges.

According to the *Maid Honor* log, which was onboard the *Vulcan* at this point, Santa Isabel Peak (the highest area of Fernando Po) was sighted at 10.00 am on 14 January. With zero hour – the time of the attack – thirteen-and-a-half hours away, all the boats could do now was stop and wait.

Their engines were restarted at 5.30 pm, and the two boats crept towards their prey as darkness engulfed the port. Once they entered the harbour, they cut their motors and drifted silently through the moonless night. Meanwhile, on shore, twenty-five men and women enjoyed dinner at the Casino Terrace Restaurant, including eight officers from the *Duchessa d'Aosta* and two from the *Likomba*. As the wine started to flow, the men settled into what would be a long and entertaining night. By 10.00 pm, Zorilla made his excuses and left the dinner table. He immediately fled from the island.

Just after 11.30 pm, the wartime blackout was enforced, throwing the town into utter darkness. The party in the Casino Terrace Restaurant continued in earnest, the officers' eyesight slowly recovering from the bright spotlights that had been shining in all evening. Back in the harbour, the *Nuneaton* came to a halt, silently dropping the two Folbot canoes into the water, with Hayes and Winter in the first, and Newington and Abell – two of the local volunteers – in the second. Both groups, who were heavily armed with tommy guns and pistols, made their way towards the *Nuneaton* with minimal noise and scarcely any visibility. The four men on the two boats arrived at the wrong target because it was so dark, raiding an unoccupied Spanish launch by accident. Soon realising they were aboard a different ship, they quickly returned to their Folbots and set off again for their actual target.

The commandos eventually got to the *Likomba*, where they were met by two sailors who believed the boats contained their drunk captain and officers returning from the shore. When they saw the Folbots were actually filled with men with blacked out faces and armed to the teeth, they did not hesitate in fleeing, jumping over the side and swimming for it.

Newington and Abell immediately searched the ship and made sure no counterattack was possible – all they discovered were two cats – while

Hayes and Winters heaved up their heavy rucksacks, containing enough explosives to blow the anchoring chains, and began setting the fuses.

Meanwhile, aboard the *Nuneaton*, Goodman was steering the tug alongside the *Likomba*, in order for the rest of the men to board. Once they were parallel, Guise and Perkins attempted to mount the *Likomba* with a towing hawser. However, they had only just set foot on the enemy vessel when one of the charges now attached to an anchoring chain accidentally went off. Fully exposed to the blast, both men were sent flying the way they had come, landing back aboard the *Nuneaton*. Neither was injured worse than a few cracked ribs, so they quickly re-boarded the *Likomba*, this time more successfully. They connected the hawser to the front of their prize, just in time for the *Nuneaton* to take the strain and start to tow the boat out of the harbour. At that exact moment, the order was given, and the remaining anchor chains were blasted, freeing the vessel.

Attached to the *Likomba* was a small seventy-ton Spanish pleasure cruiser, under half the size of the *Likomba*. Initially the men of the Maid Honor Force were inclined to cut this boat free as it had little value to them; however, while it was being searched for crew members, a picture of the boat displaying a Nazi flag was found, so they quickly changed their mind and decided to take it as well.

The explosions on the boat had caused the decoy dinner party, happening just 400 meters away, to fall silent. The naval officers peered around to see what had caused the noise, but with no sign of fire or any further sound, they returned to their meal.

During this time, the *Vulcan* had made its way alongside the *Duchessa d'Aosta*. Unlike the minimalistic boarding party of four used to take the *Likomba*, March-Phillipps was leading a group of over twenty men to take the much larger *Duchessa d'Aosta*. The boarding party waited patiently on the bridge deck, next to the custom-made platform to get them across to their prey.

Covered by two Bren guns, the men were given the order to board by March-Phillipps when the two boats were parallel. Carrying a line, Lassen connected and secured the boats together temporarily, allowing about a quarter of the raiding party to board, before the two ships crashed into each other from the swell of the sea, parting suddenly before crashing back together and allowing another six or so men to board. This went on until all the men were on the *Duchessa d'Aosta*.

Meeting no resistance on the upper deck, they quickly and efficiently searched the ship, finding only one pig and two crew members on the deck. One was arrested while the other managed to free himself and leapt over the side, smacking into the sea on his stomach before making haste towards the safety of the shore. Below deck, twenty-seven European crewmen were discovered and quickly arrested. March-Phillipps would later report that there was 'no resistance worthy of the name'. A few of the men were uncooperative, so a member of the Maid Honor Force 'had to take his [truncheon] and play a quick arpeggio on their heads'.[16] They also discovered a stewardess who had barricaded herself into her room, believing the noise was just drunken sailors returning to the ship. When the commandos kicked her door in, she immediately fainted.

With the radio room secured, so no messages could be sent back to shore, the Maid Honor Force prepared to blow the six anchor chains that stood between them and the valuable boat. With a single blast from March-Phillipps' whistle, the six chains were blasted into thousands of pieces, allowing the *Duchessa d'Aosta* to come free for the first time in eighteen months. The *Vulcan* immediately pulled forward, taking the strain of the *Duchessa d'Aosta* and dragging her out of the harbour. From the deck, March-Phillipps shouted in ecstasy, 'My god, she's free!'[17] Travelling at three knots, the *Vulcan* quickly overtook the much slower *Nuneaton*, as both ships towed their well-deserved acquisitions away, within thirty-five minutes of launching the assault.

Although the Maid Honor Force had got away with the relatively small explosions on the *Likomba*, the six explosives on the *Duchessa d'Aosta* had woken the whole of Santa Isabel, with people rushing from their houses, believing there was an air raid taking place. Guise recalled it as 'a titanic roar and a flash that lit the whole island'. Confusion was the best friend of the attackers, as rather than the islanders searching the waters, the army started firing blindly at the sky, hoping to hit an enemy plane.

Such was the confusion from the explosions in the port, followed by the rapid fire of the anti-aircraft guns, the officers of the *Likomba* and the *Duchessa d'Aosta* were so dazed after their dinner that they slowly sauntered back down to where their ships should have been, only to realise they had gone.

Captain Specht furiously marched over to the British Consulate, where he confronted Vice-Consul Godden who recalled how 'he was very drunk and quarrelsome' when asked to leave the Consulate and 'in reply, he struck me in the face'.[18] Godden responded by 'literally knocking the shit out of him' to which Specht 'collapsed in a heap, split his pants and emptied his bowels on the floor'.

Consul Peter Lake recalled that 'the following day was full of rumours ... Free French, Vichy, USA, British and even anti-Falange Spanish pirates were all equally possible culprits'.[19] Speculation was further encouraged by March-Phillipp's clever ploy of dropping a bunch of Free French caps into the sea, which were found floating in the harbour when the sun rose.

On 20 January, the stolen ships arrived in Lagos harbour to a 'tremendous reception'. M reported back to Fleming that 'casualties, our party, absolutely nil. Casualties enemy, nil, except a few sore heads. Prisoners, German, nil; Italians, men, 27, women; 1, natives, 1', as well as two ships, the *Likomba* and the *Duchessa d'Aosta*.[20] James Bond did not manage quite the same result as *Operation Postmaster*, as there were far more casualties and noise from his mission. However, the concept of sabotage like this was something 007 became famous for.

Chapter 7

Thunderball

The eighth full length Bond novel, *Thunderball,* sees 007 sent on a mission to retrieve two stolen atomic bombs, which are being used by international terrorist group, SPECTRE, to threaten world peace. In an attempt to save the lives of millions, Bond travels to the Bahamas where he meets Felix Leiter and tracks the bombs to a man called Emilio Largo. After a fierce underwater fight, Largo is killed, and the bombs are returned safely. Throughout the book, the reader is enthralled by the workings of a crack commando unit trying to recover something of extreme value, which comes directly from Fleming's knowledge on the topic.

With the success of *Operation Postmaster* and the concept of *Operation Ruthless* lodged in the forefront of his mind, Fleming was of the opinion that a permanent foraging force should be created. Rather than having to build a team from scratch each time there was a need for a pinch, he wanted something lasting.

Working on the concept alone, he set about writing a proposal to create his own team of professional robbers, something he would later term his 'Red Indians'. On 20 March 1942, Fleming placed a paper on Godfrey's desk titled 'Naval Intelligence Commando Unit', which outlined his observations of the German Intelligence's naval commandos. He described how these commandos' would always accompany the front-line troops anytime a naval facility was attacked. Because they were right at the forefront of the action, if the attack was successful, their remit was to capture as much important material – including cypher machines and codes – before the defenders had time to destroy them. Fleming recommended that NID should build a corresponding commando unit, based on a similar structure created by the Germans. Signed off with his usual 'F', Fleming handed his proposal to Godfrey for his initial thoughts. The Director of Naval Intelligence read the document, and simply wrote in pencil on it 'YES, most decidedly', and passed it back to his assistant.

Where Fleming had suggested that his commando unit should be submitted to Admiral Sir Roger Keyes, Commander of Combined Operations – meaning he would be the man to make the final decision – Godfrey crossed through it, writing instead that the principle should be 'worked out in collaboration with C.C.O.'. As with most things, Godfrey was far from supportive of handing over any control or power to anyone outside of NID, in particular to Keyes. To create something similar in isolation would not only be unpopular, it meant starting from scratch. This was a difficult task and Fleming knew it; he asked Godfrey to reconsider.

Godfrey would not change his mind when challenged by Fleming. On 13 April, Godfrey wrote a to him that 'it would be a mistake to turn over the working out of an "advance intelligence unit" to the C.C.O.' because a unit 'similar to what has been proposed' was 'bound to get a low priority' and 'moreover, to turn it over to him is an admission that he and his intelligence staff are better able to work out such an arrangement'. He therefore ordered that 'the matter be tackled' by Fleming under his supervision. With that, the decision was final. Fleming was in charge, with Godfrey's beady eye watching over him. With no option but to fall in line, Fleming called a meeting on 3 June, which according to the minutes set out the plan for 'a suitable number of trained Commando troops' to 'be detailed a fortnight before each operation for special training on their objective'.[1]

It was agreed in the meeting that the unit should be a blend of commandos and specialists. Simply having naval practitioners would not suffice – experts would need to be present to identify and inspect the loot being hunted. Although this was generally accepted at the meeting, it was agreed that said experts 'should be dressed alike and should be toughened physically and mentally in just the same way' as the commandos. The structure would be such that 'the number of regular commando troops should be reduced on each occasion by the number of specialists embodied – such specialists should never exceed 25% of the strength of the platoon' in order to make sure the group was sufficiently protected.

With the basic formation agreed, Godfrey circulated a memo around the Admiralty on 26 June, with a covering note asking those with suggestions of desirable loot to contact 'Commander I.L. Fleming, R.N.V.R, Ext. 991, [who] will be available to give any further information required on the machinery of Intelligence Assault Units'.[2] Between the 29 June and 6 August, Fleming was bombarded with requests on everything from 'German mines, hydrophones, ASDIC [Anti-Submarine Detection Investigation Committee] equipment, depth gauges, U-boat tactics from logbooks or war diaries' through to 'all kinds of books, documents, maps, charts and papers that could be found'.[3]

Having gained overwhelming support from Admiralty colleagues, Fleming suggested to Godfrey that firstly a meeting between representives of the different security services would be sensible. Godfrey agreed and on 22 July Fleming presented his idea to a selection of intelligence specialists and leaders from different departments. Present were Commander Arnold-Forster (MI6), Major Cass (double hatting for MI5 and the Ministry of Economic Warfare), Major Williams-Thompson (Combined Operations Intelligence), Colonel Neville and Captain Colvin (both of the Royal Marines). They agreed with Fleming's recommendation that his unit should consist of at least twenty men, mostly officers, and they should be accompanied by Royal Marines for protection.

According to the minutes from the meeting, those present 'accepted a scheme put forward by [Fleming] for the predation of an intelligence assault unit to participate in commando raids and to accompany the early assault waves in large scale operations, also with the object of seizing the high grade intelligence material before it could be destroyed'.[4]

That was all the approval he needed. Fleming's next task was recruitment. Three sections were to be made up by the Royal Navy, Royal Marines and Army. Although this was to be a fully naval affair, the army would be needed for any inland targets.

First to be recruited was Commander R.E.D. Ryder VC, a member of the naval training staff, who was given the remit to manage 'the creation and training of a Naval Intelligence Assault Unit'.[5]

Adding gravitas to Fleming's concept, Ryder was an ingenious choice to build a new commando group. Having joined the Navy in 1926, he served on various ships and submarines before being promoted to Commander at the outbreak of the war. During World War II he was put in command of several ships, including the 'Q Ship', HMS *Willamette Valley* which, similar to the *Maid Honor*, was disguised as a merchant vessel called HMS *Edgehill*. Just after midnight on 29 June 1940, the boat was torpedoed by a German U Boat, U-51, commanded by Kapitänleutnant Dietrich Knorr. It took two further torpedoes from Knorr to destroy Ryder's ship, which only sank an hour-and-a-half later. Of the ninety-seven men onboard, sixty-seven lost their lives and twenty-nine made it to a lifeboat and were picked up by a French trawler. As for Commander Ryder, he refused to board a lifeboat and remained on his boat as she sank, but 'rescued himself on a piece of flotsam' which he clung to for four days before being picked up by a friendly passing vessel.

Ryder was chosen to lead an *Operation Postmaster* style mission to Normandie Dock at St Nazaire. Intelligence believed that 'the most powerful warship in the world', the *Tirpitz*, would soon be headed to the Atlantic. Such was the fear of the 52,600 ton *Tirpitz*, Churchill wrote that 'no other target is comparable to it ... the whole strategy of the war turns at this period on this ship'.[6] The only feasible place to repair any damages sustained to the *Tirpitz* in the Atlantic was the only Nazi controlled deep water port in the vacinity, St Nazaire, where it would be protected behind 1,200 feet of concrete blocks and giant steel gates at each end. Without the dock at St Nazaire, it would not be sustainable to send the *Tirpitz* to the Atlantic, giving the Allies a much-needed advantage.

Leading a team of more than 600 men, Ryder commanded the operation of sixteen small gunboats, two destroyers and HMS *Campbeltown*, the latter fitted with 'a gigantic bomb' containing four-and-a-half tons of explosives controlled by 'Time Pencils', which had been placed deep below its deck.[7] Travelling at eighteen knots, HMS *Campbeltown* was being steered by its captain Lieutenant Commander Stephen Halden Beattie, straight towards St Nazaire on 29 March 1942, taking heavy fire from the awaiting Nazi defences and at exactly 1.34 am smashed straight into the dock gates. On impact, Beattie calmly looked at his watch and said 'well there we are ... four minutes late'.[8]

The ship's valves were immediately opened to sink her so the Germans would not be able to move her from the entrance to the port. Meanwhile, a group of commandos lead by Bill Prichard made their way to the pump houses on shore, which they filled with 150 pounds of high explosives. Destroying the pumps would mean the dock would no longer be able to be filled or emptied, rendering it completely useless. Of the 611 people who took part in the raid, 384 were either killed or captured. One in four of all the men sustained injuries with everything from a broken thumb through to lifelong disabilities. It was not until 11.00 am, when the Nazis thought they had secured the area and arrested any remaining

British commandos, that an explosion erupted in the port, destroying everything in its path. For this raid, Ryder was awarded Britain's highest military medal, the Victoria Cross. After the success at St Nazaire, he was approached to set up Fleming's new commando force, known as 30 Assault Unit or simply 30AU.

Ryder appointed Major W.G. Class as his joint second in command, along with Commander Fleming who represented DNI's interests. The unit was to be structured with three sections. The Royal Navy section called No. 36 Technical Troop comprising of one Lieutenant Commander, three Lieutenants and three Second Lieutenants. The Royal Marine Troop, known as No. 33, was to contain two Captains and twenty Other Ranks. Finally, the Army Troop, called No. 34, was to be led by two Captains (which would later increase to four) and twelve Other Ranks.

Ryder believed that actions spoke louder than words, and at a conference he called on 31 July 1942, 'after some discussion, the meeting agreed that [he] should initiate a trial on a small basis, with a special unit of any 20 men ... and that expansion might be found desirable if the unit proved its worth and obtained valuable results'. Therefore, 'while the question of the formation of the unit was still under consideration', a test group known as No. 40 RM Commando were sent out on the next big Allied outing, to test Fleming's hypothesis.[9] Timing was on their side, as *Operation Jubilee*, the largest cross-Channel operation up to that point, was due to take place just three weeks later.

Headed for the Normandy port of Dieppe, 700 aeroplanes and thirteen naval groups planned to take control of the German controlled territory by landing on six adjacent beaches. Along with British commandos assigned to knock out naval defences, 30AU were tasked to capture as much cypher material as possible.

Planning for *Operation Jubilee* was believed to be world class, but it was based entirely on reconnaissance which was flawed from the start. Reconnaissance flights over Dieppe had completely missed the anti-tank weapons and state of the art machine guns which lay on rail tracks hidden under the cliffs. As the 6,000 strong team of infantrymen made their way towards the target in the early hours of 19 August 1942, they had no idea of the sheer danger they were soon to face. Among them were the men of 30AU, led by Ryder on HMS *Locust*, while Fleming sat aboard HMS *Fernie*, some way behind, there strictly as an observer.

At 4.50 am, the first troops landed at Dieppe and were immediately hit with an almighty onslaught from the German defences. HMS *Locust* was quickly struck by one of the hundreds of enemy shells being fired at the ships. Before the men even had a chance to board their landing craft, they were in trouble, with one marine stating the 'explosion was gigantic … it blew all the fuses in my nervous system'.[10]

Unfortunately, due to poor communications between the Canadian soldiers who had landed on the beach and those still on the boats, the message did not filter through that the Allies were taking a battering at Dieppe. In fact, the commander on HQ ship HMS *Calpe*, Major General Roberts, received a message saying the Canadians were already inside Dieppe Casino – where the Germans had created their headquarters – and wrongly assumed it meant the troops had taken the beach. The truth was that a few brave commandos had managed to get to the casino, but the area was far from secured. Not knowing the deathtrap they were soon to enter, the members of 30AU aboard the damaged HMS *Locust* were ordered onto their landing craft and cast off.

As the men approached Dieppe they saw 'a weird rock garden of busted tanks and landing craft, with orchids of fire sputtering from bromeliads of twisted metal and the khaki dead lying about like bits of wood on the pebbles'.[11] It was clear that the beach was not going to fall and that they were travelling towards almost certain death. Giving the signal that their vessel was to be turned around, smoke bombs were dropped in the water to mask their escape and the men of 30AU desperately made their way back to the relative safety of HMS *Locust*.

More bad luck came when their landing craft was hit by an enemy shell, setting the Ford Diesel Engine on fire. Twenty-three-year-old Lieutenant Huntington-Whiteley screamed for his men to remove their kit and swim for safety, shouting 'every man do the best he can!'[12] Fleming recalled watching through his field glasses from HMS *Fernie* as 'the landing craft carrying the section was sunk and most of the men spent several hours in the water'.[13] They did all they could, some swimming literally miles before being picked up. For his newly formed commando unit, this was a complete failure, but at least all his men returned home.

For the raiding forces, losses that fateful day were huge. With 5,000 Canadians, 1,000 British and fifty American Rangers taking part, nearly 4,000 were either killed, captured or wounded, accounting for over sixty percent of those who actually landed on the beaches. The RAF took a battering as well, losing 106 planes, over double the number of Luftwaffe. Aside from the terrible loss of life and damage to reputation, Dieppe would also spell extra danger for all commando operations for the remainder of the war. The brave soldiers who had managed to take the casino accidentally left behind a British order stating 'German prisoners should be shackled'. This was the tipping point for Hitler, energised by his victory at Dieppe, who on 18 October 1942 ordered that 'all enemies on so-called commando missions in Europe or Africa ... whether armed or unarmed, in battle or in flight, are to be slaughtered to the last man'.[14]

Fleming found it difficult to add up the pros and cons' of his commando unit at Dieppe, 'but one thing was clear: [30 AU's] intelligence, planning and execution had been faultless. The machinery for producing further raids is thus tried and found good'.[15] It was recorded in the official history of the unit that 'the operation was not successful, however, as the section was unable to reach its target'; it could thus not be classed as a 'failure'.[16]

Although Fleming was happy to see action, albeit from afar, it was clear that he was in no state to have an active part moving forward. Despite his dreams of being on the front line, among his commandos, he was not cut from the same cloth as the likes of Ryder. He was simply not fit enough, with his daily intake of cigarettes and alcohol only ever increasing. This was something Fleming accepted and had no intention of changing. He put these traits into Bond, somewhat proudly, claiming that his protagonist never believed he over-indulged, despite some obvious medical concerns such as his tongue being furred and high blood pressure, not to mention his frequent headaches.

Fleming would have to settle for a war, in the most part, behind his desk. It was his fictional creation who could live his unhealthy lifestyle, while also being fighting fit.

*

Despite the fate of *Operation Jubilee*, the idea remained alive and Fleming was ordered to get 30 Assault Unit ready for the invasion of North Africa known as *Operation Torch*.

Although 30AU had not made their way successfully into Dieppe to actually gather intelligence, Fleming had been pleased with the detailed briefing his men had received on their targets and the local area. With the much larger scale invasion of North Africa in mind, Fleming and

Godfrey set up a new operation in Oxford called NID 5. The team they created consisted of 170 volunteer intellectuals who went on to produce fifty-eight volumes of 'useful background information' on twenty-nine locations which the commandos could target.[17]

As training began in earnest, Fleming wrote to Godfrey outlining the programme he proposed the unit should undergo. This, he suggested, would last for six weeks and for the last fortnight, he would be present as a trainer. He signed off the letter with a typical suggestion, saying the officers should be encouraged to read *Out of the Night* (1940) by exiled German Communist Jan Valtin, *The American Black Chamber* (1931) by Herbert O. Yardley, a book on the interwar US government cryptography department known as the 'Black Chamber', and *The German Secret Service* (1924) by Walter Nikolai, the first senior Intelligence Officer in the Imperial German Army.

Training started on 28 September 1942 at Montague House and lasted eight weeks. It was imperative that the unit would be ready for *Operation Torch*, which was due to take place at the start of November. Although this was a tight timeline, Fleming was first to remind sceptics that the Admiralty had emphasised the urgency of the requirement as long ago as March and therefore further delay was not an option.

The men chosen for the unit were from among officers who had volunteered 'for hazardous service'. First picked was Cambridge University graduate Lieutenant Commander Riley. Chosen for being particularly adept at survival, Riley had 'engaged continuously on Polar exploration, taking part in two expeditions to Greenland and one to the Antarctic' between 1930 and 1937.[18] At the start of the war, he joined up with the RNVR and was immediately sent to Finland as a secondee into the Scots Guards. However, with the Nazi advance, he was soon on his way to Norway where he took up a position within SOE. For his time in Norway, Riley was mentioned in dispatches. He returned to the UK only to be sent away again, this time to Iceland where he trained soldiers in winter warfare.

Second to be selected was Lieutenant Dunstan Curtis, an Oxford graduate, former solicitor and fluent French and German speaker. Curtis had served with Commander Ryder on the St Nazaire raid and had taken part in *Operation Jubilee*. One of his officers remembered him as 'middle height, and clearly something of a dandy whether in uniform or civilian garb ... he had an unusually agreeable voice, soft-toned, unaffected but effective in discussion, except with Fleming'.[19] As this description suggests, Curtis was not Fleming's biggest fan, commenting that 'the trouble with Ian is that you have to get yourself killed before he feels anything'.[20] Fleming's friend and later 30AU operative Lieutenant Robert Harling subsequently speculated that their reason for disliking each other was that 'the two Etonians were as suspicious of each other's ambitions and intentions as a pair of wary lynxes'. An on-going issue for Fleming was that he envied the 'gongs and achievements in action' of his men, as he remained, for the most part, behind a desk in the safety of NID.[21]

Fleming's role in 30AU, as described by one of the officers, was '[directing] operations in general terms from the Admiralty' while always getting 'first sight of our reports, to which he added comments' before they were sent on to more senior channels.[22] Despite this, he always saw himself as an outsider and longed to get his hands dirty with his men.

The third and final officer chosen to lead the unit was Second Lieutenant George McFee, formally an Incorporated Accountant, who joined the RNVR and volunteered for hazardous services. Within the Royal Marine section, Captain Herbert Oliver 'Peter' Huntington-Whiteley, who had been on the failed Dieppe mission, was chosen as troop leader and described in the 30AU records as 'a fine athlete and musician', with Captain John Hargreaves-Heap as the Administration Officer.[23]

Also selected was Patrick Dalzel-Job, a twenty-nine-year-old Royal Naval Volunteer Reservist, who had served as part of the Norwegian Campaign in 1940. When the order was issued to cease further civilian evacuations to Britain as the Nazi's advanced, Dalzel-Job disobeyed the orders, saving the lives of nearly 5,000 Norwegians and risking Court Marshal. He wrote years after the war that 'someone said that I gave the germ of the idea of James Bond' which he was quick to dismiss, stating 'I should think it unlikely'.[24] In fact, in his later years, he was somewhat insulted by the insinuation stating that, 'I have never read a Bond book or seen a Bond movie. They are not my style,' while, he continued, 'I only ever loved one woman, and I'm not a drinking man.'[25] But whether Dalzel-Job was just being modest or was genuinely indifferent, his remarks do not alter the fact that it was the traits, motivations and personalities of Fleming's unit that inspired much of the character of James Bond.

In a letter dated 8 November 1942, Chief of Combined Operations Commodore Louis Mountbatten, who on 27 October 1941 had replaced Roger Keyes, wrote to the Admiralty stating his support for the new unit:

'It is requested, please, that early approval of this establishment [should] be given, as the formation and training of the Special Engineering Unit is now an urgent operational requirement'.[26] This letter was slightly late, however, as on the same day it was written the first official outing for 30AU was already underway, with the men aboard HMS *Broke* and HMS *Malcolm* heading for the Bay of Algiers as part of *Operation Torch*.

From before dawn that day, *Operation Torch* had commenced along the beaches of Vichy French North Africa, described by historian Vincent O'Hara as 'a rushed, half-baked experiment in the art of war, full of untested ideas and amateur touches'.[27]

The objective of the 23,000 British and 10,000 American strong raiding force was 'to occupy the port of Algiers and adjacent air-fields ... and maintain communications between Algiers and Orléansville' to 'build up rapidly a striking force' that would 'occupy Tunisia at the earliest possible date'.[28]

30AU were to tag along with the 662 American men of the US 3rd Battalion as part of the 135th Regiment. Although HMS *Malcolm* looked like a conventional British Naval ship, it had been modified for a very special mission. The bow was filled with tons of concrete, turning the ship into a bartering ram. The plan was to use the boat to break through the Algiers harbour boom and allow the attacking soldiers to land. The ship flew an American flag in the hope the Free French would be more favourable to their American friends, as the British were firmly out of favour, having sunk Darlan's French fleet in 1940 to stop it falling into enemy hands.

Fleming had supplied 30AU with an incredibly detailed list of targets, so specific in fact that Curtis remarked that he was 'astonished at how much [Fleming] knew about Algiers, how extremely detailed his intelligence was, and how much thought he had given to our whole show. He had organised air pictures, models, and given us an exact account of what we were to look for once we got to the enemy HQ'.[29] The Oxford academics in NID 5 had done their job to the highest standard, giving 30AU every possible chance of success.

Lying face down on the deck of HMS *Malcolm* were hundreds of American troops along with members of 30AU, under the guise of being the 'Special Engineering Unit'. Lead by Lieutenant Dunstan Curtis, the group consisted of his handpicked team: Marine Paul McGrath, Sergeant John Kruthoffer, Corporal Leslie Whyman, Marine Leslie Bradshaw,

Marine Ken Finlayson and Marine Jack Watson. The men were all armed with a variety of weapons, some unconventional, for instance Curtis' Colt .45 automatic machine gun.

As the attacking fleet approached the harbour, HMS *Malcolm* was struck by a shell in her boiler room at just after 4.00 am. Signalling back to headquarters, the destroyer sent an urgent message that the enemy searchlight was proving 'very troublesome' and that she had 'made three attempts but failed to find the inner channel entrance'. The signal concluded that it 'would be easier if the searchlight could be put out of action'.[30] On a fourth attempt, with ten men dead and a further twenty-five wounded, HMS *Malcolm* withdrew, with one solider on board, Ken Finlayson, recalling how 'it is hellish lying still under point-blank shellfire, unable to shoot back'.[31] Curtis and his men did great work in 'unstowing ammunition and throwing it overboard' as the fire started to spread through the ship.

HMS *Broke* was more fortunate and able to pierce the boom with relative ease at 5.20 am, over an hour after it had first approached. Lead by Lieutenant Colonel Swenson, the men disembarked and took cover behind hay bales and wooden boxes, sheltering from the onslaught of three enemy companies, before running out of ammunition and surrendering at 12.30 pm. Fleming's men were fortunate not to have made it to land, as they would have almost certainly either been killed or captured. In the latter scenario, as commandos, this would have likely meant execution.

After their hasty retreat, 30AU were transferred from HMS *Malcolm* to HMS *Bulolo*, and redirected to Beer Green landing zone, located twelve miles west of their original target, which earlier that day the American 168th Regimental Combat Team's 1st Battalion and 1 Commando had taken. Arriving in the now friendly zone at 3.30 pm, 30AU quickly set off on pursuit of the Italian Armistice Commission Headquarters in *Cheragas*, situated in a stunning villa overlooking the city. Capture of their first target was easy, as the seven Italians guarding the premises happily surrendered as soon as the commandos arrived at 9.00 pm. Their prisoners ordered the local chef to cook pasta and tomato sauce for the hungry invaders.

Two hours after their arrival, the FSP (Field Security Police) turned up to take charge of the premises. Nothing of any real value was found at the Headquarters, apart from a notebook with Italian codes scribbled inside, which Curtis had confiscated from one of the prisoners. With a stomach full of pasta and their breath reeking of garlic, 30AU happily left the property in the capable hands of the FSP.

Next, they made their way around Algiers, looking for anything of strategic military value which could be pinched. Apart from a glass map of all the mines laid in Sicily, it proved particularly unproductive and uneventful until a passing enemy plane shot at John Kruthoffer. Luckily, Kruthoffer was able to dodge the flying bullets and Paul McGrath was on hand to fire back with his Bren gun, hitting the aircraft, which plummeted from the sky in front of their very eyes.

On 12 November, four days after landing, and taking with them their limited intelligence loot, 30AU were sent to Gibraltar where they sorted through it for the next two weeks. At the start of December 1942, with the intelligence now organised, and the small amount of useful material packed, Curtis and his men returned to the UK.

By this time, leadership of 30AU was relinquished by Commander Ryder, who moved on to run the Naval Force J in the North Atlantic and handed over to Commander Riley. Riley met with Fleming on his return and debriefed on 30AU's involvement in *Operation Torch*. It had been apparent, according to Riley, that certain officers 'had shown little aptitude for the type of work' expected of 30AU.[32] Partly, this was down to the limited language skills among the group, and he suggested a few, ideally three, new officers were to be recruited. Fleming needed little persuading and immediately took the request to Godfrey, who approved.

First to be chosen was Captain 'Sancho' Glanville, an officer in SOE. Having worked at an international firm of accountants for ten years, his knowledge of Europe was impressive. At the start of war, he trained the Yugoslav army on demolitions before joining SOE. Next was a pilot named Lieutenant Phillips, who had held a diplomatic post in Rome before the war. Joining SOE in 1939, he took part in operations along the Danube in Central and Eastern Europe. He spoke French and Spanish fluently, with conversational Italian. Finally, Sub-Lieutenant Davies, a Brazilian born athlete who had spent many years as Naval Attaché in Rio de Janeiro, was added to the unit, not least because of his grasp of Portuguese.

But what was turning into a huge success for Fleming nearly collapsed in front of his eyes. At the end of 1942, Admiral Godfrey was abruptly removed from his post as DNI. This was a huge blow for everyone in Naval Intelligence, who felt the change of leadership acutely. Fleming found it hardest of all, as Godfrey was not only the boss he respected more than anyone else, he had also become somewhat of a father figure. Godfrey was made Flag Officer of the Royal Indian Navy, which was not a bad job to be offered, but there was no question it was a step backwards in his career. One of Fleming's colleagues believed that Godfrey's abrupt removal from his post was compounded by 'the astounding, not to say shameful, lack of any recognition of his immense services during the war, an omission which was, incidentally, deeply resented by every member of the Intelligence Division'.[33]

Godfrey was replaced by Vice-Admiral Edmund Gerard Noël Rushbrooke, a man with an impeccable naval career. Having commanded HMS *Eagle*, he had survived the torpedoing of his aircraft carrier which sank 11 August 1942. Of his 791 men aboard, 131 drowned. After the loss of his ship, he was offered the post of Director of Naval Intelligence.

*

Following the success of *Operation Torch,* in January 1943, Winston Churchill and Franklin Roosevelt met in the recently liberated Morocco, where they agreed that their strategy moving forward should be to 'first, defeat the enemy in Africa, and then invade Sicily'.[34]

For the invasion of Sicily, Dunstan Curtis had proposed that, along with four members of the Royal Marines, he should take part in a special operation in Italy. While the main invasion was set for the south of Sicily, it was likely that the Axis Powers would mount a counterattack from southern Italy into Sicily. Therefore, there was a requirement for an intelligence unit to land in Italy and report back on any major movements of enemy troops heading south. Curtis believed that if 'a suitable opportunity occurred' 30AU could 'attempt to capture a staff car, or other vehicles, likely to contain important material'.[35] His proposal was tentatively accepted.

To do this, they would need to be dropped by parachute into Italy, as approach from the sea was too dangerous and obvious. In March 1943, according to a member of 30AU, Curtis and the men were visited by 'Colonel Stirling of the SAS, members of Popski's Private Army, the Long Range Desert Group, and some of Colonel Patch's paratroops'. They went into 'huddles with Dunstan Curtis, Red [Huntington-Whiteley] and George McFee', where they were told about the benefits of commandos parachuting to their targets.[36] This stuck in Curtis' mind, as he had put the idea forward on several occasions. According to the

The 1938 Nuremberg Rally following the *Anschluss*. (Everett Historical/Shutterstock.com)

Casino Estoril in the Portuguese Riviera, which inspired the basis of *Casino Royale*. (Alexandre Rotenberg/Shutterstock.com)

The view of Estoril from sea, a regular stopover for Fleming on his way to America. (Alexandre Rotenberg/Shutterstock.com)

An Enigma Machine similar to the type that Fleming hoped to capture with *Operation Ruthless*. (Lenscap Photography/Shutterstock.com)

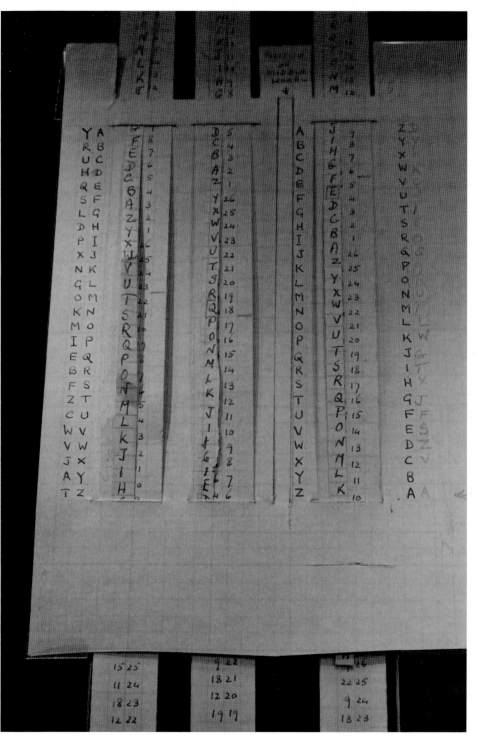

Codebreaking activity at Bletchley Park, a place Fleming would visit on several occasions. (EQRoy/Shutterstock.com)

The prize of *Operation Golden Eye*, the Rock of Gibraltar. (SCK_Photo/ Shutterstock.com)

The tunnel leading to the secret bunker which was home for the men of *Operation Tracer*. (Mitchell Eglon/Shutterstock.com)

The Rockefeller Centre, headquarters of the British Security Co-ordination in New York, where Fleming got his first taste for spying. (Jonathan Feinstein/Shutterstock.com)

Troops landing alongside Fleming's commandos, 30 Assault Unit, on D-Day. (Everett Historical/Shutterstock.com)

Retreating German soldiers in France, as the Allied forces - with 30 Assault Unit in the front line - push through Europe. (Artem Mishukov/Shutterstock.com)

Jamaica was Fleming's post-war oasis, where he built his house, Goldeneye, and would write the Bond novels. (Kavon McKenzie/Shutterstock.com)

The view from Noël Coward's house, Firefly, where Fleming was a neighbour and a regular guest. (Norman Pogson/Shutterstock.com)

Part of Fleming's love for Jamaica was the culture. Voodoo was something which fascinated him and became the basis for his second novel, *Live and Let Die*. (Vera Petruk/Shutterstock.com)

31 years after Fleming's death, Pierce Brosnan was the fifth actor to be cast as James Bond for the seventeenth instalment of the film franchise. (Denis Makarenko/ Shutterstock.om)

Daniel Craig, the sixth actor to play James Bond. (Twocoms/ Shutterstock.com)

unit's official history, on one occasion 'while waiting for favourable conditions to develop, [30AU] took part in special boat and parachute training with No.62 Commando, later known as the S.A.S Regiment'. Ultimately, the Commander-in-Chief of the Mediterranean, Admiral of the Fleet Sir Andrew Cunningham, quashed the idea, as he 'did not consider it proper employment for the unit'.

Although not playing the part Curtis had wanted, 30AU would be a central cog in the invasion of Sicily, codenamed *Operation Husky*. Lieutenant Commander Riley led nineteen members of the commando unit onto the beaches at Cape Passero and Pozzallo, the most southerly point of the island, at 5.00 am on 10 July 1943. Resistance was limited, thanks in part to Fleming's brainchild, *Operation Mincemeat*, which had meant reinforcements had been removed.

Their target was a complex of German radar stations at Cape Passero, where the Nazis had installed a long-range early warning system. As the twenty members of 30AU surrounded the station, they were greeted by surrendering guards, who were more than happy to hand themselves over. The men quickly set about clearing the area of useful material, as the invading Allied forces made their way inland. They were joined by Lieutenant Glanville and eight Royal Marines who had landed with the follow-up wave, equipped with cars and trucks. The men loaded the vehicles full of notebooks with radar courses plotted in them, operator's logs, radar sets and a Mobile Telefunken VHF set with several novel features. The convoy departed, having briefly had to act as policemen to keep away local looters, and headed towards a lighthouse at Porto Palo, which would become their temporary headquarters on the island. On 12 July, their intelligence material – having been sorted and boxed – was taken to Malta in the care of Sub-Lieutenant Davies.

Travelling north, along the winding coastal road, 30AU made several fine discoveries in Syracuse and Augusta, thanks mainly to Glanville's ability to speak Italian. The most interesting was anti-aircraft equipment, which Glanville believed 'demonstrated the ingenuity and resource displayed by the Italians in endeavouring to develop early warning of the approaching aircraft'.[37]

The men then made their way inland, heading for the west coast province of Trapani. Due to Allied aerial bombardment and the defences put in place by the Axis Powers, their journey was far from simple. With key bridges and roads now destroyed, they needed to make their way cross-country. However, the fields were scattered with mines, and the menacing sight of burnt-out vehicles that had tried to make their way through was a stark reminder of the danger. These were the 'latest German pressure mines charged with the new Hexogen explosive', which sparked the interest of Fleming and were used by Bond in *Thunderball*.[38]

Thanks again to Glanville's language skills, he was able to find a young schoolgirl who had watched the mines being laid, and offered to escort 30AU through. They arrived at the empty port of Trapani, only to find more looting underway. Such was the disorder that the Royal Marines had to 'fire over the heads of the crowd on one occasion' to stop them. The stores were found to be rich with equipment, in particular enemy mining and minesweeping technology, some of which, Glanville proudly explained, 'were previously not known to the Allies'.[39]

By 11 August, the Axis Powers started a mass evacuation from North East Sicily, four miles across the Strait of Messina to the safety of Italy. Over 70,000 German and Italian troops, nearly 15,000 vehicles and thousands of tons of ammunition were withdrawn. Deemed as one of the most successful military evacuations of the time, it did not help the Allied plans to next invade Italy.

*

On 3 September, 30AU were ordered to take part in the invasion of Italy. Sub-Lieutenant Davies was to lead the assault on Reggio Calabria, just opposite Sicily. Using his navigational skills to guide the amphibious landing craft, they arrived with little trouble or resistance.

Meanwhile, Lieutenant Commander Riley landed at Salerno, just south of Naples, on 9 September. They arrived in choppy seas, having crashed into a submerged sandbank on their way in, causing a twelve-hour delay. This gave the local soldiers enough time to burn everything of value, leaving next to nothing of use in the area. The previous day, the new Badoglio Government of Italy signed an Armistice with the Allies, meaning the destruction of such material was directly in contradiction of the terms agreed. 30AU were disheartened by the discovery of the charred remains, but Riley was quick to order his men to advance inland towards Pompeii, in the hope that such defensive measures would not yet have taken shape. Riley's men were proving a useful asset, not only with their successful pinches, but also their ability as first-class fighting commandos. So much so, the Flag Officer of Western Italy (FOWIT) issued an order that 30 Commando were 'free to operate in the area subject to giving 24 hours' notice'.

The torpedo firing site at San Martino was a key target; there were two main objectives for Riley's men: 'to remove Admiral Minisini and to capture documents and, possibly also, material relating to recent Italian torpedo practice and the development of the midget submarine'.[40] Glanville had noted previously the vast ingenuity of Italian scientists, and Minisini was at the forefront of this. Having designed the 'magnetic pistol', the most ingenious way of accurately guiding missiles to their targets, he was now working on a new type of miniature submarine. This technology was borrowed by Fleming for *Thunderball*, in which a World War II Italian underwater chariot was deployed by SPECTRE.

Conflicting intelligence made it hard to establish the strength of the defence at San Martino and taking the site would be a challenge. Riley decided that the best approach would be to attack relying on 'speed and surprise'. Doing what Royal Marines do best, they would approach from the sea, using a requisitioned Italian craft fitted with an up-to-date 'underwater exhaust' which was 'capable of a speed of 38 knots in a calm sea'.[41]

Reporting the plan back to London for approval, Fleming was ecstatic at his unit's ingenuity. He loved learning about the type of cutting-edge amphibious equipment his team were now using and the boat was also to make an appearance in *Thunderball*. Named the *Disco Volante,* the fictional boat belonging to Emilio Largo also had a similar trap door in the hull to allow Italian frogmen into the water undetected.

Lieutenant Glanville was selected to lead the party, consisting of new additions to 30AU, Captain Martin Smith and his army section, Lieutenant Berncastle and the Royal Marines, followed by a search party under Sergeant Whitby, and firing power from Sergeant Whyman on the boat.

In the early hours of 18 September, the captured Italian vessel, loaded with members of 30AU made their way silently through the still seas towards the dark port of San Martino. They arrived completely unnoticed, apart from one Italian guard who did not bother to raise the alarm. Glanville lead his men onto the jetty, where they quickly swept the area and rounded up a number of Italian workmen. Abiding by the terms of the armistice and not wanting to cause any trouble, the locals were happy to lead the commandos to Admiral Minisini's residence.

Bursting into his house, the members of 30AU found the elderly Admiral in bed with his wife, fast asleep and completely oblivious to the

Allied invasion of his launching site. Minisini refused to come voluntarily, so was declared a prisoner of war and arrested. The Admiral agreed to leave under these conditions, but insisted he was allowed to pack his belongings and take his wife, Signora, with him. Thirteen full suitcases later, and after a confused conversation between the German speaking Martin-Smith and Signora, who believed she was being taken away by the Nazis, 30AU departed on their stealth craft, heading for Capri. The captain of the boat recalled how 'a little slender woman was helped over the side' followed by 'a quite stout Admiral in a beautiful overcoat', despite it being a humid and warm night.[42] The following morning, with extra manpower having arrived in the guise of Sub-Lieutenant Davies and his unit following the successful invasion of Reggio Calabria, a full complement of 30AU carried out further successful raids.

Admiral Minisini was handed over to the OSS, the organisation that Fleming had helped to create, arriving in the United States on 21 October. He immediately sent for twelve Italian engineers and technicians who arrived on 17 December, together with forty tons of technical ordnance material which was necessary to facilitate their work. The men of 30AU were not particularly happy to see their most valuable finding be sent over the ocean to America. Fleming, who had been appointed as a member of the Combined Intelligence Objectives Committee, tasked with building better communication between the British and American intelligence service, saw this as nothing but a positive.

Along with their Allied colleagues, 30AU made their way north, taking Naples from both sea and land on 1 October, thanks in the main to the Italian resistance, who launched a mass defensive against the German soldiers on 27 September. Emilio Largo, Bond's nemesis in *Thunderball,* who 'two hundred years before ... would have been a pirate', was 'head of the black market in Naples, through five lucrative years smuggling from Tangier' and present during the uprising.

At the end of 1943, the unit returned to the UK to prepare for further operations. The work by 30AU to this point was widely praised, as they were getting their hands on Italian technical expertise before it could be destroyed. Thanks to their successes that year, Allied leaders saw the value of Fleming's unit, so much so that they grew it from approximately 50 Royal Marines and specialists to over 150 members. They were also ordered to prepare for arguably the most pivotal part of World War II, *Operation Overlord,* the invasion of Normandy.

Chapter 8

On Her Majesty's Secret Service

On Her Majesty's Secret Service sees Bond sent to Switzerland to investigate the possible existence of his arch nemesis Blofeld, who is believed to be living in disguise as Comte Balthazar on the top of Piz Gloria. Assuming the identity of Sir Hillary Bray, Bond discovers that Blofeld is brainwashing British women, sent there to cure their allergies, in order to destroy Britain's agricultural industry. After escaping down the mountain on skis, Bond partners with Marc-Ange Draco, head of Europe's biggest crime syndicate. Draco lends Bond a group of highly trained commandos to mount an air attack on Blofeld's base to destroy it.

Fleming uses his experience of working with commandos to give the reader a thrilling insight into such a raid. During the war, groups of commandos like 30AU became a staple part of major military operations.

Large-scale attacks do not get any bigger than *Operation Overlord*. Although technically every military operation that has ever been executed takes place on 'D-Day', there is one 'D-Day' that stands the test of time better than any other, and that is *Operation Overlord*, which is rightly still celebrated to this day. As one of the largest military operations of all time, historians Michael Green and James D. Brown have described *Operation Overlord* as 'the two most harrowing kinds of military operations: a seaborne landing on an opposed beach, and a night airborne assault'.[1]

The 'D' in 'D-Day' stands for the day that the operation will take place, and therefore anything either side of this is denoted by a plus or minus, for example an event three days before 'D-Day' is 'D-3' and the day after the operation would be 'D+1'.

Ian Fleming would not personally be part of D-Day, but he was a key player in the planning of the operation starting back on D-37, 1 May 1944, when 30AU was placed as part of the Allied Naval Commander Expeditionary Force (ANCXF), under the overall control of General

Dwight D. Eisenhower. It was decided that 30AU would be best placed in the Normandy and Cherbourg area, because of where the Nazi Naval Headquarters and Radar Stations were located. Therefore, Fleming's commando unit would be taking part in *Operation Neptune*, the Normandy landings.

Fleming split his force into three sub-units. Firstly, 'Pikeforce' would be led by Captain Geoffrey Pike, who was recently commissioned into the Royal Marines and 30AU, after running a care centre in Ladbroke Grove, London, for those bombed out of their homes during the Blitz. He was supported by Captain John Hargreaves-Heap, under the supervision of Major Alan Evans, and reinforced by Lieutenant Glanville, and would lead what was also termed as 'X Troop'.

'Pikeforce' was to land on D-Day on Juno Beach at Saint Aubin-sur-Mer, one of the five landing sites for the 15,000 men of the 3rd Canadian Infantry Division. Their target was the radar station at Douvres-la-Délivrande, six kilometres from the coast. The station was part of the Kammhuber Line which had been constructed across the North Coast of France in order to accurately pinpoint RAF planes for antiaircraft gunners. According to historian Tim Saunders, such was the success of the Kammhuber Line, it caused the death of so many Allied crews as to 'almost equal that of the infantry fighting in North-West Europe' at the time.[2]

Other new members of 30AU, Commander Guy Postlewaite and Lieutenant Tony Hugill were to land at H+4 (four hours after the initial landing) and make their way to the radar station to assist 'Pikeforce'.

'Curtforce' was to be led by Commander Curtis, with support from Lieutenant Robert Harling, and were to also land on D-Day at Port-en-Bessin, where they would make their way west to Côte de Nacre through Arromanches, to capture further radar stations. 'Curtforce' would consist of a lean force, including three naval specialists and a small group of naval officers and marines. Robert Harling had been drafted into 30AU as a friend of Fleming's, who hoped that he would keep close tabs on Curtis.

The third sub-unit was 'Woolforce', which would be the major 30AU force. Led by another new face, Colonel Arthur Woolley, it would consist of 'A Troop' led by Captain Huntington-Whiteley and 'B Troop' led by Captain Douglas, along with Lieutenant Commander McFee and Lieutenant Commander Dalzel-Job.

Curtis read sarcastically from a guidebook he had been given that the landing zone was 'a picturesque stretch of coastal cliff and beach which has sponsored the rise of a succession of small seaside resorts'.[3] What he was confronted with when he got there would be a far cry from this description.

*

On 4 June 1944, Pike and his men boarded TSS *Monowai*, a converted New Zealand liner. 'Pikeforce' were joined by 1,800 mainly Canadian troops and twenty landing craft. In the evening, the boat set off for their target – France.

On 6 June at 8.35 am, Captains Pike and Hargreaves-Heap led their men, into 'Mike Sector' on the shores of Juno Beach forty minutes after 3rd Canadian Infantry Brigade had landed. They had arrived on one of the landing craft, after an uncomfortable eight-mile ride. The Canadian army had landed at 7.49 am, determined to revenge the heavy losses at Dieppe, which had taught them a very harsh lesson: 'never attack a heavily defended port from the sea'.[4] Yet, the men had little choice but to end up doing this very thing once again.

The troops of 30AU were met by a tirade of bullets, shells and shrapnel ripping men apart to their left and right. Initially frozen by fear, Pike took solace from the other men around him, particularly Glanville, who 'never seemed to be frightened but just interested in what was going on' and lead his men onto the beach to find cover.[5] One member of 'X Troop', Marine Don King, turned to Glanville crouching next to him to see what his officer was pointing at with his walking stick. Seemly gesturing to nothing among the heavy enemy bombardment of bullets, he heard Glanville say, 'Look! A Black-veined White ... You don't see many of those at home.'[6] He was referring to a butterfly fluttering nearby.

Despite the heavy losses endured by the Canadian landing party on the beaches, 'by skilful beachcraft and speed of movement' 'Pikeforce' made their way immediately through the commune of Saint Aubin-sur-Mer to their rendezvous site – the local church, Eglise Saint-Aubin, 400 meters from the beach – arriving by 10.00 am.[7] Pike recalled his nervousness at the time, 'knowing half of my troops had been under fire before and I had not. You don't forget that sort of thing'.[8] 30AU had emerged unscratched, thanks mainly to the heroic work of the Canadian army, who took 961 casualties. Many of the soldiers had ignored the ruthless order to leave wounded men behind, instead turning back to the beach to drag injured comrades to safety.

Pike soon forgot his own worries; addressing his men from 'X Troop', the six foot four officer stood on a church pew and declared: 'X the unknown quantity – here we go!' He was upbeat despite the sheer destruction he and his men had escaped. Author Nicholas Rankin interviewed Marine Bill Powell, who had landed on the beach from a different craft and recalled, 'The beach was indescribable ... bodies everywhere, some dead, some wounded, others just shattered ... Yells, shouts and orders added to the mêlée.'[9] Despite being inland from the fierce fighting Powell described on the beach, Saint Aubin-sur-Mer was far from secure. It was fitted out with a heavily fortified concrete bunker, armed to the teeth with anti-tank weapons, machine guns and mortars. It was not until the arrival of an AVRE tank at 11.30 am, which made its way carelessly up the beach running over 'corpses and several of their own wounded soldiers', that the bunker was destroyed.[10]

With this going on behind them, 'Pikeforce' were afforded no time for rest, making their way further inland towards Douvres-la-Délivrande and their target. They arrived at the village of Tailleville, which one member of the unit described rather harshly as 'a dim, grey little place full of broken windows, with a damaged water tower and the local manor as its only major edifices'.[11] The first heavy resistance 'Pikeforce' met was at this local manor, Château d'Eau, in the heart of Tailleville, which acted as the base for the German Grenadier-Regiment 736 of the 716 Infantry Division and was the Nazi headquarters for the area. The nondescript building sat on the approach road from Saint Aubin-sur-Mer and was heavily guarded, with the German troops taking advantage of the many exposed fields around the village to pick off the attackers by sniper fire, as well as the dense village streets which offered the commandos little shelter.

At 12.00 pm, 'Pikeforce' and their Canadian allies came under attack about half-a-mile from the village, from 'heavy and accurate mortar and machine gun fire', which lasted until late into the evening when darkness crept in. With visibility for the defenders poor, the Allies were finally able to defeat the Nazi stronghold.[12] The battle for Château d'Eau lasted over five hours and cost the lives of thirty-four Canadian troops, wounding ninety. One soldier remarked that the Germans 'had clearly followed instructions to delay the invaders to the limit', which they had done extremely effectively.[13]

Although they were now already behind schedule, the fighting had taken such a toll on the men that they decided to dig in at the village and regroup, before heading towards their target. This proved useful for 30AU's objectives, as the men were able to search the local Nazi headquarters, discovering that the Gestapo had operated in the area and recovering useful papers.

Pike got a message back to Fleming informing him of their delay, but with the reassuring news that the unit was intact and without casualty. He informed the Commander that their target was 'not merely a radar station', but a 'major strongpoint in the system of defences', which would likely not fall for a while. Although Pike had not yet reached his objective, he took solace in the fact that his colleagues in 'Curtforce' were advancing twenty miles to their east. Unfortunately, Curtis and his men were also having their own problems.

Early on the morning of D+1, twelve hours after they intended to, 'Curtforce' landed on Gold Beach at Asnelles-sur-Mer, which had been taken by 1st Battalion Hampshire Regiment the day before. 'Curtforce' were due to have landed on D–Day as well as 'Pikeforce', but were severely delayed due to 'bad weather and heavy seas'.[14] The scene upon landing was gloomy, as the men from 30AU disembarked from their landing craft, the ruins of battle from the day before were evident, having cost the Allies nearly 180 fatalities after eight hours of frantic fighting.

'Curtforce' was fully equipped with various wireless trucks, lorries, cars, jeeps and motorbikes with sidecars. Their convoy was loaded onto two landing craft covered in camouflage netting, used the previous day for Churchill tanks. Travelling from Felixstowe, they were part of Flotilla 16 in Squadron V of Force L, aboard crafts that were designed to carry up to seventy men and were thought to be the most efficient method of crossing the channel. As Curtis and his men disembarked, machine gun fire was still sputtering out of enemy strongholds in the houses and bunkers across the sand dunes. Lieutenant Harling recollected the 'noise, noise and more noise' that 'dominated the world'.[15] As the men made their way up the narrow foreshore, all around them was the sight of disaster. Washed up trucks, equipment of all sorts and bodies. Medics were hard at work, tending to the wounded, while the deceased lay next to them, motionless.

From Gold Beach, Curtis lead an advanced party inland towards the town of Crépon, where they would form their temporary headquarters. The area had been taken the evening before by the 7th Battalion Green Howards Regiment, following a bloody exchange.

The site had two pillboxes, now blackened by smoke and stained with blood. The previous day, these had been the source of much fighting, as they had accidentally been overlooked by the company who were too keen to move inland from the beaches. Lieutenant Hugill was scathing about the lack of impact from the previous day's bombardments, later reporting 'The RAF and the Navy between them had only knocked chips off the outsides of the concrete emplacements ... the Germans inside were all right'.[16]

Realising the danger, one man, Company Sergeant Major Hollis, jumped on top of the pillbox, re-charged his magazine, threw a grenade in through the door and fired his Sten gun into it, killing two Germans and taking the remainder prisoners. Because of his heroic actions, Hollis was the only recipient of a Victoria Cross on D-Day. For Curtis, this was a stark reminder that had the weather been better, his company would have been faced with the task of disarming these strongholds the previous day.

Evoking the mass destruction, Hugill later wrote that he coldly sensed 'a kind of macabre foulness, a smell not only of blood and bad drains' but 'an aura that only the German leaves in a place he has inhabited and I hate it'.[17]

Hugill and Postlethwaite took a team to Arromanches, two miles from where they had landed, to inspect a radar station which seemed to have been completely abandoned the day before. With all the luck that any man can have, a sniper bullet narrowly missed one of the troops as they walked towards the station, lodging itself into a piece of masonry behind him. The men took cover only to find out that the area was crawling with snipers. Hours of fighting ensued, limiting the amount of searching the section of 'Curtforce' could carry out.

The fact that all the men were still alive after their narrow shave with the highly skilled Nazi marksmen would be enough luck for the day, but more would soon present itself. In an attempt to remove valuable documentation and equipment from the station, the German guards had filled a lorry with as many sensitive items as they could. Records of activity, radar gadgetry and strategy papers were crammed into the truck, which had a full tank of petrol and the keys in the ignition. The work for 30AU had already been done for them, leaving only the task of starting the vehicle's engine and driving away from the danger of sniper counterattack.

After returning to Crépon following their near-death excursion, they were greeted by a heap of messages from London wanting to know updates. Despite only being in France for a day, Curtis was already getting fed up with Fleming's 'ceaseless lunatic bureaucratic interference' which he saw as nothing but meddling.[18] He was quick to respond, telling Fleming how he felt.

Away from the arguments between Curtis and Fleming, 'Pikeforce' was also experiencing similar problems from marksmen, fifteen miles east of Curtis and his men. They had risen early on 7 June, leaving their first camp in Tailleville at 7.00 am, heading along Rue de Basly in an attempt to flank Douvres-la-Délivrande Radar Station, which was housed in the southwest of the village. However, as an official report recounts, this route afforded 'excellent cover' for 'snipers and small bodies of troops fighting as rear-guards'.[19] This same report begs the question as to why Pike and his men did not advance east of Tailleville, where they would have avoided the village and exposed road altogether.

Using Canadian Churchill AVRE tanks, the Allies tried to make an advance on the radar station, only to lose two vehicles immediately through the web of mines which lay in the fields leading to the target. Strong gun and mortar fire also destroyed a third, before the rest sensibly retreated. Hugill was jealous of how the enemy were 'comfortably ensconced in a large underground complex ... surrounded by belts of mine fields'. For now, they were not going anywhere.

An attempted second attack by the Canadians again caused heavy casualties. Licking their wounds, the infantry force, along with the members of 30AU, headed back to their stronghold in Tailleville to regroup. A meeting was held with the various officers, including Glanville and Pike, where it was agreed that the current resources were insufficient to take the Nazi stronghold. Therefore, the majority of men present would circumvent the position and press on through France, leaving a small group behind to contain the radar station. This task fell to a select group of Canadian soldiers and 30AU.

Reinforcements arrived in the guise of 'Curtforce', who had made their way from their very temporary headquarters in Crépon. Members of the unit had not felt particularly welcome in France up to this point, mainly because of the endless Allied bombing the locals had endured in recent times. However, there was a sudden and dramatic change in Tailleville, as one solider explained: 'The people here were better pleased to see us than elsewhere in Normandy, where at best they were uninterested, at worst cool'.[20] This change in attitude was due mainly to the brutality the locals had suffered under the Nazi command – something for them which was, they hoped, finally coming to an end. It was recorded officially that despite the huge lose suffered by the French at the hands of the Allies, 'the vast majority showed great understanding', although troops were warned 'not to accept any food or drink from the French in case they were poisoned'.[21]

The now larger 30AU contingent at Tailleville, 'Curtforce' and 'Pikeforce', were ordered to remain with the Canadian 4 Commando Brigade to make sure 'the target area was to be contained and harassed'.[22] For the next ten days, 30AU acted as bait for the stronghold, with occasional mortar shelling, firing sporadically at the enemy and generally making a nuisance of themselves towards the 230 Nazi soldiers holding their position.

*

Thirty miles west, the largest of Fleming's three units, 'Woolforce', landed at Utah Beach at 3.00 pm on 12 June, D+6. Moving six miles inland quickly, they set up their headquarters in Sainte-Mère-Église.

Since D-Day, no attacks had been made on assembly areas – an allotted location where those who successfully made their way across the beach would gather – as the defending forces' focus was on the frontier and approaching ships. Therefore, according to their brief, it was 'considered that adequate cover for the unit would be provided by a deep double ditch' identified inland rather than anything more substantial.[23] In any case, 'Woolforce' had landed without any picks or shovels, which were with their transport and due to arrive the next day.

After making their way across the beach, 'Woolforce' headed to their assembly point, getting to the supposed safety zone by 9.45 pm without any harm coming their way. The next hour was spent building adequate protection around the cover of a dry stream, which would serve as a bedsit for the night. Anything from bracken to oak logs was used to build up enough cover to shelter them from snipers or ground attack. Their camp was finished by 11.10 pm. Setting out the necessary sentries, Colonel Woolley ordered his men to bed down and try to get as much sleep as they could ahead of what would likely be a very long next day. Dalzel-Job wrote that he 'paid no attention when we heard the sound of bombers flying fairly low overhead'.[24]

As the men were starting to relax, a menacing roar echoed around the camp, just as Woolley saw an enemy aircraft appear out of the low cloud with six others in tow before a slurry of bombs were dropped on the unexpecting troops below. Without any deep shelters, 'Woolforce' were sitting ducks.

The Luftwaffe had dropped their latest invention, the Butterfly Bomb, or *Sprengbombe Dickwandig*. These cluster bombs were shaped like a canister when released, only to split open in mid-air creating two wings, which would then 'flutter' down to their target. Two marines, Bon Royle and Lofty Whyman were deep in conversation when they heard the planes approach and a curious whistling sound before explosions rang out all around them. These bombs had a devastating effect and were designed to cause as much loss to life as possible. Dalzel-Job remembered the explosions not lasting more than thirty seconds, in which time a third of the unit was wiped out.

Five men were killed in the attack, sixteen badly wounded and over twenty more with less serious injuries. It was a long night for 'Woolforce', as their medics tried to patch up the wounded to be evacuated. Injuries ranged from shrapnel lodged in a man's stomach, through to a chipped tooth and a missing testicle. Bill Wright had been struck by something in the back and was 'rolling in agony' on the ground. When the medical orderly examined him, he found 'a small, jagged splinter of steel' had hit Wright 'exactly on the metal centre-piece of his army braces'. Severe bruising was his only injury and he soon cheered up, exclaiming that the bomb had had his name on it but not his number.

By dawn, the injured had been whisked back to England, while a shocked and exhausted 'Woolforce' received delivery of their vehicles. News had filtered back to Fleming who, according to colleagues in NID, 'was holding himself ultimately responsible for the unit losses' which had 'clearly shaken him'.[25] For his men in France, there was no time for reflections as they made their way to Sainte-Mère-Église.

The approach through the fields and trees was strewn with the bodies of dead paratroopers who had tried to land in previous days, some hanging motionless from trees and buildings and 'several written-off gliders of the US airborne forces littered the fields' reported one 30AU soldier, which were 'further sharp reminders of the vast and casual throwaway costs' of war.[26]

Sainte-Mère-Église was a picturesque village in northwest France, popular with wealthy British tourists before the war. By the time

IAN FLEMING'S INSPIRATION

'Woolforce' arrived, it had an eerie feeling of devastation, in what was now a heavily bombed commune, still smouldering. The church in the centre of the village, which would act as the headquarters of 'Woolforce', had two large white sheets draped over the steeple. Initially mistaking these as a sign that the Nazis holding the area had surrendered, they turned out to be the parachutes of two American soldiers, who had got caught in the gargoyles while trying to land. Woolley met Colonel King and Lieutenant Colonel O'Malley of the 7th US Army Corps, who had relieved the paratroopers and taken control of what was left of the town. Woolley was pleasantly impressed that their American counterparts 'proved most helpful and undertook to give the unit all possible assistance' following their ordeal the night before.[27] For the next four days, from 13 to 16 June, 'Woolforce' split into small groups and headed on expeditions with American soldiers to hunt for possible loot.

Back with 'Pikeforce' thirty miles east at Douvres-la-Délivrande, on 16 June, No. 41 Royal Marine Commando arrived on the scene, tasked with taking control of the radar station. They were to be assisted by two squadrons of the 22nd Dragoons, who brought the most essential piece of equipment, the Sherman Crab minesweeping tanks.

The assault was mounted the next day at 5.00 pm. With twenty-eight Sherman Crab tanks sent ahead, seventeen Churchill AVRE tanks and 160 Commandos attacked. The only members of 'Pikeforce' to take part were Glanville and four Royal Marines – Sergeant Sponge, Lance Corporal Morgan, Marine Webb and Marine Booth – who were temporarily transferred into No. 41 Royal Marines. Watching from afar, Lieutenant Harling saw that the 'members of 30AU were clearly impressed by the 41 Commando performance' and were delighted to be acting as true commandos.[28] Hargreaves-Heap remained behind in order to assist with the searching of the area once it was taken. The rest of 'Pikeforce' and 'Curtforce' headed west to meet up with 'Woolforce', at 30AU's new headquarters at Sainte-Mère-Église.

With two troops of Canadian soldiers causing a distraction to the south and west of the station at Douvres-la-Délivrande, the Sherman Crabs were able to clear a path for the Churchill AVRE's and commandos to gain access to the compound. On entry, one onlooker recalled how the commandos 'threw grenades down all the alleyways and slits which led to the underground passages and soon the Germans had had enough', at which point they surrendered.[29] From the destruction, 250 Germans and six officers were taken prisoner. The Allies suffered three fatalities and sixteen casualties while six tanks were damaged.

Unfortunately for 30AU, this was where their problems really began, as the assault troops were followed by 'a horde of British soldiery intent on loot' who stole all they could, while breaking much valuable equipment including 'a glass screen map used in the plotting-room to direct fighter operations in Western Europe'.[30] This map would not have been a traditional steal for 30AU, as it would be classed as of immediate operational importance and sent to the Allied Naval Commander Expeditionary Force for their urgent attention. Arguably lives could have been spared, had it not been smashed. But despite losing almost everything, 30AU did recover a set of wheels from a Luftwaffe Enigma machine, which was on their hotlist of targets.

Harling was ordered by Curtis to escort a 750-kilogram lorry, now packed with the loot from Arromanches, Tailleville and Douvres-la-Délivrande, back to Britain. With a parting handshake, Curtis gave his junior officer little time: 'I want you [back] here', he ordered, 'or wherever we find ourselves, [by] next week'.[31]

The remainder of 30AU were now making their way, albeit slowly, towards Cherbourg, a port northeast of Guernsey. Sitting at the top of a north facing peninsula, Cherbourg was of key strategic importance to the Allies because of its deep-water port. In order to provide essential supplies to their men, most notably ammunition and food, the invading forces had erected two temporary ports to the west of Cherbourg, one at Saint-Laurent-sur-Mer and the other at Arromanches-les-Bains. Although these served their purpose well, they were incredibly unreliable and often put out of operation due to bad weather or choppy seas. Cherbourg was chosen to be the main artery for supplying the necessities to the advancing *Operation Overlord* troops. For Fleming, it also held some of 30AU's most valuable loot, as it was the launch zone for the V-1 flying bombs – technology the British were desperate to get their hands on.

While the 156,000 Allied Troops were landing in Normandy, the German forces immediately began to retreat. In what was seen as a huge Nazi strategic error, General Farmbacher, leader of the 84th Army Corps ordered his men (numbering 40,000) to withdraw behind a mile-long defensive line, effectively cutting off the Cherbourg Peninsula. He had inadvertently isolated his men with three walls of the English Channel and over 150,000 troops surrounding them. For this, he was relieved of his duties. Hitler had declared Cherbourg a *Festenplätze* – literally meaning a fixed place – and it was an operational stronghold should an invasion come. Since March 1944, reinforcements had been put in place throughout the hills surrounding Cherbourg. Hundreds of concrete pillboxes had been erected, linked with tunnels and bunkers to provide adequate cover. The Allies had intended to take the peninsular by sea, but heavy gun and shellfire from coastal batteries caused severe damage to four attacking ships, and the naval plan was abandoned.

Although the Germans were now effectively surrounded, the threat of Nazi deployment to support from elsewhere was great. Fearing this, an urgent message was sent to Fleming's men, stating that 'further threat of oncoming German reinforcements from the east' was likely.[32]

On 22 June, the Americans launched their aerial attack on the peninsular. The anti-aircraft batteries were manned by teenagers from the *Reichsarbeitsdienst*, young recruits into the German army, there on 'work experience'. As the RAF came overhead, the Germans 'fired back like madmen' a young recruit wrote, until 'an inferno descended – roaring, shattering, shaking, crashing…' This was followed by 'a horrific silence'.[33]

30AU had no option but to wait patiently as General Collins, responsible for the attack, put in place a master plan to overrun the port. The naval intelligence men followed the front-line American troops, as they made their gradual approach. Danger was everywhere, as the Germans dug into marshy land south of Cherbourg, creating a string of trenches. Two men from 30AU were killed on 24 June, as they made their way through fields under constant sniper gunfire. One soldier, nineteen-year-old Paddy O'Callaghan, was hit in the leg. The bullet penetrated his femoral artery and he bled slowly to death. Reporting back to Fleming that evening, Curtis broke the news that further casualties had been endured. On receiving the information, Fleming was reportedly 'not only perturbed by the unit's losses but also by its thwarted movements'.[34]

The next day, General Collins' main attack was launched on Cherbourg, while the surrounded Germans desperately followed out Hitler's orders that 'the Allies must find the port in ruins'.[35] Now, 30AU were no longer observers, they were in the thick of a bloody battle. While standing next to an American Sherman, Colonel Woolley was surveying his target through field glasses when a mortar struck the tank, destroying it in one hit. An 88 mm splinter struck Woolley in the head, knocking him unconscious. His helmet saved his life, but he was invalided back to Britain.

Curtis told his men that evening that Woolley 'had proved the luckiest man in France ... certainly in Octeville'.[36] Sadly, others from 30AU did not share his good fortune. While men from 'A Troop' attempted to advance with their American comrades, two Marines were shot and wounded in open space by an observant enemy sniper. When two medical orderlies rushed to the screaming men to tend to their injuries, the sniper shot them both. According to Article Nine of the Geneva Convention, written in 1906, 'personnel charged exclusively with the removal, transportation, and treatment of the sick and wounded ... shall be respected and protected under all circumstances'. Two of the men died from their wounds and two returned to Britain – for all four, their war was over.

General Eisenhower said that in times of war 'the supreme quality for leadership is unquestionably integrity'; 'without it', he concluded, 'no real success is possible'.[37] Sadly, an on-looking Marine Sergeant, who had witnessed the brutal murder of his medical colleagues, did not share Eisenhower's philosophy and decided to take justice into his own hands. After three Nazi riflemen appeared from a bombed-out building, hands high in the air and one waving a white handkerchief, the NCO opened fire with his light machine-gun, killing all three surrendering men in an instant. An officer who happened to be coming around the corner recalled seeing the unarmed Nazis' 'blood flowing in the rainwater' as the sergeant's gun smoked from the shots.[38] He calmly ordered that the soldier be 'Returned to Unit' on disciplinary grounds.

When the incident was reported back the Fleming, his response was anything but calm, yelling at the telegram in his hands, before storming out, 'his shouting fury still echoing in the corridor'.[39]

Until darkness the following day, US forces of the VII Corps took control of the port, until the last enemy bastion was captured at the highest point of the city, Fort du Roule. The city had fallen, and the port was now operational for the Allies. Within hours, ships flooded to the deep-water port, able to drop off requisitioned civilian lorries carrying essential supplies. A unique mixture of branded vehicles from all corners of the world now swarmed into France; as one member of the unit recalled, logos painted on them included 'Wun Wabbit Wun',

'Voulez-Vouz, Madame', 'Oklahoma Kid', 'Texas Boy', 'Naughty but Nice', 'Maizy Doats', 'Never Say No' and 'Try Me For Size'.[40]

Combat historian Sergeant Forrest Pogue was surprised to see 'nearly 100 soldiers queueing outside a former Wehrmacht brothel' only hours after the fall of the port, despite the fact that pockets of resistance still needed disarming. His shock was furthered when a local Frenchman walked up and down the line warning the waiting men that the 'Germans have left much disease' and the Allied soldiers paid no regard to the advice.[41]

General Collins wrote on 26 June 1944, 'yesterday was one of our great days'.[42] He was not wrong, as it proved to be a real turning point for *Operation Overlord*. With the area now secure, Curtis and his men set about searching the many tunnels under the city, as anything above ground was by now either burnt or in rubble. Dalzel-Job had come across a group of Frenchmen who explained how they 'had been engaged in excavating the tunnels under the Villa Maurice'.[43] They proved most helpful in providing 30AU with details of the layout and any hidden chambers which would be worth searching. Sixteen 'G7a' straight-running unguided torpedoes were discovered, along with specially adapted warheads, which would have been overlooked if not for the information provided by the locals.

Villa Maurice, proudly standing tall in the centre of the city, was one of the last sites to fall. It was the Marines from 30AU who actually took the surrender. The villa had been used as a military hospital for captured wounded men from the US 82nd Airborne Division, where 250 soldiers were given the most meagre of medical care. Outside a shout came that 'The Krauts've called it a day ... Turned it in!' From the tunnels under the city appeared crowds of tired enemy soldiers, one waving a gigantic white flag, which was thought to be 'one of the largest white flags seen in any war'.[44] Behind them was General von Schlieben, wearing a brand new Knights Cross medal around his neck, hundreds of which had been dropped by the Luftwaffe in an attempt to boost moral after the invasion. Of those who had surrendered, Bon Royle recalled 'We took some amazing prisoners' including a group who 'looked like nothing we had ever seen before and, after trying all sorts of languages on them, it turned out they were Georgians from Holy Mother Russia'.[45]

The hospital was put under the command of Captain Koehler, a surgeon with the 22nd Infantry Regiment, who spoke fluent German and was therefore able to order around the German medical staff. He recalled how 'the Teutonic tendency to operate on a surgical case and disregard the outcome on the life of the patient was very apparent'.[46] The high death rate appalled the doctor. As the marines entered the makeshift hospital, one remembered the smell of 'piss and pus, sick and shit!'[47]

No V-1 or V-2 rocket technology was found in the city, which ultimately had been the number one target for the unit. Fleming was furious, viewing the losses to 'Woolforce' as being for nothing. Lieutenant Harling, who was with Fleming in NID headquarters following his delivery of material from France, received the brunt of Fleming's temper. He later wrote that 'The image of Fleming's face, distorted as if in apoplexy, inflamed as if doused in red pepper, eyes blazing with homicidal fury, has remained in my memory. At any moment, I had thought, a blood vessel would burst'.[48] It turned out that Fleming was facing not only a lot of stress in his professional life, but something much closer to home.

At the start of July 1944, Harling returned to the unit who had now set up their base at Carteret, on the western coast of the peninsula, considered by Glanville as 'a suitable training area and on the road to future objectives'.[49] Curtis had requisitioned a large season mansion as their headquarters. Harling confided in the Curtis on his return that there had been 'a sudden fearsome personal tragedy for Fleming'. He explained how Fleming's girlfriend, Muriel Wright, had died in 'one of the final doodle-bug raids on London'.[50]

Born in 1909 to a wealthy family, Muriel had first met Fleming in Austria in 1935. Her father, Henry Fitzherbert Wright, was a cricket player and an active participant in local politics. Despite wanting to follow in her father's footsteps, conservative women of her time often didn't pursue an education or a career, so she instead became a successful model for outdoor recreational clothing. Fleming may have been smitten in the early days of their courtship, but it wasn't long before he started seeing other women. There is no evidence that Muriel protested these affairs, but her family was not pleased with the situation. Her brother was particularly offended by Fleming's behaviour, and went so far as to show up at his home with a horsewhip. Fortunately, the lovers were out of town on a weekend trip.

Although Muriel may not have fully held Fleming's attention during her lifetime, it was her death that stuck with him and made her his inspiration for future literary female characters. Volunteering as an air raid warden during the war, she was ironically killed at home in her nightdress in March 1944, during a V-1 air raid that sent a piece of masonry into her flat, fatally striking her on the head. Oddly, no damage was done to the property, and her body was not discovered until some days later when her dog was found outside whimpering.

Curtis was stunned by the news of her death. 'I know you thought she was one of the most delightful creatures ever,' he consoled, before adding, 'so did I.' Their grief was only partly in sympathy for Fleming, who Harling recalled as being 'shattered' by the news of her death.[51] Really, they were both extremely fond of Muriel, to whom 'every naval officer in 30AU was devoted' and had 'failed to understand why she had not become Mrs. Fleming long [ago]'.[52] More so, they resented the way that Fleming had treated such a lovely woman, who had died having returned to her flat on her motorbike from collecting two hundred of his special order cigarettes from Morlands. This personified their relationship, with a kind natured and beautiful woman, who other men drooled over, doting on a man who treated her well only when it suited him. She ran around in circles for Fleming, and in this case had died doing so.

Despite the way he treated her, Fleming was badly affected by Muriel's death. In fact, grief was outweighed by guilt. Guilt at the way he had taken Muriel for granted. His biographer, Andrew Lycett, believed 'he immediately became very sentimental about Muriel' in odd ways, including 'refusing to return to restaurants they had once visited together'.[53]

His grief was only ever really put into words when he wrote *On Her Majesty's Secret Service* in 1962. Bond, newlywed to the love of his life, Tracy, is ambushed by a flurry of bullets. Tracy is killed in the exchange. 'Bond put his arm round her shoulders, across which the dark patches had begun to flower,' Fleming wrote. Turning to a policeman who has arrived at the scene, Bond says in a clear voice: 'It's quite all right. She's having a rest. We'll be going on soon. There's no hurry. You see ... we've got all the time in the world.'[54]

Eighteen years before writing this, Fleming leant over a metal gurney in a London hospital, with the gruesome task of identifying Muriel's body. With a stoic face, Fleming turned away from his dead lover, looked the medical orderly straight in the eyes, and nodded solemnly. He walked out and would never speak of her again.

Chapter 9

Moonraker

Unlike his previous two books, *Casino Royale* and *Live and Let Die*, Fleming's third novel, *Moonraker*, is based purely in Britain with no foreign travel. The experiment for Fleming to not send Bond overseas to somewhere glamorous was not very well received by his readers. One elderly couple wrote to him in protest, 'We want taking out of ourselves, not sitting on the beach in Dover.'[1]

Before he started writing, Fleming had told his publisher that his new novel was a 'story I've had in my mind since the war … involving the destruction of London by a super V-2'. The book *Moonraker* follows Bond's mission to investigate Hugo Drax, the creator of the Moonraker, a modified V-2 rocket using liquid hydrogen and fluorine, which he has apparently built in order to protect the British from Soviet attack. Because of some suspicious activity at the Moonraker base, Bond is sent in undercover to investigate. It turns out that Hugo Drax is a Nazi supporter who intends to fire the Moonraker at London in revenge for Germany's defeat in the war. Bond is discovered to be a double agent and captured but is able to escape and foil Drax's plan.

The Oxford English Dictionary defines a double agent as someone 'who pretends to act as a spy for one country or organisation while in fact acting on behalf of an enemy'. The chances are, if you were to ask anyone for an example of a double agent, first to come to mind would be the fictional character of James Bond. Up to this point in the Bond novels, 007 is more of a saboteur than a spy. But in *Moonraker* we see Bond go undercover for the first time. Due to the very nature of their work, little or nothing is known about many of the real double agents who went undercover in World War II, or the invaluable work they did in leading the Allies to victory. But for part of it at least, Fleming was right in the middle, and would in years to come, use his knowledge to inform his books.

At the outbreak of war, the British people were gripped by what Winston Churchill described as 'spy-mania', believing that every neighbour, colleague or person passed on the street might be a 'Fifth Columnist'.[2] One way to overcome the threat of German spying in Britain was the creation of the Double Cross system, known as XX, or the Twenty Committee (because of the value of XX in Roman numerals), designed to send false information back to the enemy.

With their network growing considerably, in 1943, the Twenty Committee had brought on board an agent called Johnny Jebsen – described as a 'slight and thin' man 'with dark blond hair, high cheekbones and a turned-up nose' – who would prove most valuable.[3] After defecting to MI6 from the German Secret Service, the Abwehr, Jebson had deliberately and successfully wooed Baroness Gertzen, a married woman living in Spain. Gertzen was a secretary for Nazi manufacturers Henschel & Son, who made everything from Luftwaffe aircraft to the infamous Panzer tanks. With an estimated 42,000 German tanks destroyed in the war, Henschel & Son made a sizable profit from the conflict. Gertzen quickly fell for Jebsen, who reported back to his handlers that 'the Baroness is very much in love' and 'was easily induced to talk about the likelihood of severe bombardment of the UK'. Although bombing attacks on Britain were already an all too often occurrence, Gertzen was going into detail about a new weapon being developed by Henschel & Son for the Nazis.

Jebson told the besotted Baroness that he intended to travel to Britain, therefore putting himself in extreme danger, as the country 'might be the object of an attack by Hitler's secret weapon'. Consequently, 'She immediately promised to give all the details of the weapon,' Jebson reported.[4] When he fed back the information to his spymasters in the Twenty Committee, they were stunned. The creation of such a new weapon described by Gertzen would be devastating.

The *Vergeltungswaffe-1* flying bomb, literally translated as 'Reprisal Weapon-1' had been in design and testing phases since the start of the war. The German Air Ministry (RLM) received a proposal in November 1939 for 'a remote-controlled aircraft capable of carrying a 1000kg warhead a distance of 500 km'.[5] The twenty-five foot welded steel chasse and plywood wings, with a span of 17 feet 6 inches, was powered by an Argus pulse-jet engine and would create a sort of buzzing sound. Hence the nickname of 'the buzz bomb'.

On 13 June 1944, the first buzz bomb struck the heart of London, causing endless desolation. The evening of the first attack, the BBC reported how a 'slight' bombing of the capital had caused just a 'few casualties'.[6] This was masterful propaganda, which sent Hitler into fury at the lack of impact from his new weapon of mass destruction. The reality was a huge loss of civilian life, including Muriel Wright.

Two days later, 217 flying bombs hit the capital and by the end of June over 660 V-1s had struck London. Flight Lieutenant John Musgrave encountered a buzz bomb while on patrol in his Mosquito VI on the night of 15 June 1944, describing the experience as 'like chasing a ball of fire across the sky. It flashed past'. The RAF were able to shoot down some of the foreign weapons, including the one Musgrave saw which, after 'a terrific flash and explosion', the 'whole thing fell down in a vertical dive into the sea'.[7] However, with hundreds being launched at any one time, this type of air combat was not a sustainable solution.

Fortunately, the secret service had their own plans. Another double agent run by the Twenty Committee, Edward Chapman, also known as Agent Zigzag, was sent to Britain by his German handlers with orders to 'report on the effects of the V-1s, giving precise timings and the resulting damage'.[8] What the Germans didn't know was that Chapman was actually working for the British. This was the ideal opportunity to feed even more false information back to the Germans, who were rightly sceptical about the BBC's laissez-faire reports on the impact of these weapons.

Described by historian Ben Macintyre as 'the most notorious double agent of World War II', the German intelligence service trusted Chapman's information implicitly.[9] Chapman reported back to his German handlers that the V-1 bombs were overshooting London, using the correct points of impact for bombs which had a longer range than the others. In reality, of the hundreds of flying bombs that were striking the centre of the capital, only a handful were overshooting their target – the majority were hitting the heart of London. The Nazis fell for the ruse spectacularly, and the operators were ordered to reduce the average range of the V-1, believing this would strike the likes of Charing Cross or St Paul's, whereas the actual target was the suburbs and countryside south of London. Although this still resulted in casualties and damage to property, chairman of the Twenty Committee, John Cecil Masterman wrote: 'The deception was a very real triumph ... saving many thousands of lives'.[10]

Fleming was privy to much of the detail of Chapman's scheme, having played a small part in the deception. It would inspire the plot of *Moonraker*, in which Bond uses a similar tactic and changes the co-ordinates of the missile to save London. Fleming had only a minor role in the Agent Zigzag story as the apparent recipient of some false information, which Chapman then fed back to his German handlers. In this case, the Twenty Committee wanted the Nazis to believe the Allies had developed a new technology to detect and destroy U-boats. In reality, there was no such technology:

Dear Fleming,

I feel sure that you will be pleased as I was to hear the results of the latest squid trials. A standard deviation of plus or minus 15 feet is a wonderful improvement on the old method of depth-finding and my only regret is that our present target is incapable of greater speeds ... I thought you might like the enclosed photos of the standard remote setting depth charge fuse.[11]

The letter was signed from underwater acoustics specialist Professor A.B. Wood and included a picture purporting to be an anti-submarine 'proximity fuse'. In reality, it was a clunky and altogether unremarkable depth charge, photographed next to an adapted ruler to make it appear a third bigger than its actual size.

It was through this ruse that Fleming learned of the deception operations against the V-1 rocket. He was also privy to information on the development of an even deadlier weapon. For Fleming, this weapon was at the top of his unit's 'blacklist'. Not only was this cutting-edge technology, far more advanced than anything the Allies had come remotely close to designing, it was the sequel to the V-1 rocket, which had claimed the life of Muriel. For Fleming, this was now personal.

In 1936, the Germans had started work on the design of a long-range ballistic missile, the first of its kind. Six years of development lead to the successful launch of the first rocket of this type, the *Vergeltungswaffe-2*, or V-2 rocket, which would throw the V-1 rocket into the appendix of any history book. Technically termed the *Aggregat-4*, shortened to A-4, the single-staged liquid oxygen propelled rocket could reach an altitude of fifty-three miles and travel a distance of nearly 200 miles at a speed of over 3,000 miles per hour. The RAF's flying aces, as skilled as they were, would not stand a hope in hell of intercepting. Twenty-year-old graduate Wernher von Braun was the designer of these staggering 46-foot long rockets, weighing 27,000lb. Built almost exclusively by slave labour from the dreaded Mittelbau-Dora concentration camp, which claimed the lives of 20,000 people, more people died building the V-2 rockets than were killed by it as a weapon.

With intelligence landing on his desk about V-2 development, Fleming sent a signal to 30AU ordering that the launch sites and development bases for V rockets be their main focus, due mainly to attacks on Southern England.

Part of the information received in Room 39 excited Fleming. An urgent message was sent to 30AU, stating that 'there seemed to be a gap in the German lines which might make it possible to reach one V-1 site' and ordered a top priority investigation. Patrick Dalzel-Job was set with the task of intercepting this target. His orders included the 'urgent need to examine one of these sites on the ground' taking with him Flight Lieutenant Nutting, the ballistics expert assigned to his unit. Choosing a crack team which included 'lucky' Bill Wright, still bruised from his near scrape with death, and Sergeant Paul McGrath, who he described as 'a very good, steady man'.[12] This was the proper commando-style mission which Fleming had always imagined for his unit. Finally, they would be put to the ultimate test, penetrating the front line and making their way into enemy territory to gain intelligence from a target before it could be destroyed.

The day after receiving Fleming's order, Dalzel-Job met with American commanders on the forward line south of Normandy as the sun was just starting to rise. The Americans were less than impressed by his demands to move ahead of them. He spent a good part of an hour trying to explain 'the nature of the Unit's requirements to a succession of U.S. Army Officers who had never before heard of 30 AU'.[13] Several tense exchanges later, he had the reluctant permissions he needed.

Moving to the front, they spied the gap in the enemy line, where 'a wide, empty area of fields and woods' was 'separated by ditches and hedgerows'. This was the perfect cover for the commando unit, who crawled for several miles through the wet and cold mud of the ditches. The only time they would be able to stand was for bursts of running through open fields when there was no sufficient cover. They needed to risk the possibility of the prying eyes of snipers or machine gun posts. Their 'zig-zag progress, very seldom erect' caused serious navigation issues for the unit. Such problems would inevitably mean delays in arriving at the target, but in this case it could also mean heading straight into one of the many German strongholds they were trying to avoid. Thanks to Dalzel-Job's experience as a sailor, he was able to get back on track 'just as I would have done sailing along the coast' using a church spire and road junctions to get his bearings.

The four commandos arrived at the launch site in the early evening after a very long day. Their battledress was caked in mud and ditch water, mixed with the men's sweat. In an almost peaceful scene, they stood looking at a 'J' shaped concrete runway surrounded by trees. They noticed for the first time in many weeks that no planes were flying overhead leaving an almost 'eerie silence' behind enemy lines.

With the site completely deserted, and clear apart from the launch pad, Dalzel-Job admitted he 'could see nothing that seemed of particular interest to my untechnical mind', but the expert, Nutting, grew increasingly excited by their discovery.[14] Pictures of the runway were sent back to Britain, answering one of the key questions about the weapon: how were they launched? The answer, as Dalzel-Job's men discovered, was almost a backwards ski-jump style runway, which ran horizontally along the ground, before curving upwards at 45 degrees at the end.

*

By 12 September 1944, the Allied troops had reached the Siegfried Line, the German defensive line along the Rhine. During their sweep through France, Belgium, Luxembourg and the Netherlands, the British, American and Canadian troops had been accompanied every step of the way by Fleming's commandos. The Allied plan was to next clear what Hitler had declared his 'fortresses', strategic ports along the north coast of France and Belgium, namely Le Havre, Dieppe, Boulogne, Calais, Dunkirk and Ostend. 30AU took part of *Operation Astonia*, the assault on Le Havre, which turned out to be a bittersweet victory for the Allies. Worried about escaping Nazis, the invading troops refused to allow civilians to leave the area, resulting in the death of over 2,000 French men, women and children from the bombing campaign that formed a prelude to the attack. The ground assault, with 30AU at the centre, was a success and resulted in the capture of over 11,300 German soldiers. With less than 500 Allied casualties, this was seen as a great military achievement, but for 30AU this was one of the darkest days of the war.

While accepting the surrender of a crowd of Nazi soldiers, 'a mob of diehards came round the corner spraying bullets', one of which struck Captain Huntington-Whiteley, killing him instantly.[15] Known as 'Red' because of his ginger hair, Huntington-Whiteley had been part of Fleming's team from the very start at Dieppe, through Africa, Sicily, Italy and then France. If anyone deserved to see the success of the commando unit he had helped shape, it was Captain Huntington-Whiteley. He was buried at Sanvic Communal Cemetery, where the men who had served under him were shocked to see on the cross how young he was, just twenty-four years old. Robert Harling remembered how the 'the marines certainly cherish [or] cherished' their Captain.[16]

In an attempt to speed up the surrender and avoid further bloodshed, the RAF dropped leaflets urging the Nazis to give up. Two members of 30AU, Jim Feeley and 'Doc' Livingstone – who were briefly taken prisoner, only to be released twenty-four hours later when the Germans surrendered – told their captors that they needed to get the leaflets signed by Allied troops to allow them safety as a POW. They then made a small fortune charging their enemy 200 francs per signature, before blowing it all 'on wine, women and song'. Fleming started to get reports of the improper activity of his men, which he now referred to as 30 Indecent Assault Unit. An officer was informed by one of his men that 'I've had three fucks ... if you'll pardon the word, sir'; proudly stating that one of the women 'even had a boudoir'.[17]

*

By February 1945, 30AU had received further reinforcements, now with nearly 300 men of whom twenty-five were officers. The Americans had their own team doing similar work. Named 'T' Force, they were a pool of approximately 2,000 American combat troops who were to 'act as bodyguards to specialists required to deal with "T" Targets'. Naturally, there was concern about the crossover which would occur between a British and American force, both aiming for the same targets. As 'T' Force was mainly focused on air targets, it was agreed by Fleming that 30AU representatives would come under 'T' Force's organisation for aerial targets, but 'must retain full right of movement round outlying targets'.[18]

113

Dalzel-Job, meanwhile, was less than enthusiastic about 'T' Force, claiming they 'were often more interested in private looting than in securing enemy intelligence', an accusation which had often been made against his own men.[19]

On 3 March, 30AU entered Germany for the first time, arriving at the ruined city of Cologne four days later, where just 40,000 of the 500,000 residents still remained. On the way, Dalzel-Job had come across a belt-fed German machine gun which he secured to the front of his jeep 'to make ourselves look more aggressive and to give us rather more fire-power'. His sergeant had the unenviable task of cleaning the gun every day, which he confessed '[he] did not enjoy'.[20]

After being one of first group of British troops to cross the Rhine on 23 March, 30AU arrived at Mannheim six days later. Here, they gained valuable material from the engineering firm Brown, Boveri & Cie, who were making cutting edge motors, turbochargers and switchboards for the German Navy.

By the middle of April, 30AU had reached Naumburg in eastern Germany, 180 miles across the country from their successful scoop at Mannhiem. While searching a school building in the village which, according to locals, had housed German Naval Intelligence staff, Glanville came across a half-burnt envelope with the address: 'SKI/KA, Tambach'. Sending a message to Fleming, Glanville asked if he could find anything of relevance. It transpired that the address referred to Schloss Tambach, a large seventeenth century pink stone castle, some seventy miles from where the envelope had been found. Room 39 had heard of the coming and goings of 'lorry-loads of documents' to the castle for several months.[21] Fleming ordered his men to immediately race to Schloss Tambach, as this might be the big break 30AU wanted. Making haste, his unit stumbled across the recently liberated Buchenwald concentration camp. Glanville recalled how shocked the men were, 'not only at the skeletons and heaps of corpses and the lampshades made of tattooed human skin, but at the polished brightwork and black-leaded furnaces in the crematorium, and at the carefully tended gallows and songbirds in their cages besides them'.[22]

Disgusted and disturbed by what they had witnessed on their journey, a section of 30AU arrived at Tambach before nightfall. They found *Konteradmiral* Walter Gladisch, of the German War Historical Department, at the front of the building, almost as if awaiting their arrival.

The castle, with hardly a light on inside, did not seem to Fleming's unit to be of much importance. A quick interrogation of the German Admiral proved that theory wrong. He explained that behind the door of the castle sat a complete library of all operational logs, naval diaries, innovation reports, meeting minutes, technical blueprints and designs of all German naval business from 1870 to the present day. Glanville did not initially believe the admiral, as such a stash would be one of the biggest pinches of the war. Testing him, Granville asked to see the reports on a naval battle he knew well from November 1941. The elderly German man wandered off, returning with a fat file that contained every possible detail of the event.

Exultation was quickly followed by dread. What should the men do with such a big prize? A quick count of the windows on the north-west side of the building where they stood came to sixty-eight. With just a handful of men, there was no way they could keep the castle safe from the 'armed bands of deserters and dispossessed roaming the land' trying to burn anything they could to the ground.[23] Lieutenant Jim Besant was left with three marines to guard the building while the others raced to get help. Only minutes after they had left, a fire broke out in the library. It transpired that one of uniformed female guards, the German equivalent to the British WRENS, Fräulein Androde, had started the fire. She was apprehended before the fire could spread. It was suggested that she should be given a spanking for her rebellion, but Besant thought she 'was too beefy to go across anyone's knee'.[24]

Reinforcements arrived in the form of General Patton's Third Army, who sent 125 officers and men to secure the site. Patton had originally not been a supporter of 30AU, refusing to allow the men to operate in his front line. Fleming flew out to try and reason with the American General. Robert Harling recalled his visit:

> Fleming, attendant US officers, and Patton made their way towards his tent, or rather marquee, dominating the HQ canvas complex. I hung around. An hour or so later, the party reappeared. Judging by the widespread, pervasive smiles, everything had seemingly gone well. Fleming certainly looked relieved.[25]

Their negotiations had indeed gone well, with Patton being impressed by Fleming. When one of his men arrived asking for help, the general was only too happy to oblige.

With the castle now safe, a new threat appeared on the horizon, this time the Russians. Tambach sat within the Red Army's zone, and they were advancing towards them quickly. To supervise the packing and shipping, Fleming flew to the castle just days after VE Day was declared on 8 May 1945. He reported that 'we'll need at least half-a-dozen 3-tonne lorries to bring it all back', but did not stay to help with the logistics. Glanville and his section, 'within a few days' had completed the 'business of cataloguing and packing the archives for shipment to London'.[26]

The last major event for 30AU occurred on 5 May 1945, the day of the German surrender, when Dunstan Curtis and members of 30AU entered Kiel at 9.30 am. Their primary objective was to capture as much of the work being done by a company called H. Walter KG as possible. With no resistance whatsoever, they achieved this with ease. They even managed to arrest the proprietor himself, Dr Helmuth Walter. Walter was an expert in 'closed-cycle propulsion', which he applied to V-80 submarines enabling them to travel faster than any other underwater craft at the time. Since 1930, Walter had been working with the Luftwaffe, most notably designing the cylinder that launched the V-1 and V-2 rockets. The launch site, which 30AU had discovered earlier in the war, had been created by this very man. Present with the unit was Lieutenant Alastair Cameron, an expert in lubrication engineering. He was amazed by the 'launching mechanism for the V-1s, also for the proportioning system of the V-2s ... which were of interest to us'.[27]

This was exactly what Fleming had wanted to find. In some way, capturing Walter and his equipment was avenging the death of Muriel. He also used Walter as a character in *Moonraker*, when on his arrival at the fictional launch site, Drax introduces Bond to a black-haired, elderly man called Dr Walter, who is the second in command of the operation. (The name Drax was not inspired by anyone relevant, coming instead from a former colleague of Fleming's, the wonderfully named Admiral Sir Reginald Aylmer Ranfurly Plunkett-Ernle-Erle-Drax.)

Many Nazi scientists like Walter were arrested and taken abroad to work for the British or Americans. But many escaped and re-entered German civilian life in disguise, which was a concept also used by Fleming. In *Moonraker*, Drax is able to build his own team of fifty men by going on the hunt for ex-Nazi scientists, who were living in Germany under false identities, usually stolen from a dead soldier.

*

With the war now all but over, 30AU was disbanded and the men returned to civilian life. Fleming was released from His Majesty's Service on 10 November 1945. His time was seen as successful within intelligence circles, so much so that Fleming's original remit was now considered essential, with an internal memo stating that 'it is recommended that such an appointment should be created in any future war'.[28]

Fleming received no official recognition for his work during the war, although he had accumulated a fair few medals which his men had confiscated during their time overseas, including a German Iron Cross and the Order of the Dannebrog from Denmark. His own lack of awards was down to the type of work he was involved in. Fleming is eager to remind his readers of this, when, in *Moonraker*, Bond is told that 'the Prime Minister had [an honour] in mind for you. He had forgotten that we don't go in for those sort of things here'.[29]

For Ian Fleming, the war had been the biggest success of his life to date. Despite the exciting adventures to come, it is fair to say he was saddened by the prospect of re-entering civilian life. He added this trait to Bond as well, often referring to the fact that 007 was never quite the same after the war.

The film of version of *Moonraker* featured very few themes from the book and was instead set in space. Although the *Moonraker* in the film was actually a spacecraft, rather than a ballistic missile, in a happy coincidence the V-2 rocket designs found at Tambach and the launch equipment from Kiel would go on to become the blueprint for the Apollo rocket programme, which put the first man on the moon. Had the items recovered by Fleming's men fallen into Russian hands, the outcome of the Space Race twenty-four years later could have been very different.

Part Two

Peace

Chapter 10

Octopussy

As part of the last Bond book to be published, 'Octopussy' is the short story which follows Major Dexter Smythe, a World War II hero who has been implicated in the exploitation of Nazi gold. Bond is sent to arrest Smythe, who he discovers is living alone on a beach in Jamaica, where he swims with his beloved pet octopus all day, called Octopussy. When Bond finds Smythe, he offers him the options of either killing himself or being arrested. Smythe decides on the former, feeding himself to Octopussy.

Smythe is described as one of 'the remains of a once brave and resourceful officer' from the war, who 'when the commandos were formed he had volunteered'.[1] Like Fleming, he 'persisted in smoking like a chimney and going to bed drunk, if amiably drunk, every night'.[2] Although Fleming is clearly describing himself here, what makes this story particularly autobiographical is the setting and location.

For Ian Fleming, the one thing which was closer to his heart than almost anything else was the small tropical island of Jamaica, which became his very own oasis. It was here that he would mix his desire for reclusiveness with that of socialising among a select group of friends. This obsession started twenty years earlier in July 1943, when Fleming landed in Jamaica for the first of what would become many times. He had arrived in the Caribbean as a representative of Naval Intelligence for an urgent conference to address the crisis of German U-boat destruction in the surrounding sea. Over 200 vessels in the vicinity had been successfully torpedoed in one month alone. It was reported to the Admiralty that 'the sinkings in the Caribbean had reached a most alarming total in that year'.

Not one to rough it in some local crumbling hotel, Fleming exploited his connections by bringing along old friend Ivar Bryce, whom he had known since school, to make use of his accommodation. Bryce, acting as a liaison officer in Washington and working for William Stephenson, had received a notice from Britain to say 'ADNI [Assistant Director of Naval Intelligence] London will be attending [the conference], you are to accompany'.[3] Bryce, described by Robert Harling as 'tall, dark, handsome, amusing, thoughtful, quick to laughter and to encourage laughter in others', was ecstatic at the prospect.[4] Not only was this a chance for him to spend time with his good friend, but it also gave him the excuse to leave the underwhelming weather in Washington and enjoy something more tropical. Furthermore, Bryce's second wife, Sheila, owned the huge 'Great House' on the Bellevue Estate overlooking Jamaica's capital, Kingston. This house was perfectly situated with a panoramic view, and was an escape from the sweltering heat of the towns, privy to a blissful breeze that so many of the locals craved. With steps each side of the front of the house leading to the impressive main door, the building looked out over an impeccably well-kept and endlessly sprawling lawn, which fell away into the view of Kingston. The house had held the great and the good over the years, including Nelson himself, who 'spent some pleasant weeks there being cossetted and nursed back to strength' after coming down with a fever.[5] For Bryce the view of 'the blue Caribbean sea, sun kissed and clear-aired' was simply 'wondrous'.[6]

'Wondrous' was not how Fleming would describe his first adventure on the island, which was less than spectacular. He arrived in some of the heaviest rain he had ever experienced as well as extreme humidity. Still, he made the best of it, attending the conference daily for the next week, returning to the house in the evening with local delicacies including lots of fresh fruit – almost nonexistent in Britain during the rationing years – which he thoroughly enjoyed, although the rain did not relent. Of course, when Ivar 'secured an ample stock of gin', which he described to Fleming as 'life-saving stuff for the long evenings', things began to cheer up.

Despite a week of hard work, hideous heat, little variety of alcohol, questionable food and no female company, Fleming had caught the Jamaican 'bug'. At the end of the trip he surprised Bryce by announcing that after the war, he was going to move to Jamaica to live a quiet life spent enjoying the culture, swimming in the sea and writing books. On his departure, Fleming asked Ivar to act as his estate agent and find him a small plot of land, secluded on the coast. Somewhat unrealistically, Fleming had in mind somewhere with private access to the sea, away from any roads or towns, and ideally with its own little island. He told

Bryce that once he found the perfect spot, Fleming would design and build his dream house there. Although there was nothing offered to Bryce in exchange for his help, he gave Fleming his word that he would do all he could.

It was not until after the end of the war, over two years later, that Bryce would return to Jamaica and attempt to fulfil his promise to Fleming. Speaking to the locals, Bryce summarised his friend's requirements as 'a little place with good swimming and an island' to a local agent, Reggie Acquart.[7] It was after viewing several locations that Acquart came to Bryce with something of interest. 'I think I have found the right place for your friend the Commander,' he told him.[8] Acquart took Ivar to see the site he had come across, which was part of a redundant racecourse in St Mary, just over fourteen acres in size and owned by a local Irish-Jamaican called Christie Cousins. Positioned on the north coast of the island, almost directly above Kingston, the plot was mostly overgrown. Through the rough, Bryce found a shack which would have been used to sell snacks to racecourse enthusiasts. The parcel of land sat on top of a forty-foot cliff, which at the bottom had a small cricket pitch sized private beach. As Bryce looked out at the beautiful expansive sea, nearly 500 years before, Columbus would have been looking back, as he sailed past this spot discovering 'the fairest island that eyes have beheld'.[9] Viewing the glasslike ocean, Bryce noticed a piece of coral with some Jamaican flowers growing out of it. This would be a far cry from the island which Fleming had wanted, but everything else about the property matched his criteria perfectly. 'He will adore this place,' Bryce said. 'Tie it up tomorrow, Reggie. I can let you have whatever money is necessary for that.'[10]

Back at the Bellevue that evening, Bryce cabled Fleming to tell him he had found the perfect location. The next day, with full faith in his friend's property nous, Fleming transferred £2,000 into the owner, Christie Cousins' account. And with that, the land belonged to him.

After leaving Naval Intelligence, Fleming had secured a job as Foreign News Manager at the *Sunday Times,* under his bridge playing friend, Lord Kemsley. As the boss of over eighty correspondents around the world, Fleming had a large map erected in his office with flashing lights indicating locations of interest. Along with a salary of £5,000 per year plus expenses, Fleming's job allowed him two months paid leave during the winter every year to spend in the Caribbean, setting a routine he would follow until his death.

'Vespers are served,' he announced proudly.[15] Fleming was grateful for the hospitality of this very eccentric couple, and particularly enjoyed his first ever 'Vesper', a frozen gin and fruit concoction he was never able to reproduce. He would go on to use the name for his first Bond girl, Vesper Lynd, in *Casino Royale*, as well as using the name for his own cocktail. The Vesper Martini has an eye watering mix of three measures of gin, one measure of vodka and half a measure of Kina Lillet. In true Bond form, it is then shaken very well before being served in a frosted martini glass with a slice of lemon-peel.

By early February 1947, with Bryce and Fox-Strangways having left Goldeneye, Fleming was alone to enjoy his new house and land, spending the majority of his time in the sea. Bryce recalled that Fleming loved 'the doings on the reef' which 'filled the whole day with interest and pleasure'.[16] Fleming's knowledge and passion for the underwater life comes through strongly as he wrote 'Octopussy'. He was able to describe in detail the many different species that would be found in his bay, explaining to the reader the characteristics of each individually.

Bryce, who after leaving Goldeneye had gone back to Bellevue, where he was living full-time, took it upon himself to introduce Fleming to some of the island's dignitaries. Fleming was welcomed into the community of expats almost immediately. Similar to Major Smyth, who had earned his place in 'Government House society' and was continually invited to parties by the island's most powerful, Fleming became friends with many of the colourful and influential characters Jamaica had to offer. For example, there was Lord Peregrine 'Perry' Brownlow, who lived at Roaring River on St Ann's Bay, a short fifteen mile drive west of Goldeneye. Brownlow had moved to Jamaica following his disastrous association with Mrs Simpson, which started as friendship until the abdication of King Edward VIII on 11 December 1936, when it turned sour. He had briefly worked for fellow Jamaican landowner, Lord Beaverbrook, from 1940 to 1941 as his Parliamentary Private Secretary when Beaverbrook was Minister of Aircraft Production. Fleming had also worked with Beaverbrook for a short time during the war as part of *Operation Ruthless*, and shared mutual friends in the press, so had a lot in common with Brownlow.

With what he thought to be a comfortable house, a perfect private cove with endless hours of underwater exploring to do and now lots of local friends, Jamaica was turning into exactly the getaway Fleming had always dreamed of. He was not jealous in the slightest of those in England who, as he referred to in 'Octopussy', were still having their food rationed and living through some of the coldest winters ever recorded.

Life was now shaping up nicely for Fleming. He had been stimulated by the war, having come out with a good job and now a holiday house in paradise. But he needed someone to share this all with. And typically, he had his mind set on someone tangled in a complicated social web.

Chapter 11

The Spy Who Loved Me

For the first (and only) time in the James Bond series, the story of *The Spy Who Loved Me* is not told through the eyes of Bond, but rather a young Canadian woman, Vivian 'Viv' Michel. A large part of the narrative concerns Viv's youth, leading up to her looking after a motel one evening in the Adirondack Mountains in North America. While alone, she is taken hostage by two gangsters for insurance purposes. Luckily for Viv, James Bond arrives following a puncture in his Ford Thunderbird, kills the gangsters and seduces her. He then leaves in the night without notice, remaining in her mind as the spy who had loved her, albeit briefly.

This novel was an interesting experiment for Fleming, moving the point of view into the mind of a woman. The book was not particularly well received, especially by female readers. Fleming defended it by explaining that he wrote in this way to demonstrate to his readers that Bond was not the idol people were making him out to be. Although some of the stories told by Viv – including the way she lost her virginity in a cinema – are taken from Fleming's life, many of her characteristics reflect those of his wife, Ann.

Fleming had first met Ann before the war while courting Maud Russell, an attractive married woman in her forties, seventeen years his senior. As one observer put it, Maud 'found comfort in other places' from her husband. Fleming would be invited by Maud to various parties outside London, at Stockton, Stanway and Mottisfont, where his name appeared on several occasions in the visitor books of the houses the Russells would rent. According to Maud's niece, 'they made little secret of their affection for each other'.[1] Anyone dating Fleming needed to be aware that, as his friend Robert Harling wrote, 'Ian doesn't really like [women]: I think he even resents them because of his sexual dependence on them. He resents the way women complicate the rest of his life'

As his attitude towards his late girlfriend Muriel demonstrated, women were often dispensable for Fleming. Bond's view of women is similar – as shown at the end of *Casino Royale* when he simply remarks after Vesper's suicide that 'the bitch is dead' – although the films made him out to be more of a Lothario.[2] Bond expert Henry Chancellor calculated that Bond beds fourteen women through the twelve books, whereas he sleeps with fifty-eight in the first twenty films.

It was November 1934 while with Maud at Stanway that Fleming first laid eyes on twenty-one-year-old and recently married Ann O'Neill. Having wed Lord Shane, Baron O'Neill, that year, Fleming and Ann did not really make much of their first meeting.

In *The Spy Who Loved Me*, Fleming described Viv as the same height and build as Ann. Although he is not directly using Ann's image while creating his fictional character, for example he describes her as having blue eyes, whereas Ann had grey-green eyes (which often caused him confusion), there is still a striking resemblance. For example, like Ann, Viv had wavy dark brown hair. Fleming goes even further, drawing attention to what he saw as flaws in Ann's appearance through his description of Viv, for instance calling out her elevated cheekbones. Ann, too, had high cheekbones, with the kind of face people would refer to as 'handsome' rather than 'beautiful'. Even Ann's personality is questioned by Fleming in his novel. Viv describes herself as an independent and optimistic person, whose personality can sometimes be overshadowed by a hint of depression. For those who knew Ann, few would disagree with this sentiment.

It was not until four years later in the summer of 1938 that Fleming would lay eyes on Ann again. He had cabled his then French based friend Ivar Bryce to meet him at Graham Paige Boulonge Maritime and block out a two week period to go travelling from there. Ivar, as we have already seen, was not one to say no to his friend, and dutifully went to the meeting place. When Fleming appeared from the ferry, he was accompanied by a young, pretty American woman called Phyllis. In his younger years, Fleming had told friends that he was not the least bit interested in English women because, apparently, they would not wash regularly and were dull in the bedroom. He hoped that young Phyllis would prove that Americans were quite different. After brief introductions, he guided Ivar and Phyllis towards the vehicle he was renting. There was a stunned silence when they were shown to a two-seater sportscar. Ivar did not protest when

Fleming informed him that Phyllis was to come with them and would be taking the enviable position of passenger in the vehicle, leaving Bryce to perch on the gear stick. Two days later, Bryce still sitting between the romantically linked Englishman and his American beauty, the party arrived at Hotel Vierjahreszeiten in Munich. After what Bryce described as 'the most uncomfortable journey of my life', Fleming decided that he was now bored with Phyllis, refusing to take her any further. She wept that she was in love with Fleming after their three-day fling but he was having none of it, declaring that he had had enough of her American views and telling her to go back to Boston immediately. At that, they parted company.

It was after this episode that Ann reappeared in Fleming's life. Staying on the other side of the country in Carinthia, Ann was with fellow guest Nin Ryan, a mutual friend of the two. That summer, despite Ann being married, she noticed the 'handsome moody creature' that was Fleming.[3] Twenty years later, Ann confessed to a friend that 'the arrogant hero figure, entering the foyer, had totally ignored his teenage admirer' who was instantly taken by him.[4] Fleming soon became a close acquaintance of her husband, as the two men shared an interest in golf and bridge. Unknowingly, O'Neill was now regularly inviting his wife's new attraction to their home, where Fleming and Ann would spend time admiring each other across the room. Ann described him as 'Glamour Boy' to her female friends. One of whom, Loelia Ponsonby, exclaimed on meeting Fleming 'that's the most attractive man I've ever seen'.[5] Ann recalled in her diary that 'at some point in the not-too-distant future [she] must and would have him'.[6]

Keeping true to the promise she had made to herself, the following year, at the start of 1939, Ann plucked up the courage to suggest that she and Fleming meet alone for the first time. He agreed, and a dinner date was arranged to take place in a restaurant in the heart of London. It was not a resounding success, with Fleming flinging a book over the table to Ann upon her arrival, feigning a migraine and telling her to sit quietly for an hour until he was feeling better. Ann was understandably taken aback by his conduct, commenting in the diary that 'considering the slightness of our acquaintance' it was 'very odd behaviour'.[7] However, this did not stop the two of them consummating their relationship that evening. Fleming was completely oblivious to the fact that his arrogance and rudeness was poorly received by Ann.

In fact, he thought being dominant and controlling was something women found attractive. In *The Spy Who Loved Me*, Fleming writes that Viv was taken by Bond because he had power over her.

Following their first date, Fleming began a regular sexual liaison with Ann almost immediately, along with several visits to the cinema. Despite Ann being very sexually inexperienced – even as a young married woman – she soon started to enjoy the physical side of their relationship. Her sister recalled that when Ann returned from her honeymoon, 'she was still a virgin because her sunburn had made lovemaking too uncomfortable'.[8] On the other hand, Fleming did not have the same problem losing his virginity. Aged sixteen, he recalled how he chatted up an eager young lady in Slough, and immediately took her to the local cinema where they began to have sex. The act was cut short by the manager storming into their box with a torch, before escorting them from the building and banning them both for life. He hastened to add that although he was interrupted mid-act, his virginity was lost forever. Whereas Fleming was mildly alarmed by this experience, his lover was mortified, needing much comfort as he walked her home. In *The Spy Who Loved Me*, these exact series of events are described for when poor Viv lost her virginity.

Despite Ann being sexually slow to start, as it were, she soon caught up. For Fleming, he did not feel the emotional side of it at all; instead, as Harling had noted, he saw intercourse, and women for that matter, as purely disposable. After becoming friends, Harling 'began to assume [that Fleming] had his own special sexual entertainments, possibly mildly masochistic and/or sadistic, lacking in appeal to most of the rest of us'.[9] Fleming's view of women was less than flattering, once describing them all as only pets, whereas men were the real human beings.

Ann gave in to his ways, and according to her sister Virginia, 'they liked hurting each other' rather than making conventional love. Ann seemed to find this rather stimulating, writing to Fleming in August 1948: 'I loved being whipped by you' and 'I love being hurt by you and kissed afterwards'.[10] With Fleming's desires and fantasies rubbing off, Ann always tried to seem more sexually adventurous. For example, one evening at dinner with Robert Harling and his wife Phoebe, Ann asked the men around the table to tell the stories of their first sexual experience with a woman. After they had gone around recounting their tales, Ann stood up and exclaimed: 'Very, very interesting, don't you agree, Phoebe? Now I'll tell you all how I had *my* first woman.'

Ann, who was prone to exaggeration and eager to shock the crowd, was likely recounting a fictional story. There is no evidence of her involvement with any women, and despite her wildly sexual relationship with Fleming, she was otherwise quite reserved. A friend of the couple commented that although 'Ann had some reputation as a woman of the world, sex and all ... I always had the impression that, for her, sex was an occasional social offering or expected indulgence rather than a physical or emotional "must"'.[11]

Ann's issue was that she could not help but share every aspect of her life with others, even if she would embellish the truth. Her taste for gossip meant little of her personal life every remained private. In the instance of Fleming, Ann and her friends secretly gave him the nickname of 'Thunderbird' – because he had bought a car of the same name, identical to the one Bond drives in *The Spy Who Loved Me,* for £3,000 – but she deliberately let this slip around her social circles, to the point that everyone knew it apart from Fleming.

*

Soon after she started to engage with Fleming sexually, Ann began to conduct another affair with Esmond Rothermere, the heir to a newspaper empire. Esmond had met Ann while on holiday in Austria during August 1936. He was married to Margaret Hunam Redhead, but after eighteen years they divorced at the outbreak of war in 1938. Ann fell for Esmond almost immediately, writing in her diary, 'I had by then given up all hope of falling in love, but we fell in love with each other,' noting next to this that she 'cannot think of a more original expression!'[12] Esmond's father, Lord Rothermere, was an ardent appeaser in the build-up to the war. On 27 June 1939 he had written directly to Hitler:

> My Dear Führer, I have watched with understanding and interest the progress of your great and superhuman work in regenerating your country. The British people, now like Germany strongly rearmed, regard the German people with admiration as valorous adversaries in the past, but I am sure that there is no problem between our two countries which cannot be settled by consultation and negotiation.[13]

Esmond – who already had to deal with enough scandal in his family following his father's support for Hitler – was extremely cautious about being caught having an affair with Ann. Fleming, on the other hand, had no interest in being subtle. Ann joked to a friend how, 'Esmond's fear of scandal is fully equalled by Ian's fear of marriage.'[14] Her relationship with the three men was confusing for her, but she enjoyed the attention her different suitors bestowed.

At the outbreak of war, Shane O'Neill, after being granted an emergency commission in the North Irish Horse Guards, was sent to Tunisia. This gave Ann more time to spend with her two suitors, rather than her husband, whom she was no longer in love with: 'My marriage had become very difficult, and when I could not see Esmond I found Ian the best antidote among the friends.'[15] Fleming was only too happy to oblige and the two became increasingly close. In fact, as the war went on, there was little time they did not spend together when they were able to, which proved challenging at times due to Fleming's naval commitments. Ann had written that while 'Shane was abroad ... Ian by then spent all his leave wherever I was'.[16]

Robert Harling was privy to one such weekend of leave spent in the company of Ann. When back in London briefly, having spent time in France with 30AU, Harling returned to his desk in Room 39 to find an envelope with his name scribbled on the front in the recognisable Fleming handwriting. Inside was a rough sketch of a map, with an arrow pointing to the village of Buscot in Oxfordshire, with a note telling him to go there immediately. After an enjoyable drive on a blissfully warm summer evening, Harling arrived at a pretty cottage in the middle of the village, next to the lush village green. Knocking at the door, it was answered by Ann, a 'lively, merry and welcoming woman' he remembered, and someone he would go on to be friends with until her death.

A very perceptive man, Harling's initial thoughts of Ann proved to be absolutely correct: 'Slim, dark-haired, fine-featured, with a mildly imperious profile and presence. She was clearly a woman possessed of looks, vivacity, wit, vitality, charm – and brains ... A woman well aware of these facts and factors'.

After eating with Ann and her two children by Shane, Raymond and Fionn, and their tutor Roland, Robert drove Ann to a lodge in Buscot Park where they met Esmond, introduced to Harling by Ann as a 'long-time ... friend of mine', followed by a 'big cheese at the Mail' called William McWhirter and finally Labour politician, Frank Pakenham. Along with Fleming, the foursome had been sitting around a card table smoking ferociously over their game of Bridge. Almost immediately after the introductions were over, the men returned to their places to continue the intense game, while Ann ushered Harling to a side table where the two sat to observe quietly.

'Robert brought some Cognac,' Ann informed the others, breaking the deafening silence. Despite the glares from the card players, she continued, 'I'm assuming it's the right drink for the right moment.'

'More action, fewer words,' Fleming announced to Ann abruptly.

Esmond chimed in as well, 'Let's get on with the game', wryly smiling across the table at Fleming. Harling noted from this brief encounter how the two men clearly got on well.

Until the end of the game – which can last for many painstaking hours – there was no further interruption from anyone. When, several hours later, the game was over, quick goodbyes were made.

Robert was surprised when Pakenham announced he was heading back to his Oxford abode, Rothermere and McWhirter stayed in the lodge, and Ann left with Fleming. He wrote later, 'I had heard rumours that Ann O'Neill was Rothermere's mistress, yet here she was, sharing a cottage, and no doubt, bed with Fleming.'

When he raised this thought, Fleming defensively accused Harling of thinking like a tabloid reporter.

Their relationship continued to blossom through the war, but so did Ann's relationship with Rothermere, who by 1940 had inherited the viscountcy. His lifestyle, influence and wealth were exactly what Ann had always wanted, but the small issue of her husband still got in the way. Then, in October 1944 – by which point Ann was practically living with Esmond at his house in Ascot, but with frequent visits to and from Fleming – a telegram arrived informing her that Shane had been killed in action in Italy. Telegrams of this type were sadly all too common through the war, with the recognisable brevity of the message delivering a next of kin tragic news: 'Deeply regret to inform you that your husband Shane O'Neill Lieutenant Colonel has been killed on war service stop letter follows stop.' Her husband had been slain near Borello, northeast of Florence, while taking the commune of Tessello 'with great difficulty' according to the regiment diaries. During this operation, 'while on a foot recce' O'Neill was killed 'by enemy shelling'.

Ann was distraught at the news, as although their marriage had been on the rocks for some time, an overwhelming feeling of guilt came over her. Her first words after receiving the news were 'death is the best revenge' for her adultery. Despite all but living with Esmond at this point, she wrote in her diary that evening, 'I was extremely distressed and went immediately to Ian,' who came into his own, arranging for Ann's two children to be sent to her, one from their home with the tutor Roland and the other from school.[17]

In a strange way, Fleming could sympathise with Ann because of his own bereavement and feeling of guilt towards Muriel. Whereas Esmond could only provide attempts at empathy, the feeling of remorse towards their badly treated lovers while together brought Fleming and Ann even closer to one and other. She had said to Robert Harling once, 'I'm not sure he'll ever get Muriel out of his memory,' adding that he had 'got her out his mind while she was alive but cannot now she's dead. His sense of guilt is probably quite a help to him: now he's able to curse himself that he treated his dear Muriel so heartlessly'.[18]

The death of Shane proved an advantage for Esmond, having never entertained the idea of divorce for Ann, who in turn wrote that, 'He had always wanted to wait until the end of the war before we took any legal steps.' Now, this was not an issue as he would be able to marry Ann as a widow rather than a divorcee.

On 28 June 1945, Ann and Esmond became husband and wife. The night before her second wedding, Ann spent the evening with Fleming. While the two dined together, he told her on several occasions that he had strong feelings for her. Ann reflected that 'if he had suggested marriage I would have accepted' and not married Esmond the next day.[19] Despite this, Ann's love towards Esmond was genuine, and in some ways they were a better suited couple than she and Fleming would ever be. Their companionship even trumped Fleming in the bedroom, with Ann telling a friend that 'Esmond's a better lover: more considerate, more attentive, more unselfish' than Fleming.[20]

Life with Esmond started perfectly for Ann. They moved into Warwick House, a 'site with its terrace overlooking the park and proximity to St James's Palace' as friend James Lees-Milne described it.[21] It was here that Ann hosted what would become her infamous parties, with the likes of the artists Lucian Freud and Francis Bacon, and renowned photographer Cecil Beaton. She also spent time with notorious socialites, such as Doris Castlerosse, the great aunt of models Poppy and Cara Delevinge, and rumoured mistress of Winston Churchill, who had also conducted an affair with Beaton, despite his homosexuality.

Ann liked being the wife of a newspaper tycoon; not only did it come with a certain status in society, she was able to influence many of her husband's work decisions. Ann was an intelligent woman, who had lacked the stimulation of being a part of a business. This was, to say the least, unpopular among Esmond's staff, who gave her the unflattering nickname of the 'Monster'. One employee – Rothermere's bridge partner – William McWhirter, wrote: 'Esmond will come to the office in the morning and announce something with a tone of finality, and you know perfectly well where it has come from. Then you set to work to argue against it, all the more forcibly because you know that his pride is involved and that he will have to go home and explain to Ann why it can't be done.' Part of Ann's meddling in her husband's newspaper business was because she felt she could do it better, and to be more precise, that Esmond was not doing it very well. This was something she was very open about, even writing in a public letter in 1949 that, 'Esmond Rothermere is a much less colourful personality than the first generation; he has not the drive, the fire or the conviction.' This type of put-down towards her husband was normal for the remainder of their marriage.

Esmond was happy enough for Ann to be the leader of their marriage, and despite being a quiet and passive man, put up with all the parties hosted by his outgoing wife. But something was wrong with their relationship from the start, with one friend commenting that 'something seems to [have gone] wrong in the taxi from the registry office'.[22]

Fleming, meanwhile, was content with their situation. Clearly having one's lover married to someone else is, to say the least, unconventional. But for Fleming, it was a relief that no pressure was placed on him to make a move. If anyone epitomised the saying 'once a bachelor, always a bachelor', it was him.

Chapter 12

Dr No

One of his many books to be based in Jamaica, *Dr No* was Fleming's fifth published novel. In this story, Bond is sent to the Caribbean to investigate the disappearance of the local station chief and his secretary. Bond is led to an island off the mainland called Crab Key, which is inhabited by Dr No and his men, supposedly running a guano mine. After being captured by Dr No, Bond is forced to make his way through an obstacle course designed to test the ability of the human body. He survives the many hurdles he encounters, and kills Dr No before escaping with his accomplice, the beautiful Honeychile Ryder.

Dr No is tinged throughout with Fleming's intimate knowledge of Jamaica, recounting many of the journeys he took around the island and the people he met. For example, not only is the murdered station chief one Mr Strangways, when Bond is caught by Dr No's guards he is quick to give the false name of Mr Bryce – the two men who had helped Fleming add the finishing touches to Goldeneye.

On 13 January 1948, Ian and the recently re-married Ann travelled to Jamaica together. Their arrival at a sweltering Kingston Airport inspired Bond's arrival on the island in *Dr No*, as Ann and Ian were greeted as local celebrities, with a press photographer on standby to snap them. For Bond, as he headed for the airport exit, a press camera was thrust in his face, and it's flash temporarily blinded him. For all the gossip there was only one paper who dominated the breaking news on the island, the *Daily Gleaner*. The couple were not welcomed as politely as Bond, who received a kind smile and words of thanks from his photographer, whereas Fleming was simply moved on as the journalist tried to snap other famous faces. Their picture would appear in the *Daily Gleaner* the following day on page twelve, with the caption 'happy to be home' under the photo.[1]

Fleming would have been concerned about being seen so blatantly with Ann, referenced in the newspaper as 'the married Lady Rothermere', had they not been prepared. He had invited the Duchess of Westminster, Loelia, to join them at Goldeneye for the duration of their trip. Loelia – dark haired, tall and strikingly beautiful – described her visit as simply 'to spread a thin aura of respectability as chaperone for Ann'.[2] This tactic worked, almost too well, with the press mistakenly reporting 'how serious this flirtation [between] the Duchess of Westminster and Captain Fleming ... might be is hard to tell. Only future history will record the happenings'.[3]

Fleming and Ann took great pleasure in teasing their companion in a charming but somewhat irksome way. Fleming would steal her name for Bond's secretary in his novels. Bond is no more relenting than his creator towards her, telling her that with a name that sounded like something from an offensive rhyme, she should be prepared for endless jeering. Loelia shared a similar interest to Ann, in that she also found Fleming extremely attractive. They had spent time in a sexual relationship during the war, but this was now in the past.

The press had reported that the threesome was heading straight for Goldeneye, but their first stop was with the Bryces at Bellevue Estate. Ann made no secret of the fact that she did not like Ivar and Sheila Bryce, seeing the former in particular as a bad influence on Fleming. Their marriage was also not a happy one, and Ann feared this put Fleming the 'commitment-phobe' even further away from the idea. She confronted him on the topic: 'There seems to be some mental comparison going on in your nasty mind between a possible marriage of ours and their sad relationship.'[4] Loelia and Ann had not seen Bellevue Estate and Fleming had only been there with Ivar when 'the house was barely furnished' and 'far from beautiful inside as it later became'.[5] The vast building and sprawling grounds would only build up their expectations for Fleming's much more modest house. The threesome spent a happy day at Bellevue, before heading for Goldeneye.

For Ian and Ann, their stay at Goldeneye was blissful, but more tiresome for poor Loelia, who looked on as a sort of spare part. Settled into an enviable routine, they would rise early for a warm swim, followed by breakfast of fresh coffee and eggs, which was Fleming's favourite meal. He would often write about it in Bond, for example in *Dr No*, 'there had been a wonderful breakfast as the dawn flared up across the bay'.[6] The morning meal would be followed by reading in the sunken garden or time spent back in the sea trying to catch lobsters with long trident-like spears.

By late morning, Fleming would usually spend time with the gardener, Holmes, making plans for his land, which was the only time he wasn't glued to Ann. Lunch, prefaced by a strong Vesper Martini, was fresh local fish, steak, kidneys, liver or the local dish of curried goat. This started what would become an ongoing fiasco with the food served at Goldeneye. Violet explained how Fleming 'just like Jamaican food. He just love shrimp and fish and oxtail and liver ... not many English people like. But the Commander real crazy about'.[7] His guests, on the other hand, were less than impressed.

A well-deserved rest in the shade would follow the long lunch. The evening activity involved rubbing shoulders with the great and good on the island at one party or another. On their return to the house in the early hours, merrier than they had left, Fleming and Ann would lean over the cliff fence and gaze out to sea and admire the star-filled clear night sky. For Loelia, this was not much fun, seeing her former lover, who she was still hugely attracted to, gallivant around with Ann: 'What a wet worm I was. They were madly in love,' and would spend 'from ten in the morning to seven at night together' while she 'was left on this stick of coral to wander about among the blackamores in the village'.[8] Fleming rather cruelly also wrote of 007's fictional secretary, that she would soon become a lifelong spinster unless she were to quickly marry a man.

On 26 January, Fleming, Loelia and Ann were invited to a lunch party at King's House hosted by Lady Molly Huggins, with the Duke and Duchess of Sutherland in attendance. Possibly the most notable couple on the island, Molly was married to Sir John Huggins, the Colonial Officer for Jamaica. Although Sir John himself was not someone who stood out in the local history books, claiming the typical islander to be 'an unimaginative man with no special intellectual tastes, no enthusiasms', his wife Molly was the talk of the town.[9] She was an attractive, tall blonde lady, with a booming personality. Author Matthew Parker described how she was 'in part well-meaning and affectionate, but hampered by ignorance, arrogance and double standards' towards the locals. Despite this, she affectionately became known by the Jamaicans as 'Lady Molly', while she described them as 'sadly neglected' with 'a great deal of poverty' and decided there should be 'no colour prejudices of any kind' under her watch. For the time, this was incredibly forward thinking.[10]

Unlike Sir John's rather sheltered upbringing, Molly saw a lot of the world in her youth, having been born in Singapore in 1907 and then quickly sent to boarding school in England. As she grew from a child into a young adult, her desires turned towards influential older men and so began a string of affairs. It was not until 1929 that she settled down with the thirty-seven-year-old John Huggins, marrying him aged twenty-two in Kuala Lumpur. For the next fourteen years, the couple were posted Trinidad, Washington and finally Jamaica, by which point, they had three daughters.

When they arrived in Jamaica, Molly immediately took to restoring King's House, complete with 150 acres of land, stables and a swimming pool. Fleming describes the house in *Dr No* with extreme flattery, going into detail about Richmond Road – with King's House placed at the end – which was home to the richest and most influential people on the island. Fleming would never have traded Goldeneye for another property, but if he was ever forced to, there is no doubt he would choose somewhere on Richmond Road.

Although there is no record that Molly had been romantically linked to Fleming, she certainly admired him, claiming 'he was so good-looking in a rugged way' and visited him many times at Goldeneye. They would spend long afternoons alone together at Fleming's accommodation, where he taught her to 'swim underwater and spear fish'.[11] Regardless, they became solid friends, and Fleming was often invited – as he was on this occasion with Ann and Loelia – to enjoy the splendour of one of Lady Huggin's lunch parties.

Molly had begun a very public affair with Robert 'Bobby' Kirkwood, who lived with his wife Sybil on the Craighton Estate, in the Great House above Kingston. The affair caused her husband some embarrassment, with the influential political leader Norman Manley saying he should 'put a restraining hand' upon her and not let his wife 'roam at large' and 'do very much as she liked'.[12] This caused a stir between Kirkwood and Manley, which culminated in a heated argument at a party at King's House, where Kirkwood went on a rampage in defence of his mistress. Fortunately for Fleming and his two female companions, no such dramas unfolded at their lunch party.

*

Fleming, Ann and Loelia attended another event on the island, having been invited on 30 January 1948 to a party by Fleming's former American naval contact, William Stephenson and his wife Mary, where Lord Lyle and Mr and Mrs Tate, of sugar giants Tate & Lyle, were in attendance. For Loelia, these parties were a blessed relief from being trapped with Fleming and Ann, whose never-ending lovemaking in the room next door had left her sleep-deprived and exhausted. On this occasion, she struck up an instant friendship with Mary, as Ann wrote: 'Loelia is ensconced at the Stephenson's' and for once 'sounds happy'.[13]

By now, Fleming had become somewhat bored of his two houseguests, blaming them for indulging in too much of what he referred to as 'Mayfair talk'. He felt that by spending their whole time gossiping about people in England, his female companions were not properly enjoying the freedom Jamaica provided and was subsequently ruining it for him. To his great relief, Loelia and Ann left Goldeneye on Thursday 5 March, heading to Miami and then on to New York. Nearly two months with his guests was more than enough time, and the blessed peace was very welcome. However, after they left, Fleming was far from alone. There was a string of female guests who came to stay in his bed, still warm from Ann. She wrote to him from Miami, hoping 'the remoteness of Goldeneye won't force you to collect some sordid female to replace me'.[14] Her wish was not granted.

Most notable among his lovers that year was Rosamond Lehmann, the successful novelist, who also happened to be exceptionally beautiful. Despite being in the middle of her own very public nine-year affair, Lehmann entered a short-lived 'spiritual' relationship with Fleming, as she described it.[15] Since 1941, Lehmann had been the mistress of married poet Cecil Day-Lewis. The next year he would call a halt to their relationship and marry his second wife, the actress Jill Balcon, with whom he would have two children, including the three-time Oscar winning actor Daniel Day-Lewis.

While staying with Fleming, Rosamond Lehmann boasted that she had encouraged him to write books, having been impressed by an article she had read by him in *Horizon* magazine. Fleming's romance with Lehmann would continue on and off during his many trips to the island, where she would stay with him at Goldeneye. However, like most of his relationships, the two would have spectacular arguments. During one particularly heated falling out, an angry Rosamond threw a dead octopus into Fleming's bedroom while he was changing for the arrival of guests. Realising that she was causing too much pain staying with him, Fleming pleaded with a neighbour – who arrived later that day for lunch – to let her stay with him away from Goldeneye. Their conversation took place with Lehmann all the time standing in front of them both. His neighbour finally capitulated saying, 'I'll settle for the polaroid camera' in exchange for his new houseguest, before adding 'and the tripod'.[16] Fleming was only too willing to comply.

Despite his many visitors, Fleming was missing Ann madly, telling her in a letter that he had raced after her plane in his car as it took off. She responded in a similar spirit, while her husband was in the same hotel room, saying, 'you are a great big piece of my life and I feel amputated without you'. And 'please mean it', she added, 'when you say you will be good. It would be an interesting feat to be faithful to someone for three weeks, you have never done it before and it might make you feel very happy'.[17] For her part, she assured Fleming she would only make love to Esmond when absolutely necessary.

After departing from Jamaica, Loelia had left Ann in Miami, heading to New York where she attended various glamorous parties. Despite her review of Goldeneye being far from complimentary – stating it was 'strangely uncomfortable ... in daytime it was fine, but at night, when the lamps were lit, every insect known to man seemed to pour in from the darkness outside' – Loelia agreed to help Fleming find someone who might rent Goldeneye for the ten months of the year he was not there.[18] It was at a party with theatre producer Gilbert Miller that she met Noël Coward. Although Coward was already known to Fleming, mainly through his brother Peter's wife Celia Johnson, who had stared in Coward's film *Brief Encounter*, they were in no way close. Coward and Fleming also had a mutual friend in William Stephenson, with whom both men had worked during the war. Coward was in New York for the revival of his stage production, *Tonight at 8:30*, which consisted of nine one-act plays. Despite boasting on the flyer that the 'tour of six American cities has occasioned notable excitement among playgoers everywhere along her route between the coasts', the critics saw it quite differently. The production was a complete disaster, running for only four weeks, with each day more excruciating than the last. Writing to a friend, Coward announced that 'I fear we are a flop and I have always believed in putting geographical distance between myself and a flop'. He was therefore only too keen to hear Loelia's pitch for Goldeneye, which was a lot more flattering than she had found it. What appealed to him the most was its solitude, tucked away in a part of the world where no one would know who he was, and even if they did, he would be so secluded in the grounds of Goldeneye, no one would be able to get close. He blamed having too many people around him for the failure of *Tonight at 8:30*, claiming that 'they all want something from me and I really want nothing at all from them'.[19]

On his return journey to Britain, Fleming met with Coward in New York on 8 March to agree a price. His negotiations with Coward – with whom he would become a close friend – were tough, claiming that he had other Americans interested in using the property, which was a complete lie. They settled on the handsome price of £50 per week, which at the time of writing is worth approximately £1,750. Fleming would only need five weeks of occupancy in Goldeneye by paying guests to cover the annual staff costs of running it. Fortuitously for him, Coward took the place for two months. Fleming was content with his negotiating skills, but Coward was not over the moon about the arrangement: 'I am paying two hundred pounds a month … That includes three servants, of course, but all the same it's on the expensive side,' he complained to a friend.[20] Notwithstanding this, Coward became one of Fleming's dearest companions, a relationship described by author Matthew Parker as 'an unlikely close friendship.'[21]

Two weeks later, Coward and Graham Payn arrived in Jamaica. Payn was an actor who had starred alongside Gertude Lawrence in *Tonight at 8:30* and was Coward's lifetime partner. With Coward's expectations as high as the price he was paying, their holiday to Goldeneye did not disappoint and would change the couple's lives forever. Although Coward commented that his 'ship arrived five hours late and rammed the pier' he soon fell in love with the place, saying 'it all seems far too good to be true'.[22]

For Coward, Jamaica 'would remain a safe haven, a place to lay one's plans, lick ones wounds, and get things back into perspective'.[23] It was during those first two months spent at Goldeneye that he decided to buy his own property (he ended up buying two plots). He would go on to construct Blue Harbour, five miles east of Oracabessa, on land known as Look-Out, as it was the site that pirate Sir Henry Morgan had used for that very purpose.

Coward's house would soon become notorious. This was not only because he made a rule that the saltwater pool could only be swum in if in the nude, but for celebrity guests, including Laurence Olivier,

Vivien Leigh, Charlie Chaplin, Alec Guinness, Audrey Hepburn, Michael Redgrave, Peter O'Toole and Peter Sellers. One guest, local hotelier John Pringle, arrived at Blue Harbour to find Mr and Mrs Olivier 'naked on Noël's terrace, Vivien draped over Larry's cock'.[24]

Much of the mischief brought to the island was courtesy of Coward's influence. For example, he caused controversy away from Blue Harbour when he attended the newly opened Tower Isle Hotel in Kingston for breakfast with Lord Beaverbrook, where he offended staff by ordering champagne along with his coffee and eggs. Luckily, his theatrical acquaintance and fellow islander Errol Flynn was friends with the owner, Abe Issa, and smoothed over the issue. Issa was not a man to cross, having opened a string of high-end establishments across the island, including Myrtle Bank, the hotel Bond tells people he is staying at when he arrived in Jamaica to investigate Dr No, throwing potential enemies off his trail. The Myrtle Bank had become known to Fleming on his first visit to Jamaica during the war, as it was the venue for the 1943 U-Boat conference. He had initially got confused with the Jamaican accent, believing it to be called the 'Turtle Tank' hotel.[25] As homeowners in Jamaica, a friendship between Flynn and Fleming would have been much more likely than the latter's close relationship with Coward. After all, Fleming and Flynn both gave each other a run for their money on who was the greatest womaniser or drinker on the island. But the men never got on, and where possible avoided each other as much as they could. Flynn's widow said her late husband found the Bond author 'pretentious and full of himself'.[26]

Among other settlers was Ivor Novello, who was the next famous face to become a homeowner on the island, buying a house near Montego Bay, described by Coward in a less than flattering way: 'Ivor, with typical Welsh cunning, has almost achieved the impossible, which is to find in Jamaica a house with no view at all ... You can see the sea, which is three miles away, by standing on the dining-room table.'[27] Novello would join Coward as a well-known homosexual on Jamaica, along with fashion designer Edward Molyneux.

As the friendship between Fleming and Coward blossomed, so did their endless game of mocking each other. Fleming pokes fun at Coward throughout *Dr No*, basing the character loosely on his friend. Dr No's head was described as looking almost like an egg, with a fully bald skull and yellowish skin. Coward, although not completely bald, had combed back thin hair, which only covered part of his head, while the shinning forehead stood out. Fleming added some other traits to Dr No for good measure, explaining how he seemed to float rather than walk. He gave Bond the impression of 'thinness and erectness' and had a 'straight immovable poise'.[28] This hint of innuendo is also masked by a dig at Coward's sexuality, describing him as 'straight'. Many of Fleming's villains have this sexual orientation, whether it was the very camp Le Chiffre in *Casino Royale* or the lesbian Rosa Klebb in *From Russia, with Love*.

Fleming had in fact been deadly serious about basing the character on Coward. When in 1962 *Dr No* was to be made into a film, Fleming wrote to Noël asking him if he would play the title role. Coward's reply was 'Dear Ian, the answer to Dr. No is No, No, No, No!'[29] He gave the reason that he did not want to wear the character's famous metal hands.

*

The summer of 1948 – eighteen months after her first visit to Jamaica – was not a happy one for Ann, as she discovered she was pregnant in July that year. She wrote to her cousin and close friend Evelyn Waugh that 'this is the point of view of a heathen woman' who has ended up 'in my sad condition'. To all intent and purposes this was her first child with Esmond, but Ann knew she carried within her Fleming's baby.

Esmond and Ann went on a golfing holiday to Gleneagles in Perthshire, along with Fleming, Loelia and Ann's children in August 1948. During their stay, Ann was rushed to hospital where she gave birth a month early to a premature girl, who died eight hours later. Esmond never left her side through the whole ordeal and Fleming wrote daily. In a cruel twist to this story, still believing the child was his, Esmond named her Ann and had her buried next to Ann's mother at the edge of the sea near Aberlady.

Writing to Fleming from her hospital bed, Ann told him, 'I feel full of remorse towards Esmond and yet my grief and loss is entirely bound up with you.'[30] After the anguish of this event, Esmond took Ann to Paris and Portofino, to stay with their friends Alexander and Jenny Clifford to help her recover. But by this point he knew that the child was not his, and was in fact his friend's, Ian Fleming.

In a sad way, it was losing their child that brought Fleming and Ann yet closer. Although Ann 'was amazed how long the torture lasted', it was her 'deep love for Ian ... based on his understanding of [my] mental condition at that time', that got her through it.[31] Just as when her first husband had died, Fleming was able to do and say the right things.

In his own attempt to escape the misery of losing a child, Fleming headed back to Jamaica in September 1948, this time without Ann, who was enjoying Europe. Instead he was visiting his brother Peter and his wife. Although Ann was sad not to be with him, she wrote 'it is nice knowing you are there now and not "dipping your wick" in some horrid harlot'.

Despite Ann's confidence that her lover was behaving, Fleming was never far from a sexual relationship. Along with Peter and Celia, he went to dinner on Thursday 30 September with the journalist Elsa Maxwell. Having taken a shine to Fleming, Maxwell was catalogued by Ann's friend Mark Amory as an 'ugly energetic gossip columnist who liked Fleming'. Ann described her in a letter to Fleming as one of those 'bitches who have earned you the name of "Don Juan of the Islands" in the American press'. It is not known whether Fleming was receptive to Maxwell's advances. It is unlikely that he was, for this was the time that Fleming and Ann were probably closer than they had ever been. While the couple were not physically together, they wrote to each other daily, to the point that Fleming warned that he should disguise his handwriting on the envelopes to Ann otherwise the Cliffords – with whom Ann was a guest – would get suspicious. It was not helped that Fleming would spell the address wrong each time, so a change in handwriting would likely not make much difference.

Jamaica had become Fleming's bolthole, an oasis where he could escape everything going on around him, and now finally could indulge in his desire to be an author. Ann had written to him 'I suppose you are hating the thought of leaving'.[32] But after his routine two month visit to the island and now a second trip, he was ready to return home. He summed up his feelings in *Dr No*, where Bond also started to miss the sights and smells of London, in particular the weather and taste of English tea.

Chapter 13

The Man with the Golden Gun

The last full novel to be published by Fleming, *The Man with the Golden Gun*, follows Bond back to Jamaica, sent to kill the deadly assassin, Francisco Scaramanga, whose weapon of choice is a gold-plated Colt .45 revolver. Bond goes undercover as Mark Hazard, hired as Scaramanga's personal assistant. Helped by Felix Leiter, Bond is able to kill the assassin, but only after being shot himself. As with *Dr No* and 'Octopussy', Fleming gives his readers a detailed description of Jamaica, thanks to his intimate knowledge of the island.

Continuing their annual tradition, on 6 January 1949, Fleming and Ann visited Jamaica to the same welcome from the press as they had received the year before. This time, though, they were prepared for the photographers to meet them at the airport. As they were without Ann's loyal chaperone, Loelia, she slyly told the reporter eagerly awaiting their arrival that she was 'staying with the island's new celebrity resident, Noël Coward'.[1] She had not checked her facts properly though, as Coward was not due to arrive in Jamaica for a whole month. The reason they were attempting to be more subtle about their incredibly open affair was a result of the loss of their child. Ann's now estranged husband and Ian's friend, Lord Rothermere, had tried to get his wife's lover fired, by pleading with his fellow newspaper tycoon, Lord Kemsley, for whom Fleming worked. Kemsley was a bridge partner of Fleming, so decided not to take any drastic action. However, the intervention certainly hurt Fleming's chances of a successful newspaper career. As his biographer John Pearson wrote: 'The least [Fleming] had hoped for was a directorship. It never came ... Gradually it dawned on him that there was a reason – a private reason – for this absence of recognition.'[2]

January was bliss for the couple. With hardly any familiar faces in Jamaica, the two of them could spend time together alone, swimming off Fleming's private beach, reading in the garden, and paying regular visits to the bedroom. It was not until 3 February that Coward arrived on the island with Graham Payn. The local press was also waiting for his arrival but did not click that Lady Rothermere was meant to have been his houseguest for the past month. For the remainder of their time on the island, Fleming and Ann spent much of their visit with Coward and his partner.

Worried that their blatant infidelity would trickle through the press world back to her husband, Ann agreed to be photographed for *Life* magazine at Coward's house. This way, she thought, there would be no doubt of her innocence. However, after a heavy night on the martinis, when the local reporter arrived to interview the wife of Lord Rothermere at Blue Harbour the following morning, she was four-and-a-half miles away in bed with Fleming at Goldeneye. Thus followed what Coward described as 'a very natty high comedy scene' in which he had to keep the reporter occupied while his houseboy was sent '*chaud pied* [hot-footed] to fetch her'. Arriving flustered at Blue Harbour, Coward recalled how Ann 'kept forgetting she was a house guest and asking us what we had been doing all the morning'.[3]

After this escapade, the foursome decided they would take a trip to the west side of the island, Coward hoping that Fleming and Ann would be a little subtler than their antics to date that year. Not only was Coward looking out for his new friends' reputation, he also had a hidden agenda. He was a close acquaintance of Lord Beaverbrook, the newspaper tycoon, who lingered in the same circles as Lord Rothermere. Coward did not want to be seen as complicit, or worse, an enabler in the affair of Rothermere's wife. Years later, Coward would take credit for her relationship with Fleming, considering 'himself responsible for the whole thing' according to Ann.[4] But right now, he was far from happy at being tangled in their adulterous web. Fleming and Beaverbrook had crossed paths on a few occasions, not least during the war and Fleming's planning of *Operation Ruthless*. Both men had also stayed with their good friend Sir William Stephenson in Jamaica the previous year. Beaverbrook, on meeting Fleming, was not a fan, referring to him as 'that young whippersnapper' to Stephenson.[5]

The trip took the two couples to the luxurious Sunset Lodge in Montego Bay, on the other side of the island from their respective houses. In another feeble attempt to avoid speculation around his relationship with Ann, Fleming made sure he was photographed walking along the beach with various women, notably the daughter of Molly Huggins, Diana. Despite his efforts, the following morning the couple decided to have breakfast on Fleming's balcony in full view of everyone. Coward was incandescent about their lack of tact, reporting later that 'after this I descended upon them both and gave them a very stern lecture indeed'.[6]

Fleming and Ann were not particularly fussed about the rumour mill, which was inevitably spinning, continually fuelled by their indiscretions. They were now closer than ever, as Ann wrote to Fleming after their holiday: 'I cannot contemplate life without you but I am a frustrated romantic and you must decide ... None of this need be immediate but we will have to be brave one way or the other.'

This 'frustration' related to Ann's departure on 18 February, which was not a happy parting. The couple had argued terribly for their last week. Two days after she had gone, Fleming reflected in a letter to Ann how difficult he found it being in Jamaica without her. They had been due to leave together in several weeks, but Ann had insisted on departing early, asking Fleming to come with her. When he refused, their row only intensified.

The argument was born out of the realisation on both sides that their affair could not continue indefinitely. Either they must marry or end their relationship. To Fleming, both ideas were hideous. On the final stretch of her trip back to Britain, Ann wrote to Fleming: 'Please till we meet again think about both of us very carefully'.[7]

*

The following year, the same routine was conducted. This time, Ann and Fleming arrived in Jamaica with Robert Harling and his wife Phoebe. Harling asked Fleming straight out whether they would 'be acting as an alibi or phoney chaperon and chaperone' for the couple, whose 'tangle continued into still further entanglement and puzzlement?'

Fleming snappily responded that Robert was being too suspicious and instead should just try to enjoy the holiday. With that, the conversation was over, and having travelled aboard the BOAC via New York, the foursome was soon in the sunny paradise of Jamaica, motoring from the airport to Goldeneye. On arrival at the house, Harling was blown away, claiming to Fleming and Ann that 'it would be difficult to find any refuge from the bustling urban twentieth century to equal Goldeneye'.[8]

Fleming had organised for the foursome to take a trip to the far west point of the island, some 120 mile's drive along the north coast to Negril.

Fleming describes the sensation of their night-time journey parallel to the coast in *The Man with the Golden Gun*, as Bond enjoys hearing the waves lapping onto the beach, seeing the sprawling sugar cane fields and the dull smell of mangrove swamps.

Unlike their trip the year before with Coward, Fleming and Ann opted to stay in a private villa rather than a hotel. Harling wrote home that 'for our excursion Fleming had been loaned a house on the shore owned by one of the local tycoons'. For the next week, the group settled into an idyllic routine of swimming – for which Fleming found someone to match his enthusiasm in Harling's wife – along with drinking, eating and playing 'pencil-and-paper games' under the orders of Ann.[9] Like Bond – who arrives at the house in an unfamiliar parcel of land that he had not been to before – they were on a part of the island Fleming had yet to explore. He led Ann and the Harlings on adventures around the local hills, discovering a new part of Jamaica.

This trip marked the moment Fleming and Ann both made up their minds. Ann would divorce Esmond, in order to marry Fleming. The request from Ann the previous year that Fleming should make his mind up had finally been granted.

Ann's divorce from Esmond was announced in the *Daily Express* on 22 March 1952 and in a settlement she received £100,000, an amount she felt was far too low. She wrote to her brother that 'unlimited novel expenditure will have to cease'. She did continue to feel remorse for the way Esmond had been treated from the very start of their marriage, in particular that she led him to believe she was carrying his baby. Ann claimed that this added 'to my guilt because it cannot be integrity to leave anyone whether he is a millionaire or a dustman'.[10] Her escapades with Fleming were now coming back to haunt her.

It was not helped that Ann again found herself pregnant, with no doubt this time that it was Fleming's child. Fleming and Ann agreed they should marry and soon. As their relationship had only really started properly in Jamaica, it seemed fitting for the couple to do the deed where they were. Something simple was to be arranged, which suited Fleming well as he had no interest whatsoever in marrying Ann, or anyone to that point. Fleming decided that he needed a distraction. When asked why he had become an author, he said as a long-established bachelor soon to be married, he thought that writing a spy novel might take his mind off the prospect.

With wedding planning underway, this was the first time that Fleming would put the character of James Bond into words. By 18 March 1952, 62,000 words of the first draft of a James Bond novel, *Casino Royale*, were now written. The couple did not spend a huge amount of time together during this process, with Ann sitting in the garden painting while Fleming was inside writing, an early warning sign of the troubles they would have in their marriage.

Fleming and Ann arrived at the Town Hall in Port Maria, a ten-minute drive east of Goldeneye on Monday 24 March 1952 for their nuptials. There were more glamorous and obvious locations for the couple to get married if you headed south from Goldeneye towards Kingston. But reflecting the views of the author, James Bond comments in *The Man with the Golden Gun* that the south coast of the island is not as attractive as the north, so the location was set. Keen to have a quiet affair, the only witnesses present at the wedding were their friends Noël Coward and Cole Lesley, dressed in smart white suits, despite the former's threats to 'wear long elbow gloves and give the bride away'.[11]

The local registrar, whose only memorable feature was his bad breath, conducted the ceremony. It became so intolerable that Fleming needed to whisper to his bride 'try to keep upwind of him'.[12] Coward enjoyed the affair, writing that 'it was really rather sweet' but concluding that 'the dark gentleman who married them had the most awful breath and so the responses were rather muffled'. He wrote to Fleming and Ann afterwards in a long, witty and poignant letter a list of what they should and should not do now they were married. For example, he mockingly tells Fleming not to shout at Ann if she cooks a meal for him that he does not enjoy or not to feign a migraine and retire to bed every time Ann's friends come for dinner.

The letter was received with great enjoyment by the newly-weds, although the advice was sincere and almost a prophecy for their declining relationship in the years to come. For now, Ann had decided 'to live with someone [she] loves in a scented garden eating steaks cooked on charcoal and bananas and cream', rather than her two former, stuffier but far wealthier husbands.[13]

After the ceremony, the group headed back to Goldeneye for a feast that Fleming had organised. Their menu consisted of self-caught turtle, which Coward described as like 'chewing an old tyre', followed by black crab cooked in its shell, which Noël thought was 'like eating cigarette ash out of an ashtray' and then topped off by a cake with green icing, similar to 'bird-lime'.[14]

The celebrations continued long into the night, with Fleming's favourite drink 'Old Man's Thing' being brought out with Violet proudly explaining the recipe: 'you have the skin of orange, skin of lemon. Pour rum on top. Put sugar in dish. Put on oven, keeping stirring. Set light when coming to the boil. Put lid on the dish, then turn out all the light in the house when carry it into the guests'.[15] After this, Coward started singing:

> Mongoose listen to white folks wailin'
> Mongoose giggle, say 'Me no deaf!
> No more waffle and Daily Mailin'
> Annee Rothermere's Madame F'.

Despite all the fun, Coward wrote in his diary that he 'sensed that Annie was not entirely happy'.[16] Whether this was an early indication for how their marriage would unfold or not, Ann was certainly nervous about being a divorcee. It was something she condemned generally. She wrote to Evelyn Waugh after their wedding that 'I disapprove so deeply of divorce' so much so that she 'anticipated total social ruin' for herself.

The following day, Fleming and Ann, who were remarkably fresh-faced after their evening, flew to New York for a four-day celebration before heading back to Britain. Ann was pleasantly surprised by the warm reception they received in America and on their return home. Far from being chastised, they were treated 'as Tristan and Isolde'.

By mid-July 1952, Ann was heavily pregnant, and had 'reached the stage of permanent discomfort'.[17] It was not until nearly a month later that she was 'released by Caesarian' at 'the opening of the grouse shooting season', when on 12 August she gave birth to their 9 lbs 4oz son, Caspar Robert Fleming. In a touching letter to Ann, Fleming wrote that evening how proud he was of her bravery through a slow delivery, expressing his love for his wife and baby.

Before the birth, Fleming had asked Robert Harling, whose wife Phoebe was also pregnant, what they intended to name their third child. When Robert replied with, 'Amanda for a girl, certainly. Caspar or Caleb for a boy', Fleming was immediately disapproving. Referring to the name Caspar as a humiliation to any child and their parents, he begged him to choose something different. He confessed after his son was born that actually it had always been one of his favourite names.

Caspar's parents took time to agree how his name should be spelt, with Fleming saying to Ann after his birth that he hoped that 'Kaspar; was doing well' and then Ann subsequently writing to a friend 'we would both like it very much if you would be the female godparent to Kasper'. After a brief period of trying 'Kasbah', an Arabic word meaning fortress, they settled on the conventional spelling of Caspar.

The friend Ann was asking to be a godparent was Clarissa Eden, niece of Winston Churchill and wife of future Prime Minister Anthony Eden. Along with Clarissa, Noël Coward, Cecil Beaton, Peter Fleming and 'some stout golf player' called Sir George Duff-Dunbar were asked to be godparents.[18] Caspar was christened at the end of October 1952 at Chelsea Old Church. Fleming wrote to Ivar Bryce afterwards that the service had gone seamlessly and to plan.

In the space of a few months, Fleming and Ann went from being an adulterous pair to a married couple with small family. It is at this part of the story that they should live happily ever after. Sadly, Fleming and Ann would not have this luxury.

The last words in *The Man with the Golden Gun* sum up the Fleming's problem with relationships perfectly. He writes that for Bond, love from any woman 'was not enough for him ... It would be like taking "a room with a view". For James Bond, the view would always pall'.[19]

*

By the time of his son's birth, Fleming had completed his first novel, *Casino Royale,* which went to print the following year in 1953. With an original run of 4,750 books – which sold out in a month – it was published by Jonathan Cape, his brother Peter's publisher. Jonathan Cape himself was reluctant to accept the manuscript but did so thanks to Peter's persuasion. He said of Fleming: 'He's got to do much better if he's going to get anywhere near Peter's standard'. For a first publication, *Casino Royale* sold well, shifting 8,000 copies in the first year in the UK and 4,000 in America.

Despite these sales, the jury was out as far as the critics were concerned. Paul Johnson commented in the *Spectator* that Bond consisted of 'all unhealthy, all thoroughly English' traits, which include 'the sadism of the school bully, the mechanical two-dimensional sex-longings of a frustrated adolescent, and the crude, snob-cravings of a suburban adult'.[20] Others were more positive, for example one of the men who worked for Cape who read an early draft wrote to the publisher: 'I sat up till 1.30 last night. *Casino Royale* made me sit up. It was so exciting that I could persuade myself that I was back at the old baccarat, and the vodka and caviar were so delicious'.[21] Possibly the harshest critic was Ann, who was far from enthusiastic about her husband's literary creation. After she finished reading a proof of the book, Fleming asked if she would mind if he dedicated it to her. She replied, somewhat patronisingly, 'Surely, Ian, it's not the sort of book one dedicates to anyone?'[22] Her tune would soon change when the books brought in considerable funds.

Chapter 14

Live and Let Die

In *Live and Let Die* – Fleming's second novel – James Bond is sent to New York by M to investigate the mysterious Mr Big, a criminal mastermind using voodoo to disguise his dealings in seventeenth century gold coins to fund terrorism. Bond follows Mr Big to Jamaica, where he is able to kill him using a limpet mine after escaping from capture with Big's fortune-telling assistant, Solitaire. It is a novel of rich detail about America and Jamaica, in particular the practice of Voodoo, which fascinated Fleming.

Due to the birth of Caspar, Fleming was inconveniently delayed in going to Jamaica for his annual winter escape. It was not until the middle of January 1953 that his plane took off from London and swept him away to Jamaica via New York. This was to be the research phase for the start of his second novel. *Casino Royale* had been scribbled off almost on a whim, with no research and, as Fleming confessed in a letter to his publisher, had been written in under two months as a hobby to take his mind off the prospect of marrying Ann.[1] The next book was to be written in a different way altogether. He had sent a letter to Ivar Bryce before Christmas telling his friend to block out time in the middle of January to fly to New York, before taking the Silver Meteor night train to St Petersburg in Florida – where he intended to look around a live worm factory – then fly from Tampa to Jamaica.

Bond reflects in *Live and Let Die*, that 'there are moments of great luxury in the life of a secret agent' when 'from the moment the BOAC Stratocrusier taxied up to the International Air Terminal at Idlewild, James Bond was treated like royalty'.[2] Fleming and Bryce felt similar as they landed in the same airport in 1953. As wealthy men, at this point Bryce more so than Fleming, their transit was filled with fine food, drinks and ultimate comfort. Bryce had not only agreed to accompany his friend on the trip, but had even allowed Fleming to get his former girlfriend, now Kemsley employee, Clare Blanchard to arrange for the

Bryces' Rolls-Royce to meet them at Idlewild Airport. She thought this too vulgar, so simply asked Bryce's driver to collect them at the said time, but not in a specified mode of transport. Accordingly, 'Ian was disgruntled to find the Bryces' chauffeur at the wheel of a Lincoln rather than a Rolls'.[3] Instead of driving in the Lincoln or the Rolls Royce, for his second novel Fleming put his secret agent in a Buick with Dynaflow gears, a car Bond particularly enjoyed.

Staying just one night in New York, Fleming enlisted the help of his old friend William Stephenson to give him an 'Access All Areas' pass with two detectives in their local precinct. The night was spent sitting in the back seat of the detectives' car as they patrolled the crime-ridden streets. Post war New York was not only in a phase of industrial downturn, but the tensions among the white people in the suburbs was growing. With this cocktail of change came a drastic increase in crime, which was perfect for Fleming's research. That evening he 'witnessed with alarm the hold that drug traffickers were gaining' across the city. The detectives were kind enough to introduce the English author to a local crime boss, who explained his conspiracy theory that 'the National Association for the Advancement of Colored People was a dangerous communist front'.[4] Many of the sights from that evening made their way into Fleming's books. For example, they passed a diner called *Glorified Ham-N-Eggs*, whose motto 'the Eggs We Serve Tomorrow Are Still on the Farm' was borrowed by Fleming for *Live and Let Die*, with a slight improvement to 'the Eggs We Serve Tomorrow Are Still in the Hens'.[5] Unlike *Casino Royale,* Fleming's second novel is a feast of real life places and meticulous research.

From New York, the group travelled on the Silver Meteor train. They were amazed by the endless line of silver carriages sitting queued up in the underground station and, as Fleming described, the unforgettable noise of 'the auxiliary generators of the 4000 horsepower twin Diesel electric units [that] ticked busily'.[6] Bryce recalled the 'extra personal pleasure' he got when he realised he was such an integral part of Fleming's next novel.[7] In *Live and Let Die,* Bond travels under the false name of Mr Bryce, adding even more glee to Ivar's involvement. Their trip was enjoyable, as the train cut through Florida, past plantations and marshes, through continuous fields of citrus groves. While Ivar sat back and relaxed, Fleming scribbled endlessly in his notebook as they made their way to the Caribbean.

Joined by Ann, the Flemings arrived in Jamaica to a great amount of excitement. British Prime Minister Winston Churchill had been on the island for a two-week holiday. The seventy-eight-year-old war hero had arrived following several meetings with President Truman and President-Elect Eisenhower. The latter had been a close confidant of Churchill's during the war as the Allied Commander in Chief. Credited for being the man who won the war, Eisenhower had joined the Republican Party as presidential candidate. Unsurprisingly, he won, and considerably so, taking 442 electoral votes and winning all but nine states, compared to his opponent Democrat Adlai Stevenson who won just eighty-nine of the electoral votes. Fresh from his triumph, the President-Elect met with his old friend Winston Churchill on 5 January 1953 at the house of a mutual acquaintance, financier Bernard Baruch; a photograph of the three men appeared in the press the following day captioned 'Meeting of Three Old Friends'.

With such a high-profile event catching the interest of the world's press, there was little chance that Churchill's visit to Jamaica would go unnoticed. The *Daily Gleaner* summed up the mood, writing that although 'this island is no stranger to distinguished visitors – to royalty, statesmen, film stars, literati, millionaires' taking 'most such visitors in its stride', the arrival of Winston Churchill had 'stirred the patriot emotion of all the people of Jamaica'.

The island's Governor, Sir Hugo Foot, who stood proud in a crisp white suit next to Sir Harold Mitchell, greeted Churchill on 9 January 1953. Mitchell had been the Vice-Chairman of the Conservative Party under Churchill and had invited the Prime Minister to stay in his property, the 1,200-acre Prospect Estate, in the Great House. Living for six months of the year in his Jamaican house, as a hobby, Sir Harrold tried to reinvigorate the land, and perhaps his career, by growing everything from coconuts to pimento, keeping cattle and even planting sugar cane. Inspecting the guard of honour lined up to welcome him off the US President's private jet, which had been leant to him, Churchill was presented with a box of Jamaican cigars which he accepted gratefully. He told onlookers, 'The doctors have advised me not to swim. I intend to swim every day.'[8]

For the Mitchells, the whole trip caused a huge upheaval in their lives. They were forced to move out of the main house into one of the many properties on the estate to make room for Churchill, his wife, daughter and son-in-law, who were arriving directly from London. Despite this inconvenience, they were treated to a new road to the gates of their property, which had been resurfaced for the Churchills at considerable cost to the government.

Sir Winston and his family left on 22 January 1953, the very day Fleming and Ann arrived. As they drove from the airport to Goldeneye, Fleming noted the beauty of the journey, which he put onto paper for his novel. He explained to his readers in detail the colourful splendor of the scenery, a place he loved more than anywhere in the world.

Although their paths had not crossed in Jamaica, the Flemings were connected with Churchill in several ways. Not only was his daughter, Clarissa, Caspar's godmother, his son, Randolph, was close friends with Ann. Fleming's father and Churchill had also served together in the Great War. Fleming therefore took it upon himself to send a Bond novel to the Prime Minister, asking him rather presumptuously to write a short review of the book to be used on the jacket.

Somewhat unsurprisingly, Churchill did not respond to this very audacious letter. But Fleming had no time to be disheartened as 1953 was a year of many great parties in Jamaica. He split their time mainly between hosting at Goldeneye and attending raucous gatherings at Blue Harbour being thrown by Noël Coward.

Coward always preferred to play host, mainly because it meant no travel for him and he was also not particularly fond of Fleming's house. At Goldeneye, the house he had rented for a short while, Coward observed that 'all you Flemings revel in discomfort'[9] and was far from complimentary about Fleming's design:

> If Ian had built it on the angle to the right, he would have had a full view of all the sunsets. But he built it flat, facing the sea, and therefore it didn't get the sunsets. And the windowsills were too high, so that you sat in that lovely big room with the windowsill just about to your eye-level and you got an admirable view of the sky, and nothing else.[10]

Despite his feelings towards the house – which he compared to the discomfort of a hospital clinic, dubbing it 'Goldeneye, nose and throat' – when not hosting himself, Coward was one of the most regular visitors to the Flemings' parties.[11] He was not very flattering about the food either, which he felt 'was so abominable I used to cross myself before eating it … it tasted like armpits'.[12]

The staple for guests was housekeeper Violet's suckling pig, which she recalled would always be a 'big one roast in the oven' followed by Fleming's own special concoction, 'Poor Man's Thing'. [13] This potent drink often got the better of many of the Flemings' guests, some having to be guided to one of the bedrooms to recover. For Fleming, having Violet there was an added pleasure, as she was someone who he adored, and the feeling was mutual. Their relationship was that of Bond and Quarrel in *The Man with the Golden Gun* – his trusty local helper – which was described as that of a Scottish landowner with his gillie. If guests would stay at Goldeneye when Fleming was not there, any request that was contrary to Fleming's was met with a, 'No, Lady, I obey my Commander.' When on one occasion a particularly pushy guest rather arrogantly suggested that her request would no-doubt be endorsed by the Queen, Violet replied, 'I still don't care, Lady. I respect the Queen but I obey the Commander.'[14]

Coward composed a poem about the property and the parties, which would be performed after much 'Poor Man's Thing' had been consumed:

> Alas! I cannot adequately praise
> The dignity, the virtue and the grace
> Of this most virile and imposing place
> Wherein I have passed so many airless days.
>
> Alas! I cannot accurately find
> Words to express the hardness of the seat
> Which, when I cheerfully sat down to eat,
> Seared with such cunning into my behind.

At his nearby house, Blue Harbour, Coward was the only other man on the island to rival the recklessness of the Flemings' parties. Often, Fleming and Ann had to settle for sleeping there, as they were too drunk to make the journey back.

It was on their return from one of Coward's parties – clearly one which was less raucous – that Fleming and Ann were forced to pull their car over for the noise of 'insistent drumming and singing' caused them too much curiosity.[15] Leaving their vehicle by the side of the road, they snuck around the buildings to see what was causing the commotion. What they stumbled upon was so extraordinary that the next morning Fleming would start writing about it for his next novel. They had come across a voodoo funeral; something Fleming described in *Live and Let Die*, detailing the huge amount of smoke spreading through the pirouetting drummers. Among them were dancers, all thrusting their large buttocks while continually jerking their upper body. Behind this furore stood a gravestone and a huge black cross made of wood, with an old morning coat pinned to its front. On top of the cross was a battered bowler hat, sitting above a white drawing of a face.

This was the type of island experience that Fleming lived for. He cared more about the nature and history of the place, and much less about the socialising.

In particular, he detested some of the house guests that Ann insisted on inviting. Among them was a honeymoon couple called Tanis and Teddy Phillips, who stayed for 'twelve interminable days' at Goldeneye.[16] While Fleming tried to write, he would overhear their 'perpetual marital endearments in high drawl voices', which he found a great distraction. When Fleming reached the end of his tether, he ordered Ann to tell them 'they must not call "Lion" and "Bear" to each other while [I am] writing'. When she could not find a tactful way of doing this, Fleming announced over dinner – when Tanis referred to her new husband as 'Bearingtons' – that he would be happy for the couple to keep using the house, but he and Ann were going away for the remainder of their stay.[17] Fleming never carried out his threat, but 'Lion' and 'Bear' suitably toned down their affection for each other and even bought Fleming two bottles of whisky as an apology.

For Ann, her next guests held great excitement, for her father was due to visit Goldeneye, along with her friend, the painter Lucian Freud. Not known for his fidelity, Lucian had recently divorced – for the second time – from Kitty Epstein, having met her while conducting an affair with her aunt, Lorna Garman. Freud was a regular attendee to the various lunch parties thrown by Ann in London. Her brother-in-law, Eric Dudley, was dismayed when he found Freud at one such gathering, 'absent-mindedly munching on a bouquet of expensive purple orchids'.[18]

Guy Charteris, Ann's sixty-seven-year-old father, had re-married to Vi, twenty years after the death of Ann's mother, Frances. The three were due to arrive on the SS *Cavina*, of the Elders & Fyffes Line, direct from

Bristol on 2 March 1953. In anticipation, Fleming and Ann travelled south to Kingston where they stayed the night as guests of a rich and influential Portuguese couple called Charles and Mildred D'Costa. Such was the extravagance of their wealth, the following morning Fleming and Ann were awoken by 'three black slaves ... in starched shocking pink' arriving with 'a vast mahogany table' on which they served a breakfast on the veranda of delicious fruit and underwhelming scrambled egg which were 'a grey mush'.[19] The scene is recreated for Bond, when in *Live and Let Die* he is also treated to the same breakfast during which he marveled at the sunrise over Kingston and Port Royal.

At 9.30 am, Ann and Fleming were at the harbour, awaiting the arrival of the SS *Cavina*. As they looked out to sea, they could see the boat on the horizon, but while they stood looking, the wind picked up so much that Ann's 'hair was blowing perpendicular' and they 'could not hear each other speak'. The boat could not moor in those conditions, so for the rest of the day, the couple had to make do in the Grand Hotel lobby, surrounded by 'a sweating mass of gum-chewing Yanks'. By sundown, the boat eventually arrived at the harbour to everyone's relief. As Guy and Vi hugged and kissed Ann and Fleming, an old green Gloucestershire apple fell from Guy's pocket and smashed on the decking. He was arrested straight away by a watching customs official who explained that 'it is against the law to import foreign fruit that bring disease'. Fleming's mood by now was at breaking point, and he immediately set about defending the importation of elicit food onto the island. Ann recalled that 'while Ian argued ... I threw pieces of Didbrook apple into the sea' in an attempt to destroy the evidence. It was an exchange of Jamaican pounds that finally settled the argument and proved Guy's innocence.

Desperate to leave the hustle and heat of Kingston, Fleming was stopped by Ann who had realised among the chaos of the arrest that they had completely forgotten about their other guest, Lucian Freud.

After making some enquires with the crew, a message arrived saying 'would Commander Fleming step on board as Mr Freud [needs] help'.[20] Fleming went on the ship to find Freud banished to his cabin, as he only had 10 shillings with him and therefore could not pay the fare. Fleming settled the bill happily – anything to get out of sticky Kingston and not to be alone with Lucian Freud. Fleming disliked Freud and made little attempt to hide it. He wrongly believed that Ann and Lucian were having a sexual relationship, and if not, then the latter certainly wanted to.

In fact, when Freud married for the third time to Lady Caroline Blackwood, daughter of the Marquess of Dufferin and Ava, he asked Ann to be his best man at their wedding.

The drive north through the island was always one of the biggest pleasures for Fleming, and as the air started to cool and the sun began set, he wondered whether the stress of Kingston that day had all been worth it for this moment. Bond follows the same route in *Live and Let Die*, which he believes to be some of the most picturesque scenery in the world.

Back at Goldeneye, the Flemings, Charterises and Freud settled into a relaxing and enjoyable routine. Breakfast, as described by Bond in *Live and Let Die*, was always fresh fruit – usually paw-paw, green lime, red bananas, apples and tangerines – and scrambled eggs with bacon. All of this was washed down by cups of local Blue Mountain coffee.

After breakfast, Freud found a shaded place below a banana tree where he would paint, Ann would sit nearby with a book, Fleming was inside tapping away at his typewriter and Guy, faithfully followed around by Vi, was out birdwatching. Within the first couple of days, Ann reported to her brother that 'Papa is very happy ... he has found 50 birds'.[21]

At dinner on the second evening, Guy started to list some of the birds he had seen that day. He was particularly taken by the *Myadestes Genibarbis*, known simply as the Solitaire bird. Described by ornithologist and the real James Bond in the *Field Guide to Birds of the West Indies*, as 'Mostly grey, with rufous throat, foreneck and posterior underparts; breast much paler than back; lower eyelids and chin white; *much white on outer tail feathers; feat yellow*', Guy was delighted to have seen such a rare breed of thrush.[22]

Fleming was equally as excited, not because of the bird, but because of its name. He had been struggling to come up with an equally exciting name for his new Bond girl to 'Vesper' for his second novel. He needed look no further, for his heroin in *Live and Let Die* would be 'Solitaire', who he described in the book as possibly the most stunning women Bond had ever come across.

Live and Let Die, Fleming was proud to say, was 12,000 words longer than *Casino Royale,* finishing at 74,000 words, but had been written 12 days faster. With the success of his first Bond story behind him, Jonathan Cape agreed to print 7,500 copies in the first run, quickly followed by another 2,000. For his now growing American readership, 5,000 copies of *Live and Let Die* were printed. Fleming was quickly becoming an established thriller writer, but his notoriety to date was only a drop in the ocean of fame he would soon be sailing.

Chapter 15

Quantum of Solace

'Quantum of Solace' is a short story in the collection *For Your Eyes Only* published four years before Fleming's death. Bond is in Nassau when he is told a story of a former civil servant's marriage to an airhostess. The marriage starts to fall apart to the point that they both live in the same house but with a clear border through the middle and refusing to talk to each other. The story was written by Fleming at a time that his own marriage was breaking down, while his love for another woman was growing.

Four years of marriage was already taking its toll on Fleming and Ann. As things were deteriorating, Caspar's Godmother, Clarissa Eden, contacted Ann through the Conservative MP Alan Lennox-Boyd, to enquire whether Lady Eden and her husband, Prime Minister Sir Anthony Eden, might use Goldeneye for a holiday. Sir Anthony had been advised by his physician 'to take a complete rest' following the stress he had endured through the Suez crisis which had come to a head in 1956.[1] Eden had undergone a simple operation three years earlier, but when the surgeon's hand slipped trying to remove his gallbladder, his bile duct was severed and his health never properly recovered.

Fleming was ecstatic about the prospect. Such a noteworthy guest would do wonders for Goldeneye's letting potential and would surely raise his ever-growing profile as an author. He was miffed to learn that Ann had provided a 'woman's guide to Goldeneye' for Clarissa, including details such as the need to give two days warning in order to be able to have a bath and that the reef is 'abounded with scorpion fish, barracuda and urchins'.[2] Warning Clarissa that 'all the doctors on the island were black' Ann suggested that should the Prime Minister get 'impregnated with spines [from an urchin] he should pee on them' rather than seeking medical help.[3] Fleming was extremely angry that 'Ann had dared to say anything even slightly derogatory about [his] house'.[4]

Fleming wanted his VIP guests to get VIP treatment, so hurriedly sent off a telegram to his Jamaican lawyer, Anthony Lahoud telling him that two important friends were due to stay at Goldeneye for three weeks in November. He asked Lahoud to hire some get extra staff to help Violet get the house ready. As they hastily got everything prepared, the press got wind of what was going on, with headlines such as 'Fleming's private hideaway where Eden flies tonight'. Fleming and Ann wasted no time in getting as much publicity for themselves as possible, with Ann being overly impulsive as usual. She was quoted in the *Daily Express* on Friday 23 November 1956 as saying 'we lent the house to Noël Coward seven years ago after he had a colossal flop in New York. He went there for a few months to lick his wounds. It was very successful'. Coward was not particularly amused by this, but after Fleming recommended that Ann 'keep her trap shut' Noël was happy to play island host to the Prime Minister and his wife.[5]

The Edens arrived on 24 November 1956. On their first evening, Ann and Fleming received a telegram from their grateful guests: 'Everything here more wonderful than we expected. A thousand thanks Anthony and Clarissa'.[6] Noël Coward appeared at the gates of Goldeneye with Frank Cooper's marmalade and Huntley & Palmers biscuits which Clarissa wrote in her diary 'was not what we had been looking forward to'.[7] He was stopped by security because 'the Edens had closed the shutters and were not coming out to play'. Instead, they remained on the grounds of Goldeneye almost for their entire stay, eating only local food, with Clarissa telling Ann, 'We have finally got a line on langouste from Oracabessa.'

The only criticism from the Edens was 'all those squeaks and whizzings' that came at night, which turned out to be the rats. According to the *Evening Standard*, Sir Anthony organised a rat hunt with his security detail and happily reported that 'seven of the little beasts have been killed'.[8] Fleming again jumped to the defence of his beloved house, claiming they were only friendly field rats, not vicious house rodents. Returning to England rested and better, things were looking up for the Edens thanks to Goldeneye. However, on 9 January 1957, Sir Anthony resigned as Prime Minister, having been pushed out while staying in Jamaica. Ann wrote to Clarissa in condolence, saying sweetly that 'the security men had carved "God bless Sir Anthony" on all the trees' around Goldeneye.[9]

Clarissa is credited for her support and understanding towards her husband, and how the two stuck together throughout this particularly challenging period. This was in stark contrast to Fleming and Ann's failing marriage. In fact, when Ann wrote to Clarissa from Jamaica after Anthony's disappointing resignation, she would do her best to make it her last visit to the island.

For a while, Ann had started to grow distant from Goldeneye and Jamaica. Her letters home turned from those of excitement, invigoration and joy at being in the Caribbean to that of distain. For example, in 1955 she wrote to her brother that 'I left England with great reluctance' and 'I was tearful at leaving Caspar which broke the last vocal cord'.[10]

*

When the time came the following year for the annual visit to the island, Ann refused to come altogether. She cited her fear of flying as the main reason, but really this was just a ruse to avoid going. Travelling solo, Fleming left London on 14 January 1956, headed for Jamaica via New York as usual. Now the successful author of an ever-growing franchise, he proudly sat at the front of the plane in first class.

Fleming found it incredibly hard to be at Goldeneye alone, particularly for the first few days. He wrote desperately to Ann on his arrival, admitting that he had stolen a photograph of her and Caspar from her bedside table, begging at the end for Ann to come to Jamaica if she could.

Friends on the island were sympathetic towards Fleming's desolation at being alone and immediately organised a packed schedule of visitors, outings and meals. It was towards the end of his stay on one such outing when Fleming was invited to dinner by Charles and Mildred D'Costa, the millionaires who had let Fleming stay with them in Kingston while waiting for Lucian Freud and Ann's father to arrive. Also at dinner was an attractive, middle-aged divorcee called Blanche Blackwell. The offspring of a wealthy family, the Lindos, Blanche's ancestors had made their fortunes through owning Jamaican banana and sugar cane plantations since the seventeenth century.

Fleming was his typical charming self when introduced to Blanche, asking her straight out, 'Don't tell me you're a lesbian,' when she told him her family owned estates on the island. Blanche in return thought Fleming was 'the rudest man in the world'. Fleming's assumption that Blanche was a naïve island girl was incorrect, as after she divorced her husband, John Blackwell, in 1945, she moved to London, where she watched over her son Christopher's education at Harrow School. It was not until 1955 that she moved back to the island, where she set up shop near Goldeneye.

Although they had not met before, Fleming had been told by his friend Duff Dunbar of a woman on the island called Blanche, whom he thought the writer would get on well with. Fleming dismissed the possibility, thinking she was 'a great big black Jamaican mammy'.[11] Thus, perhaps his surprise when he met the attractive and petite white woman with dark features at the D'Costa household caused his foolish comments. Such was her beauty Errol Flynn had asked Blanche to marry him years before.

With a few days still remaining before he was due to travel back to London, Fleming invited Blanche to Goldeneye for a swim in his private bay. Despite his rudeness on meeting, she agreed, mainly through curiosity. She knew that Noël Coward was a mutual friend, making it even more surprising that it had taken so long for Fleming and Blanche to meet. The day after their first encounter, Blanche came to Fleming's house and from then they immediately grew close. Unlike Ann, Blanche was able to provide much-needed emotional support to Fleming. For some time now, Fleming had been craving the affection of another woman. His desire was a central theme in 'Quantum of Solace', where Bond wished for someone to look after him and want to spend time together.

She would take him shopping to find presents for Caspar, spend time listening to his concerns and even agreed to look after Goldeneye for the ten months of the year he was not there. She was also the epitome of what he thought a woman should be: attractive, a keen swimmer, obsessed by and respected in the Caribbean. She even gave Fleming a present, a small boat called *Octopussy*, which would inspire the title of one of his short stories.

Fleming returned to London in a better place than he had left. The excitement of a new woman in his favourite place in the world was just the stimulation he needed.

Although the timing was most likely a coincidence, Ann was also starting to grow close to someone else. By April 1956, she had got to know Hugh and Dora Gaitskell, who had been invited to dinner with the Flemings that spring. They were joined by Sir Maurice and Lady Violet Bonham Carter, grandparents of actress Helena Bonham Carter, and also Randolph Churchill, son of Winston. Hugh Gaitskell had become leader of the Labour Party, who were then in opposition, and remained in the role until his death in 1963.

In his early years, Gaitskell was often described as a champagne socialist – having attended the Dragon School, Winchester College and finally New College, Oxford – while supporting the strikers of the General Strike in 1926. Rising through the political ranks in Britain, he was briefly Chancellor of the Exchequer from October 1950 to October 1951. After Labour lost power in 1951, Gaitskell sat in the back benches of parliament, before successfully beating Nye Bevan and Herbert Morrison to be elected leader in 1955.

In an unlikely match, Ann and Gaitskell struck up an immediate friendship, with Ann enjoying his intellect and political clout, and Hugh seeking relief in her spirited personality, which contrasted the dull and dusty life of a privately educated socialist in the House of Commons. His serious public persona was a far cry from the fun-loving side that Ann would soon discover, or possibly create. The two had a mutual love for dancing and spent time together on the dance floor of the Café Royal. She started by playing rather hard to get, putting out the bait, which Gaitskell took instantly. She wrote to a friend, 'I suppose I shall go dancing next Friday with Hugh Gaitskell to explode his pathetic belief in equality ... but it will be a great sacrifice to my country'. Her tone soon changed, as he adapted to her 'style', reporting how he was 'a changed man' wanting only 'wine, women and song'.[12] It is debated to what extent their relationship was physical, but it was certainly an intimate one. Ann took to referring to Gaitskell as her 'unrewarding but ever devoted admirer'.[13]

Similar to her affairs when married to Shane and Esmond, she carried on with her new man in an obvious and almost deliberately public way. Once in 1959 she wrote to Evelyn Waugh how Fleming was seeking 'revenge because I took old Caspar and old Hugh Gaitskell to tea at the Sandwich Golf Club', at which Fleming was a member. She had paraded Gaitskell in front of Fleming's friends and contacts, and to top it off neither Hugh nor Caspar 'had combed their hair or wore ties', meaning they stood out and 'and were very unpopular'.[14]

The arrival of Blanche and Hugh marked a permanent change in the Flemings' relationship, and one which would define it for the rest of their lives. Although neither had been completely faithful through their marriage to this point, both seemed fairly content with the other's infidelity, which even became a sort of unwritten rule in the Fleming household. The difference came when Ann met Hugh and Ian met Blanche, because they went from having casual affairs with people to whom they were physically attracted, to meeting people who provided the emotional support they desired.

Fleming and Ann were simply too similar to be compatible. Ultimately, they were both selfish and not willing to compromise to the other's wishes. Fleming wrote in desperation to Ann, 'If I FIGHT my case it is just for the same reasons as you FIGHT yours. We both feel the other is getting too much of the cake.' In particular, both wanted to be noticed by the opposite sex, not for a minute wanting to be overlooked for being married.

Ann was growing increasingly close to Gaitskell through 1956, and although Fleming was pining for Blanche, their physical proximity was limiting. Regular evenings spent dancing together, meals and intense conversations became a staple for Ann and Gaitskell. It was therefore surprising that in 1957 Ann informed Fleming that she wanted to come to Goldeneye with him and to bring their four-year-old son Caspar as well. Fleming was reluctant to let his son come to Jamaica, because of the dangerous sea-life and baking sun.[15] Although he was of course quite right to point out the dangers, Fleming had been looking forward to getting to know Blanche better, and now there was the danger of Ann getting in the way. She was also starting to affect his social standing on the island, deliberately causing trouble with Fleming's friends. Noël Coward had increasingly started to dislike Ann, whose 'occasional off-handedness was beginning to grate', especially her swipes in the press.[16]

Despite Fleming's protests, Ann had made up her mind. Refusing to travel by air, she, Caspar, his nanny and her other son Raymond travelled on the *Caronia* ocean liner, although the eleven days of luxury were ruined by high winds and stormy seas. Ann wrote that while 'Nanny suffered seasickness, rheumatism and neuralgia' she 'remained mobile on Dramamine and gin' while 'Caspar woke at six every morning and [Raymond] wanted to be escorted to the night club every evening'.[17]

Fleming on the other hand opted for the BOAC flight via New York. Such was his delight at the quality of his journey, he decided to plug the airline in 'Quantum of Solace', claiming that the reason BOAC were doing so well taking passengers to Jamaica – despite the fact that their planes were slower – was because their service was the best. Getting to the island twenty-four hours before his family, Fleming was relaxed and in the perfect mindset for his holiday. The following day, on 15 January, Ann arrived in Kingston shaken and exhausted after a horrific journey, which she felt would 'qualify me for sanctuary in local loony bin',[18] only to learn that Fleming had claimed to be too busy to pick them up, so sent the Governor's aide-de-camp instead.

Thus, the tone for Ann's visit to Goldeneye was set. Almost to antagonise his wife, Fleming invited Blanche to their house for a drink on their first evening, where she explained in detail how she had helped with the Edens' visit. Ann's female intuition took over, and from the moment she saw Blanche with Fleming, she knew that her husband was having an affair and this time it was serious. Ann came to refer to Blanche as 'Ian's Jamaican mistress' and became fiercely jealous of her, despite having an equally serious relationship with Gaitskell to comfort her.[19]

Ann left Jamaica earlier than anticipated after just a month, arriving back on the UK with Raymond, Caspar and Nanny in late February. With Fleming alone at Goldeneye, he was able to spend his valuable few remaining weeks getting to know Blanche better. Their time was spent mostly in the sea looking for fish, talking on the veranda or exploring for local delicacies. They even took a trip to the neighbouring Cayman Islands, accompanied by a friend of Blanche, Anne Carr, for appearances' sake. Because of the last-minute nature of this trip, Fleming forgot to book anywhere to stay, meaning the three had to share a room at Bay View Hotel. The night was far from romantic for the new couple, not least because they had a third person watching over them, but Fleming indulged in too much gin and sleeping pills, so snored noisily all night meaning that poor Blanche had to sleep on the porch where she was immediately attacked by waiting mosquitoes.

Back in London, Ann received a letter from her husband telling her of the whole event. Describing it as 'very chaste and proper', he did not go into detail about Blanche, but described Anne Carr as repugnant and uninteresting. Despite Fleming's review of his companions, Ann was now certain of her husband's new blossoming relationship.

When Fleming subsequently returned to London, he spoke endlessly about Blanche and her virtues. He explained to Ann that she was not a local and naïve girl, as he had previously assumed, but someone who was well travelled and networked. Dropping into the conversation that she would likely be in London with her mother that summer, Ann jumped at the opportunity to find out more. Keen to understand her competition, she invited Blanche to lunch at their house in Victoria Square.

Ann's friend Peter Quennell was also invited to provide a second opinion on her husband's new lover, but Fleming was not included in the proceedings. Blanche was suspicious, but in an attempt not to seem guilty, she reluctantly accepted.

When the day came, Ann introduced Blanche to Peter as 'an old girlfriend of Ian's', which was met with a stunned silence by everyone, surprised that Ann was going for the jugular so early in the proceedings. Blanche was shocked, but managed to hold her own, retorting, 'Ann, that was a very unprovoked attack.'[20] The meal from then was a case of point scoring, with the two women trying to get one up on the other, while all the time Peter sat in the middle watching as if it were a tennis match.

By the time it came to her husband's next annual visit to Jamaica at the start of 1958, Ann had grown to detest Goldeneye even more. She wrote in her diary that 'I thought I should stay with Caspar' rather than going to Jamaica, which was only part of the truth. Although it was the place that 'had been the setting for [our] happiest days together', she was too jealous of the relationship Fleming had built with Blanche to return anytime soon. The house, and island for that matter, was the epitome of everything she disliked about Fleming. She wanted to stop him going, but he insisted that Goldeneye was the place where he could do his best writing. Appealing to what Ann cared about so much – money – Fleming explained that Ann's divorce settlement was now down to £70,000 and after a few years, this would all be gone, meaning they would need to live off income alone. Ann remarked that he had become 'an unendurable life-companion and a nervous wreck, however we shall have expenses abroad'.[21] Ann was not willing to compromise the huge income likely to be coming from Fleming's ever-growing fame from James Bond. The profits from the first three books – *Casino Royale, Live and Let Die* and *Moonraker* – according to Fleming, had only 'just about [kept] Ann in asparagus', but his next two, *Diamonds Are Forever* and *From Russia, with Love* had proved much more lucrative.[22] Fleming was therefore allowed to head back to the Caribbean to be with his mistress and to work on his next novel, *Dr No*.

In response, Ann decided to treat herself to a new property. Based between 16 Victoria Square, which she found too small and St Margaret's Bay, equally unappealing as it was surrounded by Fleming's golfing friends and Noël Coward, Ann wanted to move. Fleming was worried, begging her not to rush into a decision and waste his newly earned money on an ugly house. In truth, Fleming had no desire to move in the slightest, but he knew it was the only way he could continue with the life he was living. In an attempt to save his marriage he wrote to her from Goldeneye that she should buy anything that would make her happy, but pleading that it should at least have a small river or stream for him to enjoy.

The house Ann chose was Sevenhampton Manor. It was a far cry from Fleming's wishes of a river, 'a small box' of a house and near a golf course. There was a water source, but once dredged it turned into a pond smelling of stagnant water. Instead of the cosy house Fleming had in mind, they were now the owners of 'some huge palace that we cannot afford to heat or staff', and worst of all, Fleming was nowhere near a decent golf course.[23]

For Ann, it was perfect. Not only was she getting her revenge on Fleming, who had always had what he wanted in terms of accommodation – his oasis of Goldeneye, St Margret's Bay, where he was close to his favourite golf course, St George's, which he believed was 'the best golf course in the world', and Victoria Square, which was still a type of bachelor pad – now this was Ann's turn.[24] And she loved it. Writing to Evelyn Waugh on 31 August 1959, she exclaimed that 'we have bought a home' boasting that 'alas, there is a ballroom, billiard room and 40 bedrooms … the Carolean wings are lovely'.[25]

*

In January 1960, the Flemings' annual visit to Jamaica was a little more crowded than usual. Travelling separately were Ann, Caspar and Nanny, while Fleming took his normal BOAC flight. However, not only did Fleming have Blanche to see when he got to the island, Hugh Gaitskell was also due on the island. Ann was sad that he could not come and stay at Goldeneye, as the press 'would make jolly jokes' because of Anthony Eden's 'legend'. He feared newspaper headings claiming that Goldeneye was 'the place political careers go to die'. Instead, he and Ann enjoyed activities such as rafting along the rivers to see wildlife, despite Gaitskell being 'blind and deaf to natural beauty', and swimming, which he was very good at and usually 'disappeared for several minutes' before 'he rolled onto the shore like an amiable hippo'.[26]

Ann and Fleming had arrived in Jamaica both sick with bronchitis. Ann was quick to recover, but Fleming's turned into a fever. Ann wrote that 'happily Noël Coward came to call and proved himself a Florence Nightingale', by changing Fleming's 'sopping pyjamas, turning the mattress, and fetching iced drinks'. Ann put this down to Coward having always fancied Fleming, suggesting he had 'jumped at the opportunity to handle him'. While Coward was out collecting more ice, Fleming furiously shouted at Ann for exposing him 'to homosexual approaches'.

Coward remembered the events a little differently, writing in his diary on 29 January that he had found Fleming 'scarlet and sweating in a sopping bed in a hellish temperature' and it was down to him to look after him. He felt that Fleming and Ann's 'connubial situation is rocky. Annie hates Jamaica and wants him to sell Goldeneye. He loves Jamaica and doesn't want to. My personal opinion is that although he is still fond of Annie, the physical side of it, in him, has been worn away'.[27]

Fleming's books were now a hit, selling considerably around the world. In total, Jonathan Cape had sold 380,000 hardback copies of James Bond novels. Another publisher, Pan, sold seven million paperbacks in the UK and ten million in America. American sales had been boosted thanks to an endorsement from President John F. Kennedy, who named *From Russia, with Love* as one of his top ten favourite books of all time. His brother Robert and sister Eunice were also said to be big Fleming fans, saying 'the entire Kennedy family is crazy about James Bond'.[28] Ironically, it was also reported that the night before shooting the President, Lee Harvey Oswald spent the evening reading a Bond novel.

As the money was starting to pour in and with no need to remain in post, Fleming resigned from *The Sunday Times* in 1959. He did, however, stay on as a consultant to attend a Tuesday morning conference every week, for which he would be paid £1,000 per year. In doing this, Fleming needed to find himself a new office, which he did on Fleet Street, and hired a secretary called Beryl Griffie-Williams.

Fleming had a routine that every Tuesday morning he would rise early and motor to *The Sunday Times* conference in London. Tuesday 12 April 1961 was no different and he was particularly excited to see mock-ups of the highly anticipated colour magazine which would come into print the following year. The excitement was clearly too much for Fleming's weakening heart, and during the conference he suffered a serious heart attack. Luckily for the author, Dennis Hamilton, Editor of *The Sunday Times*, was on hand to help.

'Come on, Ian,' he shouted, as Fleming keeled over in a pale heap on the floor. 'You'll bloody well do as I tell you ... I'll get you a doctor.'[29]

Hamilton summoned help and Fleming was rushed to hospital where he would remain for a month. His illness, which he described as 'the Iron Crab', was serious heart disease and it would only be a matter of time before it killed him.[30] Hospital was boring for Fleming, who took to refusing to see visitors altogether, apart from Blanche, of course, who saw him regularly while on her summer visit to London. His new secretary, Beryl Griffie-Williams, would inform any of his correspondents that 'Mr Fleming is away at present as he is suffering from slight tension due to overwork'.[31] This was far from the truth, but Fleming was insistent that this heart attack was all but a minor setback.

He decided to make the best of a bad situation and work on a new literary project. Having read *Squirrel Nutkin* by Beatrix Potter from his hospital bed – a book he intended to give to Caspar – Fleming came up with the idea of his own children's book, *Chitty-Chitty-Bang-Bang*.

When he was released from hospital, advised by the doctors not to travel, Ann immediately accepted an invitation from Hilary Bray's friend, Edward Rice, for the Flemings to stay with them in Normandy. The trip proved difficult for Fleming's health, and upon arrival he spent most of the time resting or walking around the local woods supported by a stick. Travelling when advised against it was an unfair reflection on Ann's attitude towards her husband's health. Deep down, she worried for him and was always encouraging Fleming not to strain himself, whether with physical exertion, mental stress or overindulgence, mostly with alcohol and cigarettes. She bore the brunt of his moodiness, which mistook her caring for ceaseless nit picking. Thus, the couple grew further apart, so much so that she claimed his poor health was the only thing keeping them together: 'If you were well our marriage would be over'.[32]

Recovery was slow for Fleming, who was mostly just frustrated by his inability to play golf. His spirits were lifted in June 1961 when Harry Saltzman and Albert R. 'Cubby' Broccoli offered Fleming a film deal for James Bond, starting with *Dr No*. At an impressive rate of $100,000 per film and five percent of the producers' profits, Fleming had landed on a gold mine.

Having lobbied for David Niven to play Bond, followed by Roger Moore, who would of course go to have his chance, Fleming was not initially keen on the choice of little known Scottish actor, Sean Connery, who had started from modest means, having worked as a truck-driver, milkman, sailor, coffin polisher, boxer, model and lifeguard. Fleming invited Connery to the Savoy for lunch and was instantly taken by the handsome actor. Connery recalled the lunch and meeting the author for the first time: 'When I first met Fleming ... I saw him as a complete sensualist – senses highly tuned, awake to everything, quite amoral. I particularly like him because he thrives on conflict'.[33]

Dr No, true to the original novel in most ways, started filming in Jamaica on 16 January 1962. This coincided nicely with the Flemings' annual visit to the island. They invited Peter Quennell and poet Stephen Spender to come with them. A holiday alone would have been too much for the quarrelling couple.

Still, their trip was far from a happy one. Ann was furious at Fleming's immediate insistence of phoning Blanche as soon as they got there. She took him to task on this: 'You do not telephone your mistress the minute we arrive without talking to me about it, for however much you prefer to see her ... you do not care how unhappy I am.'[34] Furthermore, his head was turned by the beautiful actress, Ursula Andress, who was playing the first 'Bond girl' Honey Ryder. She recalled how 'he invited me to dinner in Ocho Rios at Goldeneye ... He was a very interesting man, he was intelligent, interested in culture'.[35] Really, on this occasion, he was just very interested in her.

Ann hated almost everything about the holiday, writing to Evelyn Waugh that 'God willing, I shall be home next week', having been on the island a relatively short amount of time.[36] She left early and returned to England. What followed was an unpleasant sword fight of written words between the couple, as angry letters were exchanged talking of separation. Fleming was clear that if it were not for the love he had for Caspar, he would be delighted by the prospect of divorcing her. But with their son's happiness in the forefront of their minds, the couple were trapped in an unhappy relationship.

In the last year of his life, Fleming's health only got worse. At the premier of the film version of *From Russia, with Love,* Bond's second onscreen instalment, Fleming was so unwell that he had to ask his doctor, Jack Beale, to accompany him to the event. In typical Fleming style, he had booked the entire front row of the Dress Circle for his party alone. He was now of esteemed celebrity status, selling on average 112,000 paperbacks per week.

Both Fleming and Ann spent their final years together in misery. Ann suffered the death of her alcoholic sister Mary-Rose on 23 December 1962, her brother Hugo had his gallbladder removed only for the surgeon to find an abscess on his pancreas, and possibly worst of all, Hugh Gaitskell died from medical complications on 18 January 1963. Ann had spent the two days before his death in the hospital with his wife Dora, but was not able to be with him for fear of exposing their affair. She was devastated that she could not fulfil his final wish, which was to see her.

Fleming had his own personal tragedy with the death of his mother Eve on 24 July 1964. He insisted on attending the funeral despite being gravely unwell. He was also worried sick about his brother Peter, who had had a second cancerous growth removed from his neck the previous year. Ann, meanwhile, told a family member that 'Ian's life from now on hangs on a thread'.[37]

She was right. Aged just fifty-six, on 11 August 1964, Fleming unwisely attended a committee meeting of the Royal St George's Golf Club, where he fell gravely ill. Rushed to Canterbury Hospital, he died at 1.00 am on 12 August 1964, Caspar's twelfth birthday.

Afterword

When the headline 'Bond Author Dies' appeared on the *Evening Standard* news bill, it sent shock waves through Fleming's many readers and admirers.[1] However, for those close to him, it had seemed only a matter of time before Fleming's failing health would catch up with him.

He died at the point of his highest success, and something he had spent his life craving and working towards. The third film to be made, *Goldfinger*, was released on 18 September 1964, just over a month after Fleming's death. With a production cost of $3.5 million, the film was so successful that it made its money back in just two weeks, with viewings from only sixty-four screens. A total return of $23 million made it one of the most profitable films of its time.

A further two novels were published after his death, *The Man with the Golden Gun* in 1965 and *Octopussy and The Living Daylights* in 1966, taking the Bond collection to fourteen books. By this time, Fleming had sold 27 million copies of his novels in eighteen different languages.

Despite their marriage difficulties, losing Fleming was extremely difficult for Ann. Although on the face of it their marriage was fraught with unhappiness, deep down, her love for Fleming never wavered. Three days after his death, just twenty family members attended Fleming's funeral in the St James Parish Church in Sevenhampton. Dressed in a black suit and accompanied by his mother, Caspar struggled to take in the fact that his father was dead.

The legacy left behind for Caspar was something a twelve-year-old boy can only dream of. But like his father, Caspar would often go into deep spells of melancholy and found life difficult. Ultimately, he was a very unhappy person.

A year after Fleming's death, Caspar was sent to Eton, following in the footsteps of his father and grandfather. But, as the son of the creator of James Bond, popularity and money meant he soon fell into bad habits with the wrong crowds. The police were called to the school when Caspar was found to be in possession of a number of illegal firearms. His uncle and godfather, Peter, claimed they belonged to him, thus saving Caspar from being criminally charged, but he was expelled from Eton.

From then, things went from bad to worse in the Fleming household. Caspar's moods darkened, turning from unhappiness to violence. Ann had no idea how to deal with her son and ended up simply trying to appease him. When Nanny, who had been in the household for nearly fifty years, smacked twenty-one-year-old Caspar with all her strength after he had knocked his mother to the ground in a fit of rage, Ann dismissed her.

The terms of Fleming's last will and testament were that aged twenty-one, Caspar got access to his trust fund. This was used in the most part to fund his growing drug habit. The same year, when visiting Goldeneye for the first time as an adult, he took a drug overdose and swam out to sea from the bay his father loved so much, in an attempt to kill himself. Luckily, local friends saw what was happening and managed to summon a helicopter. On 2 October 1965, after receiving electroshock therapy because of his suicide attempt, Caspar succeeded in killing himself by an overdose. He left a note for his mother in which he wrote 'if it is not this time it will be the next'.[2]

In the space of two years, Ann's sister, her lover, her husband and her son had all died. The following years were hard for her, and she never truly recovered from so many loses in quick succession. On 12 July 1981, Ann, who had been suffering from cancer for some time, died from complications after getting laryngitis.

In contrast to the members of the Fleming household, the literary Bond did not fade away with the death of his creator. In fact, things continued to grow at a rapid pace. Like the films, the books were carried on, with author Kingsley Amis being commissioned to write a new Bond novel, *Colonel Sun*, published in 1968, four years after Fleming's death.

Amis was somewhat dismissive of the honour, saying that after his divorce, he was 'so churned up emotionally' that he 'couldn't write anything more serious than James Bond'.[3] He even wrote it under the pseudonym of Robert Markham, to avoid any association with the novel. This insinuation that the Fleming books were not highbrow writing did not put off John Gardner, who was asked to write a further fourteen Bond novels from 1981 to 1996. Now, esteemed authors such as Anthony

Horowitz, Sebastian Faulks and William Boyd have added to the Bond series, all commissioned by the Fleming Estate.

Since his death, the term 'The Fleming Effect' – meaning 'the science of Fleming's fiction is in the detail' – became a common phase.[4] Fleming's attention to detail through all his books, whether it be his description of people, locations or events, were in the main, taken from his real life experiences. It was this that made his books so successful and is the ingredient in the films which make them what they are today. So many elements of Fleming's Bond still appear in the films and will continue to do so.

Even the films written completely independently of the original novels are always inspired by something from Fleming's life or his writing. For example, the film names – with the exception of *Tomorrow Never Dies* and *Die Another Day* – are all taken from Fleming's literature or life. *The World Is Not Enough* was the motto of the Bond family, discovered in *On Her Majesty's Secret Service*, and *Goldeneye* was of course in honour of Fleming's Jamaican house. The success of the films, which are arguably more popular now than ever before, rely on the 'Fleming Effect', which is something audiences still crave. Today, Daniel Craig's portrayal of James Bond is perhaps the most loyal to the books, marking a return to the character created by Fleming.

Although so much of James Bond's life and adventures seem ludicrously farfetched, when one looks at the life of his creator, it is clear that not all of it is complete fiction. What lay behind the imaginary spy was a man of great wit, who served his country with enthusiasm and imagination, and enjoyed the finer things in life. Like Bond, Fleming was far from perfect, with his drinking, smoking and attitude towards those he loved, especially women. But ultimately, he was a man who lived a life full of fascinating experiences, and thanks to his ability as an author, he put those experiences onto paper and inadvertently immortalised himself forever.

Bibliography

Addison, Adrian, *Mail Men: The Unauthorized Story of the Daily Mail,* Atlantic Books, London, 2007.

Amory, Mark, *The Letters of Ann Fleming*, The Harvill Press, London, 1985.

Beevor, Anthony, *D-Day: The Battle for Normandy,* Penguin Books, London, 2014.

Binney, Marcus, *Secret War Heroes: The Men of Special Operations Executive,* Hodder & Stoughton, London, 2005.

Bond, James, *Birds of the West Indies*, Collins, London, 1960.

Bryce, Ivar, *You Only Live Once: Memories of Ian Fleming,* Weidenfeld & Nicolson, London, 1975.

Cabell, Craig, *Ian Fleming's Secret War*, Pen & Sword Military, Padstow, 2016.

Cherry-Garrard, Apsley, *The Worst Journey in the World: Antarctic 1910–1913,* Skyhorse Publishing, New York, 2016.

Chowdhury, Ajaj & Field, Matthew, *Some Kind of Hero: The Remarkable Story of the James Bond Films*, The History Press, Stroud, 2015.

Cohen, David, *Churchill & Attlee: The Unlikely Allies Who Won The War*, Biteback Publishing, London, 2018.

Dalzel-Job, Patrick, *Arctic Snow to Dust of Normandy: The Extraordinary Wartime Exploits of a Naval Special Agent,* Pen & Sword Military, Padstow, 1991.

Day, Barry, *The Letters of Noel Coward*, Bloomsbury, London, 2007.

Durnford-Slater, John, *Commando: Memoirs of a Fighting Commando in World War Two,* Greenhill Books, London, 2006.

Duncan, Paul, *The James Bond Archives*, Taschen, London, 2015.

Eden, Clarissa, *Clarissa Eden: A Memoir – From Churchill To Eden*, Weidenfeld & Nicolson, London, 2007.

BIBLIOGRAPHY

Fleming, Fergus, *The Man with the Golden Typewriter: Ian Fleming's James Bond Letters*, Bloomsbury, London, 2015.

Fleming, Ian, *Casino Royale*, Jonathan Cape, London, 1953.

Fleming, Ian, *For Your Eyes Only*, Jonathan Cape, London, 1960.

Fleming, Ian, *You Only Live Twice*, Jonathan Cape, London, 1964.

Fleming, Ian, *Diamonds are Forever*, Jonathan Cape, London, 1956.

Fleming, Ian, *Dr No*, Jonathan Cape, London, 1958.

Fleming, Ian, *From Russia, with Love*, Jonathan Cape, London, 1957.

Fleming, Ian, *Live and Let Die*, Jonathan Cape, London, 1954.

Fleming, Ian, *Moonraker,* Jonathan Cape, London, 1955.

Fleming, Ian, *Octopussy and The Living Daylights*, Jonathan Cape, London, 1966.

Fleming, Ian, *On Her Majesty's Secret Service*, Jonathan Cape, London, 1963.

Fleming, Ian, *The Man with the Golden Gun*, Jonathan Cape, London, 1965.

Fleming, Ian, *The Spy Who Loved Me*, Jonathan Cape, London, 1962.

Fleming, Ian, *Thunderball,* Jonathan Cape, London, 1961.

Goldstein, Richard, *Helluva Town: The Story of New York City During World War II*, Free Press, New York, 2010.

Green, Michael & Brown, James D, *War Stories of D–Day: Operation Overlord: June 6, 1944,* Zenith Press, Minneapolis, 2009.

Harling, Robert, *Ian Fleming. A Personal Memoir*, The Robson Press, London, 2015.

Henderson, James, *Jamaica and the Cayman Islands,* Cadogan Island Guides, Kingston, 1996.

Hodges, Andrew, *Alan Turing: The Enigma,* Vintage, London, 2014.

Horn, Bernd, *A Most Ungentlemanly Way of War: The SOE and the Canadian Connection,* Dundurn, Toronto, 2016.

Hugill, J.A.C, *The Hazard Mesh*, Faber and Faber, London, 2011.

Jeffers, H. Paul, *Taking Command: General J. Lawton Collins from Guadalcanal to Utah Beach and Victory in Europe,* New American Library, New York, 2009.

Jeffery, Keith, *MI6: The History of the Secret Intelligence Service 1909–1949,* Bloomsbury, London, 2010.

Keene, Tom, *The Lost Band of Brothers*, The History Press, Stroud, 2015.

Knowles, Elizabeth, ed., *Oxford Dictionary of Quotations*, Oxford University Press, Oxford, 2004.

Lett, Brian, *Ian Fleming and SOE's Operation Postmaster: The Untold Top Secret Story*, Pen & Sword Military, Padstow, 2012.

Lycett, Andrew, *Ian Fleming*, W&N, London, 1995.

Macintyre, Ben, *For Your Eyes Only: Ian Fleming and James Bond*, Bloomsbury, London, 2008.

Macintyre, Ben, *Agent Zigzag: The True Wartime Story of Eddie Chapman: The Most Notorious Double Agent of World War II*, Bloomsbury, London, 2007.

Macintyre, Ben, *Double Cross: The True Story of The D–Day Spies*, Bloomsbury, London, 2016.

Macintyre, Ben, *Operation Mincemeat: The True Spy Story that Changed the Course of World War II*, Bloomsbury, London, 2010.

Malapi-Nelson, Alcibiades, *The Nature of the Machine and the Collapse of Cybernetics: A Transhumanist Lesson for Emerging Technologies*, Palgrave Macmillan, Toronto, 2017.

McCormick, Donald, *17GF: Life of Ian Fleming*, Peter Owen Publishers, London, 1993.

Millard, Andre, *Equipping James Bond: Guns, Gadgets, and Technological Enthusiasm*, Johns Hopkins University Press, Baltimore, 2018.

Milton, Giles, *D-Day: The Soldiers' Story*, John Murray, London, 2018.

Milton, Giles, *The Ministry of Ungentlemanly Warfare: Churchill's Mavericks: Plotting Hitler's Defeat*, John Murray, London, 2016.

Norton-Taylor, Richard, 'Months before the war, Rothermere said Hitler's work was superhuman', *Guardian*, Friday, 1 April, 2005, available at: https://www.theguardian.com/media/2005/apr/01/pressandpublishing.secondworldwar (accessed 3 February, 2019).

Nutting, David, *Attain by Surprise: Capturing Top Secret Intelligence in WW II*, David Colver, London, 2003.

O'Hara, Vincent, *Torch: North Africa and the Allied Path to Victory*, Naval Institute Press, Annapolis, 2015.

O'Reilly, Charles, *Forgotten Battles: Italy's War of Liberation, 1943–1945*, Lexington Books, Lanham, 2001.

Page, Norman, *The Thirties In Britain*, MacMillan Education, London, 1990.

BIBLIOGRAPHY

Parker, Matthew, *Goldeneye. Where Bond was Born: Ian Fleming's Jamaica*, Hutchinson, London, 2014.

Pearson, John, *The Life of Ian Fleming*, Bloomsbury, London, 2013.

Penketh, Anne, 'Secret plan to bury soldiers alive inside Rock of Gibraltar', *Independent*, Sunday, 4 February 2007, available at: https://www.independent.co.uk/news/uk/this-britain/secret-plan-to-bury-soldiers-alive-inside-rock-of-gibraltar-434984.html (accessed 22 March 2019).

Phillips, Lucas, *The Greatest Raid of All*, Heinemann, London, 1958.

Pile, Jonathan, *Churchill's Secret Enemy,* CreateSpace, 2012.

Rankin, Nicolas, *Ian Fleming's Commandos. The Story of the Legendary 30 Assault Unit*, Oxford University Press, Oxford, 2011.

Robertson, Connie, ed., *Dictionary of Quotations*, Wordsworth Editions, London, 1998.

Ross, Steven T., *U.S War Plans. 1938–1945*, Lynne Rienner Publishers, Boulder, 2002.

Saunders, Tim*, Commandos and Rangers: D–Day Operations,* Pen & Sword Military, Padstow, 2012.

Simmons, Mark, *Ian Fleming and Operation Golden Eye: Keeping Spain out of World War II*, Casemate Publishers, Oxford, 2018.

Smith, Adrian, *Mountbatten: Apprentice War Lord 1900–1943*, I B Tauris & Co, London, 2010.

Stevenson, William, *Man Called Intrepid: The Incredible WWII Narrative of the Hero Whose Spy Network and Secret Diplomacy Changed the Course of History*, The Lyons Press, Lanham, 2009.

Thomas, Andrew, *V1 Flying Bomb Aces*, Osprey Publishing, Oxford, 2013.

Usher, Shaun, *Speeches of Note: A celebration of the old, new and unspoken*, Hutchinson, London, 2018.

West, Nigel, *Historical Dictionary of Naval Intelligence (Historical Dictionaries of Intelligence and Counterintelligence)*, Scarecrow Press, Lanham, 2010.

Notes

Foreword

1. Pearson, John, *The Life of Ian Fleming*, Bloomsbury, London, 2013, p.281.

Chapter 1

1. Lycett, Andrew, *Ian Fleming*, W&N, London, 1995, p.220.
2. Lycett, p.220.
3. Fleming, Ian, *Casino Royale*, Jonathan Cape, London, 1953, p.1.
4. Quoted in Pearson, p.7.
5. Quoted in Lycett, p.12.
6. Pearson, p.6.
7. McCormick, Donald, *17GF: Life of Ian Fleming*, Peter Owen Publishers, London, 1993, p.23.
8. Quoted in McCormick, p.24.
9. Quote in Macintyre, Ben, *For Your Eyes Only: Ian Fleming and James Bond*, Bloomsbury, London, 2008, p.20.
10. Quoted in McCormick, p. 27.
11. McCormick, p.30.
12. Pearson, p.75.
13. McCormick, Donald, p.35.
14. Quoted in Pearson, p.87.
15. Pearson, p.5.
16. Quoted in McCormick, p.42.
17. Quoted in Pearson, p.94.
18. Quoted in Pearson, p.113.
19. McCormick, p.46.
20. Pearson, p.ix.
21. Macintyre, 2008, p.48.

Chapter 2

1. Robertson, Connie, ed., *Dictionary of Quotations*, Wordsworth Editions, London, 1998, p.83.
2. Quoted in Cohen, David, *Churchill & Attlee: The Unlikely Allies Who Won The War,* Biteback Publishing, London, 2018, p.105.
3. Quoted in Page, Norman, *The Thirties In Britain,* MacMillan Education, London, 1990, p.123.
4. Quoted in Simmons, Mark, *Ian Fleming and Operation Golden Eye: Keeping Spain out of World War II*, Casemate Publishers, Oxford, 2018, p.6.
5. National Archives, ADM 223/297.
6. Macintyre, Ben, *Operation Mincemeat: The True Spy Story that Changed the Course of World War II*, Bloomsbury, London, 2010, p.26.
7. Quoted in Cabell, Craig, *Ian Fleming's Secret War*, Pen & Sword Military, Padstow, 2016, p.xxiii.
8. National Archives, ADM 223/297.
9. McCormick, p.51.
10. Quoted in Pearson, p.124.
11. McCormick, p.49.
12. Quoted in Macintyre, 2008, p.62.
13. National Archives, ADM 223/297.
14. Quoted in Stevenson, William, *Man Called Intrepid: The Incredible WWII Narrative of the Hero Whose Spy Network and Secret Diplomacy Changed the Course of History*, The Lyons Press, Lanham, 2009.
15. Smith, Adrian, *Mountbatten: Apprentice War Lord 1900–1943*, I B Tauris & Co, London, 2010.
16. Milton, Giles, *The Ministry of Ungentlemanly Warfare: Churchill's Mavericks: Plotting Hitler's Defeat*, John Murray, London, 2016, p.106.
17. Lett, Brian, *Ian Fleming and SOE's Operation Postmaster: The Untold Top Secret Story*, Pen & Sword Military, Padstow, 2012, p.27.
18. Milton, p.106.
19. Milton, pp.18–19.
20. Jeffery, Keith, *MI6: The History of the Secret Intelligence Service 1909–1949,* Bloomsbury, London, 2010, p.ix.
21. Quoted in Simmons, p.85.
22. Quoted in Lett, p.22.
23. Quoted in Pearson, p.125.
24. Fleming, Ian, *For Your Eyes Only*, Jonathan Cape, London, 1960, p.55.
25. Lett, p.22.

26. Quoted in Lett, p.23.
27. Quoted in Macintyre, 2008, p.26.
28. Fleming, Fergus, *The Man with the Golden Typewriter: Ian Fleming's James Bond Letters*, Bloomsbury, London, 2015, p.6.
29. Quoted in Macintyre, p.7.
30. Macintyre, 2010, pp. 6-7.
31. Macintyre, 2010, pp. 6-7.
32. McCormick, p.64.
33. McCormick, p.63.
34. Quoted in Pearson, pp.136–137.
35. Pearson, p.140.
36. Simmons, p.18.

Chapter 3

1. National Archives, ADM 223/463.
2. Pearson, p.149.
3. Quoted in Lycett, p.125.
4. Quoted in Simmons, p.84.
5. National Archives, ADM 464.
6. Quoted in Cherry-Garrard, Apsley, *The Worst Journey in the World: Antarctic 1910–1913,* Skyhorse Publishing, New York, 2016, p.x1.
7. National Archives, ADM 464.
8. Fleming, 1960, p.31.
9. National Archives, ADM 464.
10. Cherry-Garrard, Apsley, p.xxxix.
11. Penketh, Anne, 'Secret plan to bury soldiers alive inside Rock of Gibraltar', *Independent*, Sunday, 4 February 2007, available at: https://www.independent.co.uk/news/uk/this-britain/secret-plan-to-bury-soldiers-alive-inside-rock-of-gibraltar-434984.html (accessed 3 February 2019).
12. Simmons, p.93.
13. National Archives, ADM 464.

Chapter 4

1. Chowdhury, Ajaj & Field, Matthew, *Some Kind of Hero: The Remarkable Story of the James Bond Films*, The History Press, Stroud, 2015, p.83.
2. Rankin, Nicolas, *Ian Fleming's Commandos. The Story of the Legendary 30 Assault Unit*, Oxford University Press, Oxford, 2011, p.58.

NOTES

3. National Archives, ADM 223/297.
4. Quoted in Rankin, p.58.
5. Hodges, Andrew, *Alan Turing: The Enigma,* Vintage, London, 2014, p.186.
6. Quoted in Malapi-Nelson, Alcibiades, *The Nature of the Machine and the Collapse of Cybernetics: A Transhumanist Lesson for Emerging Technologies,* Palgrave Macmillan, Toronto, 2017, p.108.
7. Rankin, p.62.
8. National Archives, ADM 223/463.
9. Quoted in Cabell, p.23.
10. West, Nigel, *Historical Dictionary of Naval Intelligence (Historical Dictionaries of Intelligence and Counterintelligence)*, Scarecrow Press, Lanham, 2010, p.23.
11. Cabell, p.23.
12. Quoted on the jacket of the first edition of *From Russia, with Love* (Jonathan Cape, 1957).
13. Macintyre, 2008, p.30.
14. Pearson, p.142.
15. Quoted in Cabell, Craig, p.21.
16. Lycett, p.122.
17. Lycett, p.122.
18. Quoted in Macintyre, 2008, p.30.
19. Lycett, p.124.
20. Fleming, Ian, *From Russia, with Love*, Jonathan Cape, London, 1957, p.128.
21. National Archives, ADM 223/463
22. National Archives, ADM 223/463
23. Cabell, pp.23–24.

Chapter 5

1. Quoted in Fleming, 2015, p.37.
2. Quoted in Pearson, p.150.
3. Quoted in Pearson, p.151.
4. Lycett, p.127.
5. Stevenson, pp.28–29.
6. Pile, Jonathan, *Churchill's Secret Enemy,* CreateSpace, London, 2012, p.45.
7. Horn, Bernd, *A Most Ungentlemanly Way of War: The SOE and the Canadian Connection,* Dundurn, Toronto, 2016, p.50.
8. Pearson, p.154.
9. Fleming, Ian, *Diamonds are Forever*, Jonathan Cape, London, 1956, p.80.

10. Quoted in Pearson, p.154.
11. Quoted in Pearson, p.154.
12. Quoted in Pearson, p.154.
13. Pearson, p.154–155.
14. Pearson, p.156.
15. Lycett, p.129.
16. Pearson, p.157.
17. Bryce, Ivar, *You Only Live Once: Memories of Ian Fleming,* Weidenfeld & Nicolson, London, 1975, p.53.
18. Quoted in McCormick, p.63.
19. Pearson, p.157.
20. Bryce, p.54.
21. Quoted in Lycett, p.130.
22. Lycett, p.130.
23. National Archives, ADM 223/297.
24. Quoted in Millard, Andre, *Equipping James Bond: Guns, Gadgets, and Technological Enthusiasm,* John Hopkins University Press, Baltimore, 2018, p.143.
25. Quoted in Lycett, p.130.
26. McCormick, p.67.
27. Quoted in Lycett, p.131.
28. Quoted in Millard, p.76.
29. National Archives, FO 1093/172.
30. McCormick, pp.10–11.

Chapter 6

1. Milton, p.132.
2. Lett, p.5–6.
3. Lett, p.39.
4. Keene, Tom, *The Lost Band of Brothers*, The History Press, Stroud, 2015, p.61.
5. Lett, p.62.
6. Lett, p.44.
7. Quoted in Lett, p.61.
8. Milton, p.130.
9. Quoted in Lett, p.88.
10. Milton, p.131.
11. Quoted in Lett, p.95.
12. Milton, p.133.

13. Quoted in Lett, p.121.
14. Quoted in Lett, p.135.
15. Quoted in Keene, p.100.
16. Milton, p.139.
17. Lett, p.170.
18. Milton, pp.140–141.
19. Quoted in Binney, p.140.
20. Milton, p.143.

Chapter 7

1. National Archives, HW 8/104
2. National Archives, HW 8/104.
3. Rankin, p.134.
4. National Archives, HW 8/104.
5. Rankin, p.159.
6. Quoted in Milton, p.146.
7. Milton, p.154.
8. Phillips, Lucas, *The Greatest Raid of All*, Heinemann, London, 1958, p.124.
9. National Archives, HW 8/104.
10. Quoted in Rankin, p.5.
11. Rankin, p.9.
12. Rankin, p.15.
13. National Archives, HW 8/104.
14. Quoted in Rankin, p.9.
15. Quoted in Rankin, p.19.
16. National Archives, HW 8/104.
17. Rankin, p.138.
18. National Archives, HW 8/104.
19. Harling, Robert, *Ian Fleming. A Personal Memoir*, The Robson Press, London, 2015, p.41.
20. Quoted in Lycett, p.152.
21. Harling, p.43.
22. Dalzel-Job, Patrick, *Arctic Snow to Dust of Normandy: The Extraordinary Wartime Exploits of a Naval Special Agent,* Pen & Sword Military, Padstow, 1991, p.116.
23. National Archives, HW 8/104.
24. Dalzel-Job, p.116.
25. Quoted in Macintyre, 2008, p.55.

26. National Archives, HW 8/104.
27. O'Hara, Vincent, *Torch: North Africa and the Allied Path to Victory*, Naval Institute Press, Annapolis, 2015, p.3.
28. Ross, Steven T., *U.S War Plans. 1938–1945*, Lynne Rienner Publishers, Boulder, 2002, p.163.
29. Quoted in Rankin, p.153.
30. Quoted in O'Hara, p. 96.
31. Quoted in Rankin, p.151.
32. National Archives, HW 8/104.
33. Millard, p.151.
34. Rankin, p.161.
35. National Archives, HW 8/104.
36. Quoted in Rankin, p. 165.
37. National Archives, HW 8/104.
38. Fleming, Ian, *Thunderball*, Jonathan Cape, London, 1961, p.109.
39. National Archives, HW 8/104.
40. National Archives, HW 8/104.
41. National Archives, HW 8/104.
42. Quoted in Rankin, p.200.

Chapter 8

1. Green, Michael & Brown, James D, *War Stories of D–Day: Operation Overlord: June 6, 1944,* Zenith Press, Minneapolis, 2009, p.5.
2. Saunders, Tim, *Commandos and Rangers: D–Day Operations,* Pen & Sword Military, Padstow, 2012, p.181.
3. Harling, p.69.
4. Beevor, Anthony, *D–Day: The Battle for Normandy,* Penguin Books, London, 2014, p.131.
5. Nutting, David, *Attain by Surprise: Capturing Top Secret Intelligence in WW II*, David Colver, London, 2003, p.172.
6. Quoted in Rankin, p.229.
7. National Archives, HW 8/104.
8. Quoted in Nutting, p.172.
9. Quoted in Rankin, pp. 227–229.
10. Beevor, p.132.
11. Hugill, J.A.C, *The Hazard Mesh*, Faber and Faber, London, 2011, p.31.
12. National Archives, HW 8/104.
13. Harling, p.72.

NOTES

14. National Archives, HW 8/104.
15. Harling, p.70.
16. Hugill, p.31.
17. Hugill, p.25.
18. Harling, p.86.
19. National Archives, HW 8/104.
20. Hugill, pp.28–29.
21. Beevor, p.133.
22. National Archives, HW 8/104.
23. National Archives, HW 8/104.
24. Dalzel-Job, p.122.
25. Harling, p.77.
26. Harling, p.85.
27. National Archives, HW 8/104.
28. Harling, p.74.
29. Durnford-Slater, John, *Commando: Memoirs of a Fighting Commando in World War Two,* Greenhill Books, London, 2006, P.195.
30. National Archives, HW 8/104.
31. Harling, p.74.
32. Harling, p.79.
33. Quoted in Beevor, p.218.
34. Harling, p.78.
35. Jeffers, H. Paul, *Taking Command: General J. Lawton Collins from Guadalcanal to Utah Beach and Victory in Europe,* New American Library, New York, 2009, p.99.
36. Harling, p.86.
37. Usher, Shaun, *Speeches of Note: A celebration of the old, new and unspoken,* Hutchinson, London, 2018, p.346.
38. Rankin, p.242.
39. Harling, p.80.
40. Harling, p.85.
41. Beevor, p.222.
42. Jeffers, p.99.
43. Hugill, p.51.
44. Harling, p.89.
45. Quoted in Rankin, p.244.
46. Quoted in Beevor, p.221.
47. Harling, p.90.
48. Harling, p.80.
49. National Archives, HW 8/104.
50. Harling, p.83.

51. Harling, p.87.
52. Harling, p.84.
53. Lycett, p.152.
54. Fleming, Ian, *On Her Majesty's Secret Service*, Jonathan Cape, London, 1963, p.325.

Chapter 9

1. Quoted in Parker, Matthew, *Goldeneye. Where Bond was Born: Ian Fleming's Jamaica*, Hutchinson, London, 2014, p.45.
2. Macintyre, Ben, *Double Cross: The True Story of The D-Day Spies*, Bloomsbury, London, 2016, p.33.
3. Macintyre, 2016, p.8.
4. Macintyre, 2016, p.213.
5. Thomas, Andrew, *V1 Flying Bomb Aces*, Osprey Publishing, Oxford, 2013, p.4.
6. Macintyre, Ben, *Agent Zigzag: The True Wartime Story of Eddie Chapman: The Most Notorious Double Agent of World War II,* Bloomsbury, London, 2007, p.265
7. Thomas, p.1.
8. Macintyre, 2007, p.265.
9. Macintyre, 2007, p.3.
10. Macintyre, 2007, pp.281–283.
11. Quoted in Macintyre, 2007, p.291.
12. Dalzel-Job, p.125.
13. National Archives, HW 8/104.
14. Dalzel-Job, p.125.
15. Rankin, p.269.
16. Harling, p.95.
17. Rankin, p.269.
18. National Archives, HW 8/104.
19. Dalzel-Job, p.162.
20. Dalzel-Job, p.154.
21. Harling, pp.187–188.
22. Quoted in Nutting, p.260.
23. Rankin, p.291.
24. Rankin, p.297.
25. Harling, p.92.
26. Rankin, p.314.
27. Quoted in Rankin, p.315.
28. Quoted in McCormick, p.53.
29. Fleming, 1955, p.304.

Chapter 10

1. Fleming, Ian, *Octopussy and The Living Daylights*, Jonathan Cape, London, 1966, p.14.
2. Fleming, 1966, p.5.
3. Bryce, pp.69–70.
4. Harling, p.235.
5. Bryce, p.78.
6. Bryce, p.71.
7. Quoted in Parker, p.16.
8. Bryce, p.79.
9. Henderson, James, *Jamaica and the Cayman Islands,* Cadogan Island Guides, Kingston, 1996, p.74.
10. Bryce, p.80.
11. Parker, p.22.
12. Bryce, p.83.
13. Bryce, p.84.
14. Bryce, p.87.
15. Parker, pp.39–41.
16. Bryce, p.85.

Chapter 11

1. Quoted in Lycett, p.61.
2. Fleming, 1953, p.213.
3. Quoted in Lycett, pp.92–94.
4. Harling, p.117.
5. Amory, Mark, *The Letters of Ann Fleming*, The Harvill Press, London, 1985, p.35.
6. Harling, p.117.
7. Lycett, p.96.
8. Quoted in Lycett, p.94.
9. Harling, p.239.
10. Quoted in Parker, p.61.
11. Harling, pp.238–239.
12. Amory, p.37.
13. Norton-Taylor, Richard, 'Months before the war, Rothermere said Hitler's work was superhuman', *Guardian*, Friday, 1 April, 2005, available at: https://www.theguardian.com/media/2005/apr/01/pressandpublishing.secondworldwar (accessed 3 February 2019).
14. Quoted in Harling, p.117.

15. Amory, p.37.
16. Amory, p.41.
17. Amory, p.42.
18. Quoted in Harling, p.117.
19. Amory, p.42.
20. Quoted in Harling, p.118.
21. Amory, p.48.
22. Amory, p.45.

Chapter 12

1. Parker, p.62.
2. Parker, p.65.
3. Quoted in Amory, p.65.
4. Amory, p.66.
5. Bryce, p.72.
6. Fleming, Ian, Dr No, Jonathan Cape, London, 1958, p.304.
7. Quoted in Pearson, p.186.
8. Quoted in Amory, pp.61–62.
9. Parker, p.21.
10. Parker, pp.27–28.
11. Parker, p.51.
12. Quoted in Parker, p.59.
13. Amory, p.67.
14. Amory, p.65.
15. Parker, p.69.
16. Amory, p.75.
17. Amory, pp.65–66.
18. Parker, p.66.
19. Day, Barry, *The Letters of Noel Coward*, Bloomsbury, London, 2007, pp.538–539.
20. Day, p.541.
21. Parker, p.73.
22. Quoted in Parker, p.71.
23. Day, p.542.
24. Quoted in Parker, p.86.
25. Bryce, p.71.
26. Parker, p.51.
27. Day, p.543.
28. Fleming, Ian, *Dr No*, Jonathan Cape, London, 1958, p.205.
29. Quoted in Chowdhury, Ajaj & Field, Matthew, p.65.

30. Amory, pp.69–70.
31. Amory, p.101.
32. Amory, pp.66–76.

Chapter 13

1. Parker, p.76.
2. Pearson, p.207.
3. Day, p.546.
4. Amory, p.119.
5. Parker, p.23.
6. Day, p.546.
7. Amory, pp.77–78.
8. Harling, pp.230–232.
9. Harling, pp.236–237.
10. Amory, p.111.
11. Day, p.573.
12. Lycett, p.218.
13. Amory, p.111.
14. Quoted in Lycett, p.218.
15. Quoted in Parker, p.151.
16. Quoted in Lycett, pp.215–218.
17. Amory, pp.112–117.
18. Quoted in Amory, p.119.
19. Fleming, Ian, *The Man with the Golden Gun*, Jonathan Cape, London, 1965, p.200.
20. Quoted in Macintyre, 2008, pp.178–179.
21. Quoted in Pearson, p.293.
22. Quoted in Pearson, p.xvii.

Chapter 14

1. Quoted in Fleming, 2015, p.16.
2. Fleming, Ian, *Live and Let Die*, Jonathan Cape, London, 1954, p.1.
3. Lycett, p.236.
4. Lycett, p.237.
5. Fleming, 1954, p.37.
6. Fleming, 1954, p.107.
7. Bryce, p.108.

8. Quoted in Parker, p.143.
9. Quoted in Amory, p.55.
10. Quoted in Lycett, p.148.
11. Quoted in Amory, p.55.
12. Quoted in Macintyre, 2008, p.152.
13. Parker, p.151.
14. Quoted in Lycett, p.303.
15. Parker, p.151.
16. Fleming, 2015, p.51
17. Amory, p.136
18. Quoted in Lycett, p.172.
19. Amory, p.125
20. Amory, pp.124–125.
21. Amory, p.125.
22. Bond, James, *Birds of the West Indies,* Collins, London, 1960, p.177.

Chapter 15

1. Lycett, p.302.
2. Amory, p.188
3. Amory, p.188.
4. Lycett, p.302
5. Amory, p.189.
6. Lycett, p.304
7. Eden, Clarissa, *Clarissa Eden: A Memoir – From Churchill To Eden,* Weidenfeld & Nicolson, London, 2007, p.201.
8. Quoted in Lycett, p.305
9. Eden, p.201.
10. Amory, p.150.
11. Lycett, pp.279–280.
12. Quoted in Lycett, p.296.
13. Amory, p.227.
14. Amory, p.237.
15. Quoted in Lycett, p.262.
16. Lycett, p.285.
17. Amory, p.191.
18. Amory, p.191.
19. Lycett, p.322.
20. Quoted in Lycett, p.322.
21. Amory, pp.210–219.

22. Fleming, 2015, p.36.
23. Amory, p.238.
24. Pearson, p.x.
25. Amory, p.237.
26. Amory, p.250.
27. Amory, pp.278–279.
28. Quoted in Macintyre, 2008, p.91.
29. Quoted in Lycett, p.384.
30. Pearson, p.xv.
31. Quoted in Fleming, 2015, p.160.
32. Amory, p.302.
33. Quoted in Chowdhury, Ajaj & Field, Matthew, p.63.
34. Amory, p.301.
35. Quoted in Chowdhury, Ajaj & Field, Matthew, p.67.
36. Amory, p.298.
37. Amory, p.349.

Afterword

1. Quoted in Harling, p.352.
2. Quoted in Lycett, p.451.
3. Quoted in Macintyre, 2008, p.203.
4. Millard, p.184.

Index

INDEX

INDEX

INDEX

INDEX